THE
HUMANITARIAN
JOURNEYMAN

(a personal journey through the dangers
of humanitarian interventions)

by

Philip Jones

Grosvenor House
Publishing Limited

This book is published by
Grosvenor House Publishing Ltd
Link House
140 The Broadway, Tolworth, Surrey, KT6 7H
www.grosvenorhousepublishing.co.uk

A CIP record for this book
is available from the British Library

ISBN 978-1-83975-409-8

Dedicated to Val

My wife of over 31 years, who supported me through two careers with
the dangers and problems they presented.
Reliable, caring and loyal; a true lioness and best friend.
Couldn't have done this without her at my side.

Contents

Foreword

The names of organisations and of real people in this book have been changed to protect them for various reasons. The locations and situations are all based on actual experiences and real events.

Philip (Phil) Jones was born in Liverpool in 1962. His family moved to Cavan Road, which sat on the then tri-district border of Norris Green, West Derby and Clubmoor, when he was two years old. He attended school at Broad Square County Primary and later, West Derby Comprehensive. Phil left school not knowing, nor caring at that time, about his exam grades. He didn't like school at all.

On leaving school at sixteen, Phil's first job, which didn't last long, was with an industrial cleaning company, followed by an apprenticeship in carpentry at Price-Wise joinery.

At seventeen and a half years of age, being disillusioned with life, he left his job and joined the army, and went on to serve a full 22-year career. Phil enjoyed the operational tours and the constant challenges and risks. He also spent two periods, each lasting two years, training recruits, primarily as a corporal and latterly as a sergeant.

Phil left the army in 2002, with his certificates of military education[1], basic and advanced levels, as the only educational

---

[1] Education for Promotion Certificate, EPC and EPC-A (Advanced) consisting of numeracy, management, army in the contemporary world and literacy (English). Basic level required for promotion to sergeant, and advanced level for promotion to warrant officer.

certificates he had, and began his 'life journey' and second career within the humanitarian sector.

Initially, he was a project manager, then after a change in circumstances, he became acting country director and finally safety and security adviser. Most notably, he became Save the Children UK's first full-time safety and security global adviser in 2005, as part of the organisation's emergency section.

This role gave Phil a thorough understanding of the sector and its personality, flaws, attitudes and weaknesses. It was a fantastic but steep learning curve which eventually led to Phil becoming an independent safety and security consultant, delivering training, advice and direction to many of the world's leading international non-governmental organisations (INGOs) in hostile, unstable, natural disaster, health epidemics, war and post-war environments.

Conducting work in many locations worldwide often put Phil directly in harm's way as he worked to ensure the safety of the field teams and successful delivery of humanitarian programmes.

Phil believed in his work, to try and develop a sense of individual and collective ownership of safety and security, which he assessed in the early days to be lacking for the teams operating in the field in some of the most difficult and dangerous locations in the world.

Leading by example, delivering training using real-time experiences and making the field teams fully aware of their environment, the risks, the threats and their vulnerability to them gave him the training mantra of: "If you are well trained and fully aware, you can work safer for longer."

During the years that followed, Phil became a constant traveller, and spent much time away from home. The list of global locations was impressive, as was the list of conflict zones he would work across, as well as the natural disasters which spanned tsunamis, earthquakes and hurricanes/tornados. He also supported interventions into epidemics, such as cholera and Ebola.

Phil worked among some of the poorest and most deprived populations on the planet. Hunger and poverty were almost ever present throughout his journey.

Phil eventually retired from working in hostile locations in December 2014 on return from Sierra Leone, following his contribution during the major Ebola outbreak.

Phil is now the operations director in an international export supply business founded by his wife. Together they own the company, which also employs their two grown-up children.

Phil is married to Val, and together they have a daughter, Vikki-Lea (aged 30), and a son, Ryan (aged 21). Vikki works full time in the family business and Ryan is currently in his final year at Loughborough University, studying International Business. He helps out with the family business during university breaks.

Not forgetting Benny the Pugalier, the family mascot.

Their family home is in Ruskington, a small village in Lincolnshire.

This book is finally being written, after years of prompting and prodding, during the global COVID-19 pandemic of 2020.

Preface

It has been very difficult to accurately portray the experiences I had during the 15 years I worked within the humanitarian sector without identifying areas that, in my opinion, were either mismanaged or avoided. I was thrown in at the deep end and had a very steep learning curve to deal with.

The large majority of humanitarian workers are selfless, hard working, courageous, thoughtful and kind.

They give up their home lives to help others and to intervene in far-flung locations, often working and living in terrible conditions and sometimes suffering the same conditions as those who they assist. These are generally known as the emergency teams, deployed quickly to natural disasters, such as earthquakes, tsunamis, floods and hurricanes, and war and post-war environments, bringing rapid support to famine, disease and displaced people in affected places.

However, there are also some interventions that are the absolute opposite. For example, as part of an emergency response, I attended the cyclone disaster in Myanmar (Burma). The cyclone was called 'Nargis'; just as hurricanes are named, so, too, are cyclones (which are the same as hurricanes and just as destructive, but differ in name due to the locations in which they occur).

For this intervention, we were accommodated in a very plush hotel in a nice part of Yangon (also known as Rangoon). This was largely dictated by the military government who wanted to, and did, control all movement of foreign-aid workers and keep them in a place of their (the government's) choosing.

The worst affected locations were quite a long way from Yangon. The Irrawaddy delta region was the hardest hit, with the most destruction and fatalities. (Over the three days of storms, around 138,000 were killed and tens of thousands injured, resulting in around 2.5 million people homeless.)

Aid agencies were not initially allowed to visit the delta region without first obtaining permission from the government through the police and having received papers stating who you were, where you were going and which organisation you represented. Police checkpoints along the routes into the delta region were there to check that you had the right documentation. But the main issue was that you started your journey from a point of obvious comfort, a nice hotel room, then went to a location completely destroyed, where people had lost everything and were struggling to survive. A big contrast.

Other examples are programmes that are referred to as 'developmental programmes'. These are long-term programmes, often over decades, where the populace is constantly suffering from famine, extreme poverty or very long conflict-driven issues. Many, but not all, developmental country programmes emanate from emergency responses. Such is the effect of a 'rapid-onset' crisis, that it needs years of direct support, hence the 'developmental approach'.

The main aim, while alleviating suffering, is to try to make each intervention as sustainable as possible. The ideal is to ensure that the good work done initially, however long that takes, can be continued once the INGOs and humanitarian workers have all gone home. During most of the interventions, national staff are trained to replace international staff, leaving behind a skill base that can continue and become self-supportive. Much of this depends on donor funding, without which it becomes very difficult to sustain.

Many international staff remain with the developmental programmes for years. They can, depending on the local security situation, be accompanied by their spouses and children, living in accommodation provided by the organisation they work for. In many locations, they will have a vehicle provided, a cleaner for their house and may even, in some cases, have a cook too.[2]

In the many years before I became involved in humanitarian associated work, there was, of course, hardship for its workers, but generally, there was very little in the way of direct targeting of aid workers, not dismissing the fact that there were killings of aid workers before this time. Many 'missionaries' (as they were often referred to) were killed due to their religious beliefs and other associated issues during interventions in conflict zones.

Since 9/11, the targeting of aid workers became a serious and deadly risk. One, in my humble opinion, the sector was slow to respond to.

Listening to many seasoned aid workers, and with my own observations, I drew several conclusions as to how and why people operated, particularly in hostile conflict locations.

There are undoubtedly those who selflessly dedicated their lives to helping people, in both emergency and developmental programmes, for many years, not facing or experiencing any direct targeted aggression. They were generally allowed to deliver their programmes of famine and poverty relief, primary healthcare delivery, education and livelihood support, with a much lower level of threat and risk to themselves.

---

[2] Cooks, cleaners, drivers and other ancillary staff are employed from within the local community, who are often deprived of employment, have large extended families to support and, for the most part, are living in extreme hardship. The employment they are given is very well received, as the wage they get is often a lifeline for them and their families. This is a very carefully planned strategy to help the local community by creating employment opportunities where, in some places, none exist.

Some of these people believed that they were immune to attack because they were helping everyone; being impartial, non-governmental, independent and transparent in their work. Seldom were they targeted because they were European, American or any type of foreigner; this all changed after 9/11 to a devastating effect.

It still took, in my opinion, an extraordinarily long time for some of the 'old and bold' to adjust to the change, and several I came across were often of the opinion that if it hadn't happened to them or they hadn't experienced such aggression over many years in the job, then it wouldn't happen now; a complete head-in-the-sand approach.

I was luckier than most coming into the humanitarian sector. I had good mentors who became very good friends. I had a solid background of being in conflict locations and an understanding of the risks involved. My training over 22 years (in my previous life) had given me a much needed and welcomed head start on many of those I would go on to work with over the coming years.

Change is inevitable. Those who refuse to accept change often suffer as a consequence; those who do accept it in this sector are often more aware, effective, safer and far better managers and leaders of their teams.

Regardless of the type of intervention, emergency or developmental, never be tempted to believe in the stereotyped term 'tree-huggers' that is often and wrongly bestowed upon humanitarian workers. While in other walks of life this reference to 'fluffy do-gooders' may be accurate, my experience of the people in the humanitarian sector that I have worked with is far from the 'tree-hugging' stereotype. Some are the most courageous, hard-working, determined, generous and selfless men and women I have ever been associated with. My hats off to them all.

My Caveat

Now this is why it is hard to tell this story. Let me explain.

Over the years, there has been an unwelcome and misguided group of people who successfully apply for work within the sector. These people are collectively known as 'disaster tourists' or, as some call themselves, 'disaster junkies'. These are people who appear to thrive on being in disaster locations, not for the help they can deliver, but to take photos of suffering, destruction or death and share the horror stories with their friends back home in the pub.

It is hard to identify these people at the application and interview stage, as they tend to know what they have to say to make themselves sound compassionate, dedicated and an appropriate fit for the job. Many are (very) well educated, but, as I quickly found out, having a degree or a master's degree doesn't mean you are a correct fit for the job (or that you have any level of intelligence for that matter).

From my observation, these people do exist in the sector. Sometimes it is hard to recruit the right number of people for any given response, as manpower scale-up can quickly outstrip the reserves of experienced people.

They tend to become recognisable pretty early into any emergency deployment; they always want the gory details and they take photographs of the things they shouldn't (not for historical records or for any practical reason, but to 'wow' their friends back home; the 'look at me, aren't I brave?' type of approach).

Once identified, they are usually sent home, but it always leaves added pressure on the team remaining, as someone has to pick up the slack until a replacement is found.

As in any sector or walk of life, there are those who are seen as autocratic, dictatorial and bullies. There are those who take the glory of others for themselves and there are people who bluff their way through life because they have the attributes I have just mentioned. This book contains, in my opinion, some people like these.

On the flip side, there are those who are good leaders, good managers and humble, compassionate and hard-working people who (thankfully) far outnumber those 'bad eggs'. Leading by example, in my opinion, is the best way. Great if you can talk a good talk, but actions speak much louder than words. Be judged on what you do rather than what you say.

Finally ("Phew!" I hear you say), I am not an expert in the workings, policies or internal politics of the humanitarian sector. I am also not a historian. I have some knowledge, but it is limited to the organisations I have worked for and the places I have worked. I have a lot of practical experience from my past life and the following 15-plus years I worked in the sector, and my particular area of expertise is in the practical aspect of safety and security in hostile locations, doing all I can to try to keep people safe, and planning for what to do when things go wrong. In a nutshell, that's it![3]

---

[3] Many confuse my role with Health and Safety. It's not. My role is about keeping people aware and safe while delivering programmes in high-risk locations, planning procedures for emergency evacuation, training people to recognise when they are being targeted (including what to do if you are shot at, caught in a minefield, involved in a bombing, have been abducted, are at potentially hostile checkpoints) and many other skills and protocols that might be required within the context of the location I am working. I also act, where possible, as a go-between negotiator with rebel groups. This is a very carefully planned and thought-through process. Being liaison between the aid organisation and a rebel group can be precarious in the extreme, but it should be noted that not all rebel or opposition groups are the baddies. Some governments are far worse.

This book is written from my perspective, using my observations, my experiences and my memories. I dare say some of my own weaknesses may be apparent in this book as I have been as honest about myself as I have been about others.

At no time in the writing of this book have I intended to offend, discredit or be unjust to any person or situation, but no doubt someone somewhere may have an opposing opinion and that is fine. This is my clearest recollection of what happened and how it happened. For clarity, I have expanded upon some descriptions to ensure that those who have no knowledge of the workings of the humanitarian sector, particularly the hostile environment interventions, get a clearer understanding of the situation as it develops and why some things are more important in a wider context than may appear at first glance; not always so obvious.

Humanitarian interventions are complex. They almost always involve some level of hardship. They can often be in a very high-risk and dangerous environment. The good people I have met and worked with are special and are truly unsung heroes for delivering the life-saving work they do.

We in developed industrialised nations have the military, the police, the fire service, the ambulance service, doctors, nurses, care workers and all of the emergency services (sorry if I have left anyone out), who are rightly held in the highest esteem. I would like the reader to place high on that list those who give up their time, their home and their family life for long periods; those who are courageous and willing to sacrifice their lives for people in hardship and difficulty, for people they have never met, across the world.

These amazing people working in the humanitarian sector should be highly ranked in society. They are without doubt fantastically dedicated people.

I hope my book, warts and all, can give everyone a little bit of insight to an unfamiliar world and break the unwanted, stereotypical 'tree-hugger' millstone that has wrongly hung around the neck of the sector for years.

Acknowledgements

Val, my wife, for all her love and support during the many years that went into the making of this book.

Vikki Lea Jones and Ryan Jones for their constant encouragement, pushing and nagging to get me to write this story.

Debbie Sinnott and Emma Barry for their time and unbiased comments while reading the draft copy for market research.

Norman Sheehan for giving me my first opportunity in the sector, I am forever grateful.

Gareth Owen for having belief in my ability and being there for advice when I needed it in the early days.

All those who volunteer to work, help and support those who are in difficulty through war, post-war, natural disasters, poverty, famine, epidemics and pandemics. To those who give up their time to live in harsh locations, putting their lives at risk for those they don't know. For those aid workers who made the ultimate sacrifice and never truly came home. To you all, the world owes you a debt that can't be repaid. I hope our recognition and thanks are enough.

Chapter 1:

Start of a Journey – Setting the Scene

At 40 years of age, a new life was beginning; no structure and no set direction. A reliance on my gratuity payment and the wages from my wife's job was just about the limit of our financial resources.

After leaving the army after 22 years, I was now in totally uncharted territory. Getting used to a new life and, more importantly, trying to make it work was now my 'mission'. (Note to self: new life, new setting, new environment, so cut the militaristic jargon. It might help me settle in!)

So, here I sit in the house we'd bought a few years before I left the forces (a great decision otherwise I might be homeless now!), pondering just what the hell to do next. I had absolutely no idea, no plan, and with the end-of-service date only just having passed, I had no real motivation to rush into anything else just yet.

As a family, we had holidayed several times over the years in Frejus, on the Cote D'Azure, in the south of France, and had toyed with the idea of investing in a few of the mobile holiday homes on the Holiday Green site... New business for a new chapter?

So the idea took its next step, and off we went for a month to the south of France for a recce (bloody military terms again!).

The recce proved what I had really suspected all along: too expensive to make it viable. But we had a great month-long holiday, including a stop off at Disneyland Paris. The kids loved it, and in truth, we did too, but no plan emerged from it, so back to square one; again.

As time drifted on, I got bored of what seemed like an eternal leave period. (Shit! There it is again. Is it so ingrained in me that I just can't shift it?)

In my latter days in the army, I became (what I thought) a bit of a whiz on the computer. Having had a DOS-based (for the non-geeks among you, DOS, or Disk Operating System, was a really basic computer programme which worked the computer) word processor, the Amstrad PCW 9512 with the loudest dot matrix printer ever, to cut my teeth on. I later sold it and progressed to a second-hand desktop of questionable origin, operating a very early version of Windows, and via the phone line I could access the internet (when I had time to sit and wait for the images to load pixel by pixel in a greyish, black and whitish horizontal stream of very slow lines). At the time, it was a true sneak peek into the future; a major technological breakthrough. Well, at least in our household!

Using a few years of experience experimenting, buggering up and losing documents (that I had spent hours putting together), I became quite the expert in producing training certificates and training programmes and writing letters and CVs, getting quite inventive and artistic. I decided to put those self-taught skills to the test. I started a self-employed business targeting new and small businesses. I designed and printed logos, business cards, advertising flyers, menus and anything else I could persuade people they needed.

After a small investment (from my shrinking gratuity pot), I bought a desk, a laptop and a decent printer (at least I thought it was at the time). I printed off some samples and set off locally to gain some business. It worked for a while. My new company was proudly called 'Personal Designs'. I had gained a few repeat customers, some of whom I had designed unique business logos for. It was a minor success, and kept me occupied for quite a few months.

Personal Designs very quickly became mind-numbingly boring; not being used to being desk-bound, it was having a really negative effect on me and the 'can't be arsed' syndrome quickly took hold.

Moving from my desk and into the living room to watch TV (telling myself I needed a break), I began to spend more time away from my work and either going out running or for long tabs (and there it is again... I was doing well. I meant walks) in different places with a mate from next door. I was starting to think I needed something more, something with a hint of excitement and risk. Being drawn back into my last life, or at least the operational sense of it, I needed, or rather longed for, a change. Little did I know it would come from daytime TV.

*

Chapter 2:

Be Careful What You Wish For

Being bored off my tits, I moved from my desk into the living room with a steaming brew and a few biscuits in hand. I sat down and switched on the TV. Flicking over the channels, I stopped as an interview with a famous comedy actor came on the screen. Ha! A bit of comedy to brighten my day, or so I thought.

Wrong! He was talking about a UK-based charity, The Child-Focused INGO (UK). As a patron, he was talking about their international interventions and some of their work around the globe. My mind flashed back to my last operational tour of Kosovo when I had been involved in some liaison work between the military and civilian aid groups, one most notably was The Child-Focused INGO. I had already undertaken some post-conflict aid to the civil community in conducting rapid assessments of issues that needed addressing in Pristina; everything from engaging the local councils and private construction companies to come together to fix infrastructure damage, such as the major drains under the city. Other projects were the removal of growing mountains of household waste that was rapidly accumulating and posing real health hazards. But the projects I took to most were those that directly benefitted the children who had gone through a horrific and very recent war. They were not back at school, and their play areas had been destroyed. It was here that I met Jane and Sue, who were running child-focused programmes for the children of Kosovo and had projects in and around Pristina.

I shared some of my assessments with them, including a new play area in the open space between blocks of flats in the Sunny Hills area of the city. The Child-Focused INGO conducted their own assessment and agreed that this was a need that could reach many children in the area, then funded and project-managed the task. I also directed them to what I called 'the lost children of Pristina' who were families consisting of only kids. Being looked after by older siblings, they relied on the generosity of neighbours for food but this wasn't consistent.

There was one particular child who was slowly going blind due to a strange growth on his eyeball. I mentioned this to The Child-Focused INGO team, and it was much later that I learned that they organised a medical intervention that saved his sight. A fantastic result.

After listening to the comedic actor and seeing his obvious and infectious enthusiasm for the organisation and its work, I thought I would make contact with them; firstly, to ask about Jane and Sue and their progress in Kosovo, but also, in the intervening days, I had searched their website and noticed that they advertised jobs in several countries. Maybe, I thought, I could register my interest, but at the time, it was purely a call out of curiosity about the programme update.

The phone was answered by a lady called Shirley. I introduced myself, and told her the story of Kosovo and my involvement with both Jane and Sue. I also mentioned that I'd had a very brief conversation with a guy called Paul during a chance meeting in Pristina.

I found it strange that Shirley, who I had never met, appeared to know quite a lot about me and my dealings with the civil communities in Pristina, and had praised my work that had crossed with Jane and Sue. Anyway, after a brief chat, she said she would put me through to Paul, who I now knew, via their website, to be the CEO of The Child-Focused INGO.

With a click on the phone line, a soft Southern Irish accent enthusiastically asked, "Is that Phil the Scouser from Pristina? How are you?"

Slightly startled, but pleased he not only remembered my name but also that I was a Scouser, I replied, "Hi, Paul. Yes, it is. How are you?" A light-hearted conversation was struck, and after several questions about my situation outside of the army and my diverse business interventions, Paul, asked if I would come to London on Wednesday? He would take me to lunch to have, in his words, 'a grand catch up'.

As it was only Monday, I thought it was doable, so I agreed to meet him at his office in Kentish Town, and that was it.

I sat with my wife, Val, that evening, telling her about the call and how they appeared to be well informed about me and my time in Kosovo. Was it just a nice coincidence, I wondered? I thought no more of it.

Wednesday arrived. Not liking the underground, I debussed the train (there it is again... no one says debuss... ARRRGH) at King's Cross and took a taxi to The Child-Focused INGO office. It was rather dark and dingy, but the walls were decorated with photographs from projects in unknown (to me) locations. The Child-Focused INGO logo was ever present wherever you looked.

I was greeted by a lady who stated, "You must be Phil?" Confirming that I was, she told me she had spoken to me on the phone and her name was Shirley. She then ushered me through to meet Paul.

I was welcomed with a hearty, firm handshake and a huge smile. Paul's body language was relaxed, and his conversation was enquiring but very informal. Paul had charisma in bucket loads. He was very passionate, practical and enthusiastic about his job and the organisation. He had little time for 'red tape' and prohibiting regulations, but was a clear thinker and a direct-action type of guy. I liked him a lot; I thought we may have much in common.

As the Iraq War (the second) was coming to its conclusion and coalition forces were in Baghdad, Paul told me of a team he had ready to go into Iraq, Nasiriyah to be more exact. The team was waiting in a hotel in Kuwait City for the fighting to conclude and the all clear to be given to progress under the UN and coalition into Iraq.

Put bluntly, Paul asked if I would be interested in joining the team. He told me to think about it and if I was interested, they could formally interview me at the office that same day and get things moving...

Two hours later, I was phoning Val to tell her that I had got a job, agreed a salary and would be travelling soon. Well, on Friday to be exact!

On the way home on the train, I received a call from Shirley who was now coordinating my movement plan. She told me the flight details, what I needed to take with me and the time to arrive at the office before going to the airport on Friday. And as a throwaway line, she told me I had a salary increase; I hadn't even started the job yet!

At home, I was now saying my goodbyes, passing on all my contact details and going through, in detail, my plans with Val, should anything go wrong. After all, she was the only person in the world (and still is) who I could trust to initiate my action plans if things went tits up. Luckily I have not needed to call on that after all these years.

After arriving in Kuwait and refamiliarizing myself with the place I'd last visited during the first Gulf War (Operation Granby), I met the team and discussed their ideas and plans with them, for when the programme was given the go-ahead.

The appointed country director was a young lady who was a qualified dentist. She was a little unsure of her authority and was often driven in her decision making by the logistician guy, who had a bit more experience but his background was in the music industry. Another team member was a young guy who, judging by his appearance, was still living in the punk era, but he turned out to be a very clever and likable guy. He often had some very practical and sensible inputs but was not forceful enough to have his ideas fully appreciated or listened to, and when challenged, he quickly withdrew and became quiet. He was always unwell, and it eventually led to his withdrawal from the programme. The others could have learnt a lot from this guy. I did.

As we waited at the hotel in Kuwait, I made a connection with members of another aid organisation who had moved into the rooms next to The Child-Focused INGO. I became good friends with their country director, and we sat for hours chatting about programme direction and implementation. I discussed a joint contingency plan with him as well, as he, too, was going to Nasiriyah.

An uneasy cessation of war fighting was underway. Saddam Hussain and his family were on the run, the Iraqi army was in disarray and had surrendered, small groups of fedayeen (Fedayeen Saddam is a guerrilla force of so-called elite fighters formed as a militia) were still attacking coalition-forces' bases and convoys. They provided a regular threat across Dhi Qar Province and beyond. During this uneasy period, the green light was given and the great aid convoy via Kuwait's border made its way north.

The area and district of Dhi Qar was in the south-central region of Iraq, and Nasiriyah was its regional capital. Sitting on the Euphrates, it had a very important and strategic location.

The fighting here during the conflict had been intense, and many reported that the battle for Nasiriyah was among the fiercest fighting of the war, in part due to large amounts of fedayeen based in the region.

After a brief and uneasy stay in the American field base at the Tallil Air Base, called Camp Whitehorse, we moved out to stand on our own and to find accommodation and office space, which would preferably be two very separate locations so that one could relocate to the other if the situation deemed it necessary.

As a project manager, I had several irons in the fire concerning new projects. I spent the first night in our new compound, which was close to the outskirts of the city. Sitting in the candlelit gloom with the team discussing our next steps gave me an uneasy feeling, and we all wondered if the fragile peace would be short lived.

Sitting in an open courtyard at night with no light pollution, the stars appeared extra bright and the sky extra dark. The idyllic scene was punctuated often with automatic gunfire from just beyond our compound walls and the arc of the red tracer rounds could be seen disappearing into the deep black sky.

Understanding the difference of celebratory gunfire and direct, targeted gunfire, I took to informing the team of the principle of 'crack and thump'.[4] Having been around all types of weapons and being a weapons instructor in my previous life, I was used to the sound, but it did make me giggle watching the reaction of others. I would often shout 'take cover' just to see what reaction it would get; it was childish and not very clever, but bloody funny at times.

---

[4] Crack and thump: The sound of a bullet passing close and past you is a sharp 'crack' as it breaks the sound barrier, followed by a dull 'thump', which is the sound of the weapon recoiling after firing. The time between each sound equates to the distance the firer is from the target. Very roughly, one second equals about a hundred metres.

In those first few days, partly because of my role in my previous life, I took to educating the team on the sounds and effects of small arms fire (yep, there it is again! I mean hand-held weapons such as pistols, rifles, machine guns and some anti-tank rocket launchers), talking through the theory of small arms fire (yep... noted. Sorry!), discussing what constitutes effective cover and dispelling the TV war and cowboy movie myths that an upturned wooden kitchen table is bulletproof.

I also took it upon myself to discuss, plan and execute our emergency procedures. Everything from hibernation planning to escaping by vehicle, on foot and, if needed, by heli-extraction. It very quickly went from just a list of advisories to a full-time role of safety and security management alongside my project manager role.

Documents were sourced from the global generic organisational emergency plans and turned into real-time action plans with detailed 'actions on'. (Yep, I know, but give me this one, as it is really appropriate!) I had a liaison role with the American Marines HQ in Nasiriyah using my experience and understanding of their operational capabilities and more crucially, establishing connections with those individuals who could make things happen if we needed it. Important relationships were made with the logistical troops alongside the warfighting tactical arm. When the crap hit the air-conditioner, could I rely on these troops to save our bacon? (Turkey bacon BTW. Keeping culturally correct.) I was never more than 60 per cent sure of that, so a different plan ran concurrent to the link with the US Forces and briefly it was split as follows:

1. Emergency hibernation planning when it's impossible to move on the streets and you are not the obvious or intended target of any attacks. (Independent action)
2. Local evacuation within the city from current location to a safer location. (Independent action)

3. As above, but in partnership with other aid organisations.
4. Country evacuation pre-planned. (Collective with other organisations and military assistance)
5. Country evacuation immediate move. (Independent action)
6. As above, but in partnership with other organisations.

While the above are just general headings, the actual planning was detailed and required ownership from everyone involved. It was easier to get buy-in with some people than with others. Some can make the simplest plans appear as difficult as plaiting diarrhoea. It was a serious situation, and many aid workers in Iraq at that time were inexperienced working in an active hostile location. Although 'officially' the war was over, sporadic fighting on a large scale was still happening.

The safety and security management was by far the most difficult task I engaged in during this period of my new career. Project managing the individual programme sectors was a doddle in comparison.

We hadn't been in our new home in Nasiriyah for long when the team started to fall apart. Our intelligent punk rocker was medically evacuated back to the UK, not to be seen again; the dentist country director either quit or was fired (I don't know which, but she left); the logistician, who developed a bad rash on his torso, bailed out too. That left me, Phil the Scouser, on my first humanitarian intervention, with less than a month in the job, running the place with our locally recruited programme manager, Nasir.

I was quickly promoted to acting country director, senior programme manager, logistics manager, finance manager, safety and security manager and HR/recruitment manager for the bakery we were building. Oh, I nearly forgot, head of civil/military liaison and sole attendee of a million meetings each week. I very quickly decided which meetings were worth attending and which were just some people telling other people just how well they were doing and what a great job they were all collectively doing for the locals... 'Waffling bullshit meetings' I used to call them, with little structure, next to no information worth listening to and bugger all use to the lowlife like me.

Finding meetings that had enough accurate information that could be analysed and used to benefit our communities was a skill in itself. They *were* out there: people talking sense based on fact and offering real-time programme collaboration. They were worth their weight in gold.

As the days passed, Nasir and I formed a very close friendship, and he became my local eyes and ears. He was a family man who was a real grafter, had a great sense of community and wanted, via The Child-Focused INGO, to help as many people as he could. He was totally dedicated; something I came to test and rely on over the months that followed.

Our primary and biggest project was the building of a bakery to produce vitamin-enriched flatbreads to the local schools, hospitals and vulnerable groups in Nasiriyah.

Land was acquired, the building was constructed and the baking machinery was imported from Beirut, Lebanon. During the pre-programme briefing, I thought we would be operating a series of old but simple pizza-type ovens with pull-down fronts. I was amazed to see this was very modern automated equipment where you load the dough mix in one end, it moves the large lump to be pressed, rolled and cut, then on to a series of moving conveyor belts (the proving stage) and flattened, then another a conveyor belt through an oven, out the other side and onto a series of cooling conveyor racks, finally sliding down a chute to where the packers put the still-warm flatbreads into The Child-Focused INGO's logoed bags, 12 breads at a time, ready for distribution. It was a fantastic set up, and if we had the ingredients, we could run the bakery 24/7. However, the road to achieving this was far from easy, and as it turned out, required a lot of 'favours' to be taken and given before production could start.

I was learning on the hoof, and it was a very, very steep learning curve. I had great respect for the authority that Paul had given me and the trust he had in me to get things done regardless of my inexperience. In many ways, the work-based methodology was similar to what I was used to in my previous life, in that it was task orientated and required a practical approach; in other ways it appeared to be a polar opposite.

The world of international non-governmental organisations (INGOs or NGOs for short) was a complex new environment for me. My thinking was simple (naively so at times): we are all volunteers, and we all want to contribute to make life for those affected by war, natural disaster, poverty or health issues, such as epidemics or pandemics (cholera and Ebola, I would get to know), better and more bearable. You would, as an outsider, think all organisations would be pulling in the same direction and be mutually supportive, yes?

Well, yes *and* no. I observed that if two INGOs were running the same programmes, i.e. health interventions (the setting up of clinics and primary health care), they shouldn't be run in the same 'space'. Confused? Yep, I was. There is a 'thing' called 'operational space' which I understood to mean: "This is our turf. We are doing health, so go and redesign your programme to do something else or move out of our 'space'." This led to some organisations avoiding full cooperation with others, often causing some ill feeling between them. I later (much later) had it explained (in a very roundabout way, which at times was as clear as mud) that much of this issue rotated around donor funding. If an organisation was already running an emergency health programme, for example, in a particular 'space' then another organisation asking maybe the same donor to fund them to do something similar would often mean a refusal due to duplication.

INGOs are fierce about their funding streams, as it is their lifeblood. As a charity, they rely on external funding, and invest huge amounts of time and effort in planning and writing proposals for programme funding to donors. From my personal and somewhat naive perspective, I thought then, and still may have similar thoughts now, that the whole competition for 'space' and all that was involved in it, was not quite right. I often wondered if the reason for the actual intervention was at some point being lost a little. So, to avoid duplication, organisations had to find 'gaps' in the 'space' and attempt to fill them with the right intervention. Laugh? Yep; I did, as it can at times become absurd.

I must add, though, that once 'space' has been decided, the emergency work that the INGOs do is fantastic on many levels. It's not without criticism, for sure, and at times they do reinvent the wheel many times over, but for the conditions they tolerate, the low pay they receive and the hardships and sometimes extreme risk they face to help others, it is absolutely admirable.

It was in my early days in Iraq with The Child-Focused INGO that I first encountered the United Nations in a non-military capacity. (I had been part of UN military forces in Bosnia and Cyprus.) UNICEF, UNWFP, UNOCHA and so many more were quite new to me. More so, it was the first time I'd heard anyone say anything derogatory about them as an organisation. I'd thought (naively again) that they were the saviours who appear and put the world to right wherever needed. Again, as I was constantly told: "WRONG, WRONG, WRONG!"

While the mandate for UN interventions is different in almost every country in which they exist, they do have their own ethos to do good and make difficult situations better in many ways. But their interventions, according to many seasoned INGO workers, are tainted by hugely inflated wages for staff (often seen as the wrong incentive to do this type of humanitarian work) which are passed on to locally hired staff at a rate way beyond the national average wage levels. This creates (I am told) an artificial economy around their sometimes huge bases, and when they leave, the artificial economy collapses. The UN can be in place for many years, depending on the mandate they were 'invited' into the country under.

Some of their international staff have (in many people's opinion) been over promoted from a lower-level job in their own country (referred to as 'national staff' or 'national hires'), to the international staff job list in another country, and their status is massively boosted, as is their pay scale. With some (not all, I must add), the power and ego boost can lead to overzealousness, poor decision making and overall bad management. Many INGO workers refer to the UN as the 'dark side', a phrase given to the not-so-nice people in the Star Wars movies; maybe a tad unfair but there is a level of truth in some of the comments made.

The UN are notoriously famous for their boundless red-tape bureaucracy. Laughingly, a friend of mine who worked for them stated that you must produce five pages of forms and two written explanations just to go the loo. Why submit just one concise document for anything when ten will do? (Just loved the sarcasm).

I, too, became involved in a situation with the UN that almost stopped our bakery programme in its tracks. Pulling in the same direction? Just not so sure.

Prior to the actual deployment of The Child-Focused INGO to Iraq, an agreement was struck between the UNWFP (UN World Food Programme) and The Child-Focused INGO (UK). The bones of the deal meant The Child-Focused INGO would build, equip and staff the bakery project in Nasiriyah and UNWFP would provide the vitamin-enriched flour that would be used to benefit the schools, hospitals and vulnerable groups at a time when there was much food insecurity.

My recollection is based on the meetings I had in Nasiriyah with the UNWFP, the documents I had received from the London office of The Child-Focused INGO and the verbal explanation of the process from Paul (who had flown out to join me to help with programme activity and to give much-needed assistance on the financial management of the programme. He promised that recruitment was going ahead to find more staff to join me, took direction from me, worked hard and then flew back to the UK). I thought it was a great plan and a much-needed intervention supported by all.

During the interim time, while the bakery was in its last throes of completion (and concurrently we had supplied children's satchels/ backpacks with books, pens, pencils and other much-needed items for the pending return to school... AND we had printed off enough exam papers for all the schools in Nasiriyah to take their exams which had been cancelled due to the war (Note: Nasiriyah was the first city in Iraq to be in a position to sit exams, and that was largely due to The Child-Focused INGO's education interventions providing not only the exam papers but equipment for schools and pupils too)), we had the local staff hired for the bakery, had them trained by the Lebanese engineer who came out with the equipment and now we were close to starting production.

All we needed was diesel fuel to power the ovens, and the flour delivery from the UNWFP. This is where my nightmare (or one of them) started.

I drove from the accommodation to the UNWFP office, which was housed in the local grain storage warehouse on the edge of town. I went into the office, which I had done several times before, to ask about delivery of the promised flour. The attitude changed from the very friendly, warm greeting I had previously received to a cold, almost unfriendly, 'Good morning.' I immediately thought that something was wrong, so instead of the polite preamble to business, I got straight to the point. I asked when the first batch of flour would arrive at the bakery? It was met with a long, drawn-out, rambling response which led to the issue that she had no paperwork to support any flour delivery agreement with The Child-Focused INGO. I offered my copies of the minutes of the Rome meeting and referred to conversations I'd had with her previously about this subject, with no problems ever having been voiced. After over half an hour of rambling explanations and denial of knowing about the agreement, I left her office to call London.

Talking to Paul, I could hear that he was as baffled as I was. He promised to get on to Rome and sort the problem out. We were days away from completion and had lots of interest from those we had assessed to be beneficiaries of our much-needed breads, who were waiting for us to begin production. We would be in the deep and smelly with the local population if we didn't deliver. The Child-Focused INGO's credibility would no doubt suffer if this went down the pan! I needed a plan 'B'.

When looking for regional support, I had made contact with a very important guy from the Kuwaiti charitable organisation. He was friendly and had offered to be of assistance if we ever needed it; the kind of comment we use often in our lives but seldom are we called upon to deliver. Now was the time to challenge his kind offer and see if he could indeed help.

I called the office of the Kuwaiti charitable organisation and spoke to my important guy (I was seriously hoping he really was important!) about arranging a meeting. It was agreed, and the following morning I was driving to the Kuwaiti/Iraqi border at Safwan.

We had a very pleasant meeting in his air-conditioned office, drank some tea and engaged in small talk until I reached a point that I thought it was correct to approach the matter at hand.

As soon as he asked how the programme in Nasiriyah was progressing, I told him of our 'flour' problem. We talked about the UNWFP and he spoke of programmes he had been involved in and some of the (totally unrelated) difficulties he had faced and triumphed over. I was beginning to think that while it was a good-natured meeting, it was going nowhere. Suddenly, he stood up and left the room. About five minutes later, he returned and beckoned for me to follow him. Showing me out, I thought.

He stopped outside a rather grandly carved doorway and said, "Before you leave, I would like you to meet the president of a Kuwaiti charitable organisation." Without any time for a response, he opened the door and in we went.

The president was a very elderly man, but was perfectly groomed and manicured. He spoke in Arabic and my host acted as an interpreter. Sitting at a very large desk in an immaculately clean and highly polished office, he began talking, catching my eye on occasion and smiling, but I had no idea what was being said. My interpreter was slow and ponderous in his translation, obviously taking care to be accurate (I think) but I must admit, I wondered if he was translating all that was being said.

After this bemusing and unprepared meeting, I left the president's office and was led to the doorway I had originally entered through. My host put out his hand to shake mine and as he did, he said that if I agreed that a delegation from the Kuwaiti charitable organisation could visit the bakery in the next few days, he would bring a sea container full of the flour we needed and a further three containers would follow as a donation.

Well fuck me! He was important after all. I agreed, and thanked him many times over.

Phone call to London:

"Hi, Paul. How did you get on with Rome?" I asked.

"They are stalling on any commitment, saying the deal was never formally agreed and they can't find any contract relating to it. I have an MOU (memorandum of understanding) but they say it's not enough and the protocol is—"

Blah, blah, blah... (as it sounded to me). I interrupted. "I have potentially secured several container loads of flour—"

"WHAT?" Paul said in a very surprised tone.

"I have got the promise of—" I started but didn't finish.

Paul interrupted. "How the fuck did you get that? Have UNWFP come good on the deal?"

"No!" I replied. "I have a contact in Kuwait, and he has agreed to give us what we need if he and his staff from the Kuwaiti charitable organisation can visit the bakery. It's a major donation. There will be some strings attached somewhere but at least all we have to do is get fuel now..."

"WHAT? You've got no fuel?" Paul exclaimed with the same level of surprise in his voice.

I explained, "Not yet. The council in Nasiriyah promised us enough fuel to run the bakery, but the fuel shortages and riots at the petrol stations and refineries have put the kybosh on that. But I think I have a plan. Call you tomorrow."

"Hey, you blue-Scouse bugger. Well done! Do what you need to get us producing. Talk tomorrow."

The surprise in Paul's voice had subsided, and he hung up.

On the Thuraya satellite phone, that conversation was the most expensive phone conversation I've ever had; $30 to say very little! (Note to self: cut the waffle!)

The drive from Safwan back to Nasiriyah was long and boring, interspersed with the high risk of being shot by the American soldiers escorting the military convoys going north. Our white vehicle had the Child-Focused INGO logo on it, and I always carried a small Union Jack flag to put in the windscreen to aid with the 'friendly' identification; more than once as a trigger-happy American machine gunner would 'cock' his weapon ready to fire, I had to stick my head out of the window and shout that I was English and working for a charity. Several close calls. The Americans, in particular, were nervous and suspicious of everything and everyone, much to the detriment of their own safety; they just pissed everyone off by being constantly in a war-fighting stance, being overly aggressive and shooting at anyone who looked at them in a funny way (whatever that was).

By contrast, in Basra, the British troops (including members of my old regiment) had come down from their war-fighting stance to begin to win the peace. Discarding the helmets for berets and carrying their weapons in a non-threatening manner (meaning not always pointing them at the general population) they were adopting the strategy of winning hearts and minds by engaging rather than alienating. Basra stayed peaceful much longer than the American-controlled areas of Iraq, due mainly to this strategy.

Being an INGO/NGO, fundamentally a charitable organisation, there is a very particular set of rules that you as an individual and as a collective within the organisation must adhere to, safeguard and demonstrate at all times.

The humanitarian imperative states the obligation to provide humanitarian assistance wherever it is needed in whatever form is required without disparity. The guiding principles are humanity, neutrality, impartiality and independence; add to that a transparency of your intent and actions.

These very noble guidelines can at times be very difficult to apply and uphold in a clearly understood way.

It is easy to become confused about their actual meanings, and sometimes that meaning can be lost in times of conflict and hardship. Trying to do the right thing by the many and not singling out the few, or the one, is a very difficult thing to do sometimes. But to fail could be the undoing of the individual or the collective in terms of both consequence and reputation. Get caught out on this, and it could mean expulsion from the country you are working in, or at worse, it could result in aggressive targeting of the organisation and its staff, often resulting in tragic, if not fatal, outcomes.

Sometimes rules get in the way. Let me tell you about Rasha Kamil.

*

Chapter 3:

The Story of Rasha

One of the early interventions I was involved in with The Child-Focused INGO in Iraq was the support to the orphanages within Nasiriyah. Three orphanages had been identified very early on after arriving in the city. The three orphanages were a boys' orphanage, a girls' orphanage and a babies' orphanage. All three were, of course, residential buildings where the children lived, played and were schooled. The buildings, all war damaged, needed repair, and much of the equipment had been looted. The pre-war staff had largely disappeared, and the new volunteers were doing their absolute best for the kids.

The Child-Focused INGO supplied support in terms of basic equipment for cooking, cleaning and beds. There was also some work to be done to repair the damage to the buildings that had been caused by fighting during the war.

Many of the children had lost both parents and several members of their extended families. Some were initially cared for by aunts and uncles, but as food and other supplies ran short, they were left either to fend for themselves on the streets or they were 'delivered' to the orphanages in the hope that they would be taken in. Some still had one parent alive, but due to their mental state after the war, they were unable to look after their children, so they were abandoned.

The age range of the children varied across the orphanages but the eldest I observed was about 16 years old. The youngest in the baby orphanage was measured in months. The total number of kids varied from day to day, but on average, there were about 25 to 30 per building, with the babies numbering roughly 15.

The most in-need orphanage was the girls'. It had the most occupants and the least equipment. Nonetheless, while visiting, the children always looked happy, full of smiles and were doing what kids the world over do: running around, being noisy and generally trying to have a good time.

During one visit I entered the girls' orphanage through the damaged wooden front door accompanied by Nasir, my ever-present interpreter friend and adviser. We went into the manageress's office and were met by a woman who was very pleasant, polite and caring. At a guess, she must have been in her early thirties, but she looked as if she was in her late fifties; such was the stress and strain of her job, looking after all the kids in her care. She oversaw all three orphanages with a small team of female helpers that endlessly rushed around making sure everyone was accounted for and that they were safe.

Today I noticed (for the first time) a young girl, roughly about 13 years of age, sitting alone at the far end of the corridor. She was dressed in a long flowery skirt that reached the floor, a cream-coloured blouse and a faded pink knitted cardigan buttoned fully to the top. Her head was covered in a scarf.

Over her right eye, she had a large gauze padding covering most of her cheek. She sat alone and looked very sad. I had a daughter at home roughly the same age as this girl, and while I was talking with Nasir and the manageress, I was constantly breaking off and glancing over at her, trying to figure out why she was alone when everyone else was playing, shouting and generally being... kids.

I stopped the conversation as my curiosity got the better of me.

"Nasir, please ask what is wrong with that girl sitting over there," I said, pointing along the corridor at the lonely figure.

Nasir asked the question, and immediately the manageress's face changed, her shoulders slumped and her eyes filled with tears. I could see immediately that she was fighting the urge to cry… but she did.

She then shouted loudly, so as to be heard above the other children, and beckoned the lonely girl to come to her.

The girl stood and walked down the narrow, yellow-painted corridor slowly, in stark contrast to the running children pushing past her as she came.

As she got near, the manageress opened her arms and gave her a loving hug as she gently held her scarf-covered head in her hands. She held her very close but not too tightly. A tear slipped out of her eye and rolled down her face. She quickly wiped it away and spoke softly. I asked Nasir what she had said. He replied, "Sorry."

Nasir and the manageress began a conversation. Usually I would stop Nasir if it went on too long and ask him to translate, but this time I sensed that would be inappropriate, so I just let the conversation between the two continue, while I tried hard to catch the odd word and make guesses based on body language.

The conversation stopped, and the manageress gently took the girl's face in her hands and removed the gauze covering her eye and almost half her face. It revealed a grossly misshapen eye socket, with the eyeball almost totally exposed. There was a large lump close to the eye socket, but it was mainly just below her eye on her cheek. It appeared to be this lump which was causing the distortion of her eye socket. She gently replaced the gauze and spoke softly to the girl before lifting her arm and pushing back the sleeve to expose her forearm. This, too, had large lumps under the skin; four that I could see. She then gently pulled the girl to her again, and with her back to Nasir and me, she lifted the girl's blouse and cardigan from the elasticated waistband of her skirt to expose two large lumps nestled right up against the young girl's spine, which appeared to be pulled out of shape and was badly distorted. One lump was roughly the size of a tennis ball and the other was almost twice the size and was elongated, following the contour of her spine.

I was dumbstruck. I had a lump in my throat that prevented me for a minute or two from speaking, and my eyes became bleary as my tear ducts sprang into action. I turned my face away from our little congregation and composed myself.

Questions. So many questions were running through my mind I knew that neither the organisation nor I had a medical mandate. We had no health programme, and could do very little for this girl; all we could do was make the orphanage as nice and comfortable as possible. I felt low. Very low.

I looked at the girl, who was now holding hands with the manageress and looking at the ground.

I turned to Nasir and told him to interpret exactly everything I was about to say, without addition or exclusion. I crouched down so my head was at the same height as the girl's. I quietly said, "Hello." She looked up and her expressionless face looked at mine. "What's your name?" I asked, and Nasir interpreted.

"Rasha," she quietly responded.

"Very nice to meet you, Rasha," I continued, allowing a smile to cross my face. I asked her if she knew who we were and what we were doing for the orphanage. She spoke very quietly, but as Nasir translated, she said that she did know that we had come to help the manageress fix the orphanage for the children. "That's right," I responded. "To make it nice for you and all the other children."

I was suffering badly; I was holding back what could have turned out to be a flood of emotion. I smiled again, and stood up to address Nasir and the manageress. As I went to speak, Nasir, taking my arm and looking me in the face, said quietly, "Not now." He told me we must leave. He spoke to the manageress and said his farewells for both of us, and he led me out into the courtyard, through the metal gates and to our vehicle.

Once in the car, we started off back to the office. I told Nasir to tell me everything that had been said during his conversation with the manageress.

It appears that Rasha was driven to the orphanage by her uncle. Her father, who was badly injured in the war, had died from complications related to his injuries. Rasha's mother was killed in a bombing raid during the war.

Three years before, lumps had started appearing on Rasha's body. Her parents were poor, and couldn't afford much in the way of treatment. Remember there had been UN sanctions on Iraq following the first Gulf War, and the hospitals were grossly understocked with almost everything, including basic medications. When the second Gulf War started, the hospitals were ransacked for what little they had left. Rasha had been left undiagnosed and untreated since the very first painful lumps appeared. It was this that forced her uncle to drive her to the orphanage, telling the manageress she was dying anyway.

"Nasir!"

"What?"

"Stop the car. Stop now!"

That was the start of an intervention I undertook; one I should not have done, as I had no mandate to do so. But it was one

I undertook anyway, accepting any and all consequences that could follow. I would do exactly the same thing again.

So, here's what happened next...

It took maybe ten minutes to convince Nasir that I had a plan, and I could make it work if he agreed to help and, more importantly, if he kept quiet about what was going to happen. He agreed.

We turned the vehicle around and headed back to speak with the manageress again.

She was surprised to see us as she rose from behind her paperwork-strewn desk to politely greet us for the second time.

I gave Nasir very strict instructions on how he was to interpret my conversation. Usually, I would allow Nasir to add more to my communication, to account for cultural correctness, to ensure we were always on favourable terms and to make sure that the correct greetings and explanations of who I was, etc. were used. This time, I just needed accuracy and clarity; culture on hold, just for the moment.

The conversation began by asking if the manageress had any medical records at all, even a doctor's note, for Rasha. I also asked if she'd had any recent treatments or seen a doctor in the last two months.

The answers were as direct as my questions. She replied by telling me that Rasha's uncle had left some medical documents, but they were too complicated for her to understand. She continued by telling me that an American army doctor was dropping in every other day to change the dressing on Rasha's eye. She needed the dressing as she couldn't close her eye, and without it, she couldn't sleep.

I asked Nasir to tell the manageress to sit down and listen very carefully to what I was about to say. I took a deep breath and told her that while I couldn't make any promises or guarantee any success at any stage, I was going to explore the possibility of finding some help for Rasha; at least to get her diagnosed properly. It seemed that the manageress was under the impression that Rasha had six months or less to live; that was what the uncle had stated when he'd dropped her off. If that was true, then at a rough guess (as dates were not recorded), she had only four of those months left.

I asked if Rasha had been told that she might have a terminal illness. Sadly, she said she had been in the room when her uncle clearly laid bare her condition to the manageress, and told of Rasha's expected life span. She knew, but didn't quite know what it was that was possibly killing her.

That lump reappeared in my throat again. I forcefully swallowed it down and continued. I told her not mention to Rasha or to anyone else what I had said. This must be kept quiet, so we don't raise any undue or unrealistic expectations. I was now, in my head, planning steps two, three and four without yet knowing how I would make it all happen.

I promised I would return in two days to let her know what we would do next. She wept; she wept without control. She came around to the front of her desk, took my hand and thanked me over and over again.

I told Nasir to reaffirm that I might not be able to do anything so not to expect a miracle. He told her, and she said, "Insha'Allah," a phrase I had already learnt, meaning God willing. And she was right; I thought that might just be the level of intervention I needed.

Through the various meetings I had attended in Nasiriyah, Basra and Baghdad, I had made quite a few useful connections with people who can 'get things done'. In Basra, I'd met with a British army colonel from the Royal Army Medical Corps, an experienced guy who, for a Rupert (Oops! Sorry! It's been a while. I meant officer... Jargon again), was a really down-to-earth, practical type of guy. We'd spoken at length about our individual situations and what we thought would be the long-term issues for Iraq plus a load of other small-talk stuff. I had his satellite phone number, so he was going to be my first point of contact. Several times over a period of about an hour and a half, I got no answer, but then it clicked, and he answered. I reacquainted myself. Luckily, he remembered me. I gave him the scenario...

"Okay, it's like this," I began (white lie number one coming up). "I, on behalf of my organisation, was trying to link some of the major hospitals in Iraq together. Using a young girl with unknown tumours on her body as a test case, I would like to see what is available throughout the country, and see if a referral scheme can be initiated. If it is successful, (Shit! I was convincing myself that this was actually a brilliant idea), we could lessen the burden on smaller local hospitals by referring patients elsewhere to receive the care and support they deserve."

I was in full creative-waffling-bullshit mode now and was rather convincing but it did have its dark side in that, for starters, I could be found out at any time. I could also create a very high expectation for many people, most of all Rasha, and do reputational damage to my future employability. Stakes were, indeed, extremely high but the life and well-being of one little girl was, in my opinion, worth it. Some may see it differently; some will strongly disagree. Even now, some of you reading this book will be shocked and quietly call me a few bad names. At that time, and during the moments of white lie telling (and some were not so white; rather they were clearly big, dark whoppers!), I had one clear mission (yep, more military jargon... get over it. I am starting to): if not to save Rasha's life by useful intervention, then to make her final time as comfortable and as happy as possible. That was my drive.

Still on the phone, I was told by the colonel that a new commander medical (commander med for short) had just arrived in Basra, and that he (the colonel) would approach him with the idea, as he had been, in the distant past, under his command in a field hospital unit. He would also talk to the local Iraqi doctors and gauge their response to the idea. Bingo! Some movement in the right direction.

Later that day, I took a call from 'Commander Med' himself. (Big surprise!) He told me he would agree in principle to support the 'referral' idea, and had spoken to a doctor who had just arrived in the country from Lebanon. This doctor was a cancer specialist. (I thought he refrained from using the word 'oncologist' just in case I had no clue as to what it was. I did know. I had a younger brother who'd had a brain tumour which sadly took his life a few years later). The commander med said to me, "You have an appointment with him tomorrow at 1400 hours. His time is extremely precious. He has a lot to do. He will have two local Iraqi specialists with him, and that is the best I can do for you I am afraid. Best of luck." With that, he hung up.

The phrase 'be careful what you wish for' was ringing inside my head. "Wow! Things are happening fast," I thought. "I need to get organised; need to do that now!" Nasir was getting ready to go home when I stopped him, told him of the plan and asked him to take me to the orphanage straight away.

Nasir smiled, agreed and got in the car with me. It was just starting to get dark, so I needed to be quick and extra vigilant. Attacks on coalition forces and Iraqi police were escalating all over the country but I still felt the support of the local population was with us; for now anyway.

We arrived at the metal gates to the orphanage and let ourselves into the compound. The manageress, having heard the clunk of the gates and seen the vehicle headlights, had come to the door.

Nasir and I walked over to her, and Nasir told her the details of what was needed to be done.

The manageress told us it was impossible and that Rasha could not go. She said it would not be possible.

WHAT? NO! I was gutted. My plan to help this little girl had fallen at the second hurdle. I was devastated. I was probably too engrossed in the plan falling apart before it really got started, to think clearly. On the other hand, Nasir was already taking action and was discussing something with the manageress. Suddenly, Nasir smiled and told me it was possible. He said that we should arrive at seven the next morning to collect Rasha and her chaperone. Nasir saved the day, and not for the first or last time.

On the drive back, Nasir had told me that the reason it was impossible was only because the manageress had wanted to accompany Rasha, but due to other issues in the orphanage, the timing wasn't right; so no chaperone, no visit. Nasir had pursued the conversation, asking if there was anyone else who could accompany Rasha so this precious opportunity would not be wasted. It turned out that one of the workers in the orphanage was a young lady who was vaguely related to Rasha, and Rasha trusted her. The manageress, in a light-bulb moment, had agreed that this could now happen and she'd said that she would arrange for this lady to be ready to go in the morning.

Phase one: getting established. Done. Phase two: the preparation for the first medical consultation. Underway. YES!

Just before Nasir collected his bag ready to go home (again), I asked him if we could take a few minutes to catch up on all events that we needed to cover for the entire programme. We discussed the educational interventions; the school bags filled, and the many that still needed filling for the next round of distributions; and the new proposals for safe play areas and a drop-in centre for children who wanted to talk and have some support of a psychosocial nature, and the recruitment to staff it. Now the bakery... OH SHIT! THE BAKERY! We still needed fuel, and we had to arrange a visit too. Bollocks!

The bakery was to be the priority on return from Basra. I had calls to make during the journey down, so as Nasir had been volunteered to drive, it gave me valuable planning time to get back on track. If I failed with the bakery, I would for sure be wearing my bollocks as earrings. My second career would be over before it started.

Sleeping that night was difficult. I wanted to keep working, but those who I needed to contact would already be loudly snoring and would not be very receptive to any favours I might need. I made notes, and eventually fell asleep.

I woke at 5am, grabbed a cup of tea, took a shower, trying hard to catch every slow drip as it came out of the showerhead. (Plumbing here was awful. With no water pressure, and sometimes no water, flushing the loo was an experience to be quickly forgotten too.)

As I emerged into the courtyard with my notebook and radios in hand, I was hit by very bright sunlight and greeted by a smiling Nasir. He had been there for about 15 minutes. He'd ensured that the four-by-four was fuelled up from our stock of reserve fuel, and was testing the Codan, vehicle-fit HF radio set, conducting radio checks with other INGOs and the UN radio room. All was 'five by five', so we were tickety-boo and ready to go.

We arrived early at the orphanage, but the manageress, Rasha and her chaperone were already waiting. After a brief conversation, we set off.

I told Nasir to tell our precious passengers to relax and maybe get some sleep, as it was likely to be an awfully long day. This day was noted as being special; it was the first time I saw Rasha smile.

I had lots to do on the journey down to Basra. Most important was fuel. I needed at least 20,000 litres of diesel to fill the empty tank (which had been taken off a road tanker, adapted and cleaned, and hoisted onto a high metal frame on the external wall of the bakery ready to supply the fuel for the ovens).

I had not wasted my early days in Iraq, and I had met a US soldier at Camp Whitehorse who seemed to be a real wheeler and dealer. He was a New Yorker, and his attitude was: 'nothing in the world is worth worrying over. You're born to die, and everything in-between is a bonus.' He was in a logistics role, and even in the early days, he would offer me stuff that I had no real use for. But he was always willing to help if he could. As I spoke to him regularly, or rather he to me, I thought he would be the best person to start the fuel acquisition trail with.

Dealing with the military. Any military in any country can and often was misconstrued as collaboration which could be seen as an indicator that your neutrality and transparency was not as it should be. Military forces are by design representative of governments, so working with them openly could lead to a false perception that you aligned with that particular government's policies, etc. Today, it is much more accepted but the line is still very vague and it can easily be misinterpreted, which may cause an added threat and risk to you as an individual or to your organisation. You can very quickly become a soft target; easy to locate and to hit. Sad but true, as the next few months and years would show in the extreme.

I spoke to my contact. He was enthusiastic and willing to help. After hearing my request for such a large amount of fuel, which I thought he could contribute a bit towards, he said, "Sure, not a problem. I can get a tanker to deliver it to you today."

In my head, I screamed, "NO! NO! NO!" but I calmly told him I wouldn't be there today and asked if he could do it late that night or very early the next morning when it was still dark. He agreed, as if it was as easy as giving me a cup of coffee. He told me to just let him know when and where and he would get it done. Was this going to be that easy? I had very limited options, so I guessed we should go with the plan in the hope that it wouldn't fail. If it did, then we would have to find an alternative, which would involve sweet-talking the local governing council in Nasiriyah again. All we could do was wait and see.

I had been getting messages from several sources that the attacks across Iraq were increasing. Convoys were being attacked in hit-and-run battles and VBIEDs were being used. (Oh sorry! I stopped apologising for jargon earlier on but this needs explanation. Vehicle Borne Improvised Explosive Devices; car and truck bombs in short. Caught up? Okay, let's continue.)

Basra and other areas in the south, apart from a few isolated incidents, were still relatively calm, and the 'hearts and minds' strategy was still holding. For how long was an unknown, but for now it was good, or at least much better than elsewhere in the country.

I also had an idea to stop off at the port in Um Qasr. Almost everything that was coming to Iraq post-conflict was coming into Um Qasr port, as it was the only deep-water, functioning port where container ships could dock. The port security was at this time being run by the British Royal Marines and an army logistics group. Again, making good contacts here early on was now hopefully going to be fruitful. But first I had to get Rasha to the hospital.

There had been a spate of individually targeted attacks recently in Basra, aimed directly at doctors and health workers. The ideology was that militia groups were kidnapping doctors and surgeons etc. to treat their own fighters, as they were taking a beating all over the country and had little in the way of medical support; so what else could they do other than kidnap what they needed?

Some of the kidnap attempts were quite sophisticated. They would watch hospitals for days, sometimes weeks, to identify their target and to establish their arrival and departure patterns, then follow them to see where they were accommodated. They would then choose a time and location within that pattern when the victim was most vulnerable.

Others were less sophisticated and very random. If you were obviously not an Iraqi national, for instance an English, American, French or other European, or due to dress and skin colour represented such, you would be taken without any verification. If you turned out to be someone who was of no use to them, you would be killed and they would repeat the process until they got lucky.

This led to doctors, etc. spending as little time in the hospital as possible, and setting up office in what was becoming heavily guarded hotels and guest houses. As we drew close to the city limit, I called the number of the contact I had for our appointment in order to give our ETA (estimated time of arrival).

At this point, I was told not to go to the hospital as previously arranged, but to go to a hotel. The details were given, and I agreed. Phone down.

I was not totally convinced that this was the right thing to do. So many collaborators with the militias were working in key locations, and with the kidnap situation being an extremely high and realistic threat, I decided caution was best.

I got Nasir to stop a few streets away from the hotel. I told him to keep the engine running and to stay on the hand-held VHF Motorola radio handset, and I would call him when I needed. I got out of the vehicle. The roads were quiet; not many people were about but a few kids were running around. It was an ordinary scene. I walked the short distance to the hotel then stopped and observed. There were no parked cars and no malingering people and it didn't appear that we where being watched. I waited five minutes, then walked to the entrance. A very smart suited doorman smiled at me and opened the door. I went inside. It appeared normal, like any mid-sized hotel I had ever been in anywhere in the world.

The guy at reception smiled and politely asked if he could help. I told him I was there to meet with someone at 2pm. He smiled and confirmed I was to be meeting my Lebanese doctor and his associates. He directed me to a table and told me to wait.

I asked about car parking, and was told that the car park was to the rear of the building and that it was safe and guarded. I radioed Nasir, told him to park up and to come inside. I spoke to reception, informed him that Nasir plus two would be joining me and asked him to prepare some tea or coffee and some light food for them. With a huge smile, he said, "Of course, sir," and called over a waiter.

While I was talking and from the moment I stood outside the hotel, I was observing routes in, routes out, traffic flow, escape routes, locations to run or drive to... My mind was constantly going through the 'what if?' scenarios. I couldn't let anything happen to Rasha; nothing at all.

Inside the hotel, I was looking for the emergency exits, stairways and fire doors, and how they appeared to be secured or locked. I noticed at least two, what appeared to be Iraqi private security guys at opposite ends of the foyer, both trying unsuccessfully to hide their AK-47s (assault rifles of 7.62mm short round ammunition) from view. They both seemed quite disinterested, and I am sure one of them was nodding off in his chair.

While I stood waiting for the doctors to arrive, I called Nasir over and relayed my emergency plans A, B and C to him, pointing out discreetly the exit points, guards and obviously locked doors, and places to take cover if any shooting started. I thought that being accidently shot by the two guards was probably more likely, but I kept that to myself. Nasir was smart, a quick- and forward-thinking guy. I had trusted in him totally in Nasiriyah, his home turf. Here in Basra, I sensed his anxiety, but I knew that whatever happened, within his capacity, he had my back. It was just reassessing his capacity in this new situation and strange location that gave me a little cause for concern, but it proved misplaced.

A group of three men emerged from a corridor that led to the hotel rooms. Two were Iraqi and one, who looked Italian in appearance but was Lebanese, went over to reception and spoke to the guy behind the counter, who then directed them over to me.

I introduced myself, listened carefully to the names of the three as they introduced themselves and I directed all to a table in the corner of the café, just off the main reception. Old habits die hard, so I had positioned my seat in the corner with a solid wall on two sides of me, allowing the best position for protection and observation. I had pre-placed my notebook on the table to reserve my preferred seat. I left Rasha, her chaperone and Nasir where they were for the moment and I engaged the three in my proposed plan, gave some explanation of Rasha's condition and the history of her story as I knew it.

I spoke about the idea of hospital referral mechanisms and the issues I was hoping to establish with this 'test case'. I kept it simple and allowed just enough detail to keep all interested, but not so much as to overstretch the case, potentially causing me to become lost in questions I had no hope of successfully navigating. After much nodding of heads, the Lebanese doctor took over the conversation with a smile. He asked if he could see Rasha.

I called Nasir to bring her and her chaperone over. The doctor smiled at Rasha, and in Arabic, he asked her how she was feeling and if she knew why she was here. The gist of the conversation that followed was the doctor talking to and relaxing Rasha, and asking relevant questions relating to her condition. Rasha answered clearly but very softly.

The doctors said that they needed to examine her and look at the tumours. (This was the first time I had heard them referred to as this, although sadly, it was what I already knew them to be.)

We moved from the café, down a corridor and into a room. It looked like any other hotel room until we walked past the bathroom and into what would have been the bedroom. The bed was gone, replaced by an examination table, several chairs, two desks and piles of books and paperwork. It was clean but a little worse for wear. There was some peeling paint and some scuff marks here and there, but it served its purpose well.

The Lebanese doctor took the lead, with the other two looking on and listening intently to what was being said. The entire examination was done in Arabic. A couple of questions from the Iraqi doctors as they examined Rasha were put to the Lebanese Doctor. Sometimes his face would show his disagreement and other times he appeared to concur with what was being said.

Eventually, Rasha, who remained calm and almost unfazed by what was happening, was told to rearrange her clothing and wait back in reception with her chaperone, where Nasir would meet them both. I remained with the doctors, and once the door closed after Rasha left, I asked a simple question: "What can be done, and is the previous prediction regarding Rasha's lifespan realistic or not?"

One of the Iraqi doctors smiled and looked at me and said, "Her lifespan estimate is not correct. I would suggest a year or more, depending on treatment." His Iraqi counterpart reluctantly agreed, although I sensed he would have answered differently if he had spoken first. The Lebanese doctor, with his huge, almost ever-present smile, looked at me and told me his father had had similar, if not the same, symptoms and similar tumours. None had been quite as pronounced as the two on Rasha's back, but after being diagnosed, his father had lived for another 15 years. The caveat was getting the right treatment at the right time.

In my mind, I was confused as to whether I was going to get good or bad news as final closure on the examination process. In my head I was shouting, "CAN YOU SAVE HER OR NOT?" but outwardly, I was fighting to stay composed.

The Lebanese doctor, after a quick and quite aggressive (or so it seemed) conversation with his two Iraqi colleagues, told me that Rasha would need to stay at the hospital for at least two days, maybe more, for further and more detailed tests. But there was hope. How much, I didn't know. But some was better than none, wasn't it? (Question to myself, with no answer.)

We walked back to the café, where Nasir was enjoying a tea, Rasha an orange juice and her chaperone was drinking what looked like riverbank mud. It was coffee: thick, black and very sweet.

I sat close to Rasha, and the Lebanese doctor explained to her that she was going to stay in the hospital for a short while so they could figure out the best way to help her. I expected Rasha to be horrified, and possibly to refuse, but it was just the opposite. She smiled, wider than I had previously seen, then nodded her head in agreement, turned to me and very quietly said, "*Shukraan Lakum.*"

"You are most welcome," I replied with a smile, until I looked at Nasir who with his eyes and shoulder movement was telling me to use my (very) limited Arabic. So, I looked back at Rasha, and in my best formal Arabic I said, "*Ant murhab bik.*"

Rasha looked at me and let out a little giggle. She must have been thinking how awful it was to be a Scouse Arab. The accent was truly terrible; well mine was. It was at that moment that Rasha really stole my heart and I was more determined than ever to make her life better, regardless. (But I *did* wonder if it would bite me on the arse at some point!)

This great opportunity now presented me with another problem. I couldn't stay in Basra. Not for long anyway; overnight at most. But at the same time, I couldn't leave Rasha here alone. What about her chaperone?

After a quick conflab (jargon: a conversation, quick and to the point) with Nasir, a solution was reached. I spoke to the doctors and asked them that if Rasha was to stay, could her chaperone stay with her? The answer was yes; it became apparent that this was normal for someone of her age. I took out my wallet and gave the chaperone $40 for food and any other expenses they may have, and promised I would return to collect them both as soon as the tests were done.

Nasir had already called the manageress at the orphanage and told her of the situation. Nasir said that she cried again and sent a thousand thank yous to me and the doctors.

We took Rasha and her chaperone to the hospital, and found the ward she was to be on. It was dim even though sun still shone brightly outside. Net curtains hung across two of the three windows, looking like a good wash was in order, and the metal bed frames had thin mattresses (no sheets, no blankets and one pillow that had seen far better days, and God knows how many heads had rested on it). But this was immediate post-war Iraq after years of UN sanctions and a collective ransacking during the war. We should be thankful the hospital existed at all. We got her settled in and ensured her chaperone had our telephone numbers (I left her with my personal mobile phone).

I got Nasir to talk to one of the nurses to ensure that both Rasha and her chaperone were looked after and got anything they needed; we would sort out any further payment on return. Nasir disappeared and returned moments later with two blankets. He explained the situation to Rasha and the nurses. Nods and smiles were given and received, we said our goodbyes and we left.

Walking back to our vehicle, I thought of how vulnerable and delicate Rasha was, but she seemed to have the heart of a lion. Here she was, having never been outside of Nasiriyah, being possibly terminally ill, in a strange city and being left for a few days, facing tests that may be uncomfortable, but she smiled.

Now that was done, I had a few errands to run. Firstly, to Um Qasr port. I arrived at the port entrance wanting to just see, if possible, what was being stored and what was being unloaded; maybe to even talk to a few Brits and get some information that could prove useful for the future.

I spoke to a young marine at the gate of one of the warehouses and asked what was going on. Typically a squaddie! (At this point, a marine and any other young soldier guarding a building are all the same: bored out of their minds, and hot and sweaty, but alert to the possible threat and the likely direction it could come from. He was pleased to be engaged in conversation with someone relatable yet not in his command structure, so he could 'constructively whinge like a good'n'.)

It turned out that his location was almost full of flour. It had been unloaded a few days before and had not moved at all. He was told that the warehouse would be emptied for distribution almost as soon as it was unloaded. "Looks like it will be a few days more before it goes anywhere," he said. "We have been told we have to remain at post until it's gone... Doesn't appear to be any time soon," he finished.

Interspersed with the desert-camouflaged uniforms, and some still in the green 'camo', were civilians with UN ID cards on blue lanyards placed around their necks; some appeared to be checking and accounting for quantities of items on the dockside, while others just seemed to be talking casually, holding clipboards and notebooks, but doing diddly-squat (Yep, jargon, meaning nothing) with them.

I thought that if I had a truck, I would blag my way in and take a load of this back to Nasiriyah myself.

As that thought entered my head, a guy came over to me and asked who I was and what I wanted.

I showed him my ID and said I was looking for a consignment of vitamin-enriched flour from the UNWFP for distribution to Nasiriyah.

Without even looking at his important clipboard, he told me none of the flour had been allocated for distribution yet, so he couldn't help. I asked him if my organisation was on his list. He said, "Sorry, I can't help." He then turned around and walked away.

I was fuming! What a 'jobsworth' he was. Some minor pen-pusher with a bit of self-imposed authority, looking down his nose at me; a mere rep from an INGO. UN Twat!

I got in the vehicle with Nasir, and we set off to find the Shatt al Arab Hotel, a location where members of my old regiment had been located since the war ended.

I got to the gate manned by a young soldier.

"Hey, son," I began. "Your RSM still on camp?"

Taken by surprise that a civilian was talking to him in a military manner threw him slightly,

"Yes, sir. He is," he responded.

"Where do I park and book in?" I asked, remaining authoritarian in my tone.

He pointed me towards the large car park and to the guard room, where I would need to book in. I winked and drove off.

As I parked up, I saw an old friend of mine. He hadn't seen me yet, so I came up on his blind side, and in my best military voice, I called him a 'useless excuse of a hairy-arsed soldier'. He spun around, almost looking for a fight. He looked at me, wearing a t-shirt, dusty jeans and longer-than-usual hair, with a good suntan too. Looking at me, he did a double take, then smiled and called me many unprintable names... "Scouse, you old bugger. What are doing here?" he finally spluttered.

It was understandably the last place anyone would expect to see me, so it was good to regale them with stories of life after discharge and what was waiting for them after they finished up playing soldiers. Lots of laughing was done. We were invited to lunch in the mess. Nasir was dumbstruck; he had never experienced this type of brotherhood and companionship, slagging each other off and calling each other some very bad names but at the same time smiling and loving every minute of it. He was baffled by it all, but confessed to enjoying the moment.

It was here I tapped into some real-time intelligence and analysis. Having been a unit intelligence officer, I understood in detail the process of information analysis for intelligence. I spoke a while on what the prospects were likely to be in the near future; none of the assessments sounded good. But it was good to reacquaint with old friends in such a strange, unexpected and broken environment. But after some great storytelling on both sides, I had to leave.

It was getting late. It would be dark in a couple of hours, so we had to decide: head back and arrive in the dark, late in Nasiriyah, or stay over and set off early in the morning.

I had written the security protocols, so I knew full well that travelling anywhere after dark was prohibited. Just because I was the acting country director, safety and security manager and everything else didn't mean I could change the rules. They were written for a very good reason and for that, I would have to abide by them, so back into town we went. We found the hotel we visited earlier, and luckily there were two rooms available. A chance for a good shower, a much-needed dump and some food. Bliss!

After an early breakfast of bread, cheese and coffee, Nasir and I made the decision to depart and head back to Nasiriyah.

The journey is very boring: two- and three-lane motorway for the most. The scenery remains largely unchanged and is a dull light brown desert with few trees and very little in the way of habitat. Lots of burnt out vehicles, some military and some not, still littered the laybys along the route.

Hijacking was becoming more commonplace along the route: usually waiting for the large coalition military convoys to pass, then hitting any following vehicles. It is usually four-by-four type pick-ups that they take and convert into mobile, heavy machine-gun platforms. Our twin-cab Toyota was just the type they would like!

As luck would have it, we joined the main highway travelling north, just as a military convoy lazily pulled onto the road ahead of us. The downside of following one of these convoys is twofold: if the convoy is attacked, as they often were, you get caught up in the crossfire, and sometimes the soldiers, particularly the Americans, tend to shoot at anything that moves, and that could include us!

Secondly, they were painfully slow and could contain many vehicles; they didn't like vehicles like mine overtaking.

Our vehicle was white and had a logo in English on the bonnet and on each of the doors. We also had put one on the roof for identification from the air. I also had my little Union Jack clearly on display on the windscreen. We were easily identifiable, or so I thought.

Having spent nearly an hour on the empty highway about 200 metres behind the convoy's rear vehicle (which was a Humvee with a machine gun mounted in a turret on the top doing a maximum of 40 miles an hour), I became impatient, due to the time this was adding to our journey on this monotonous road. I told Nasir to close the distance between us and the rear vehicle, but to do it slowly and gradually. Nasir expressed his anxiety at doing this, but I assured him it would be okay.

As we closed, I could see the soldier on the machine gun focusing on us. His machine gun was now pointing at us, but he wasn't aiming, just observing. I took my Union Jack and held it out of the window so there was no mistake identifying it. I gave a wave and a 'thumbs-up' to him, waiting hopefully for him to acknowledge and return the gesture. Luckily, and much to Nasir's obvious relief, he did. I asked Nasir to get closer, and with a nervous glance, he did.

"That's close enough," I told him. I put my head out of the window to shout a message to the gunner. "Hey, mate!" I shouted as a test to see if we were in earshot. He waved again. I urged Nasir to get a little closer and called out, "Mate, are you in radio contact with your convoy leader?"

He nodded and gave a thumbs-up.

"Can you get his permission for us to pass the convoy, as we need to get to Nasiriyah, Camp Whitehorse, quickly?"

I used the 'Camp Whitehorse' as a reference I hoped he would know; therefore, giving us a little authentication and credibility, in the hope it would clear us to pass. We had no intention of going to Camp Whitehorse at all.

He gave a thumbs-up and then an open hand signal to stay where we were.

After about 10 minutes, he waved at us to come closer, which we did. He shouted to us from behind the armoured turret that we could pass at a speed of a 100km/h (about 60mph) and that we should pass on the outside of the convoy only.

I shouted my thanks and gave a confirmatory thumbs-up, instructed Nasir to move on and passed safely.

I had previously seen convoys blocking the road to stop vehicles overtaking (therefore, stopping any potential attacker from breaking into the convoy), so we steadily made our way up alongside them and passed without further incident. I waved and gave a thumbs-up to any soldier that caught my eye and held a weapon; not because I wanted to be their friend, but to hopefully keep them calm and firmly enforce the fact that we were not a threat. A smile and a wave works wonders on many levels. Good old 'hearts and minds.' A 'blue on blue' (Yep, jargon time again! Means friendly fire. Shooting at someone who is friendly by mistake... Should be called 'unfriendly' fire, I suppose!) would really ruin my day.

Once we had passed the lead vehicle, I told Nasir to put his foot down and get us back. The road ahead was clear, and visibility was almost as far as you could see on both sides of the highway, so we tore off like a race car... only slower!

I made a few phone calls on the way back into Nasiriyah to make sure there were no active incidents that we may have run into as we returned and just to get a general 'sit-rep' (abbreviation for situation report and a widely used term when asking, usually over a radio, for information (for example, "Send sit-rep, over."). A full up-to-date situation report would then be transmitted to you. This jargon also became 'telephone talk', and even in general conversation it was normal to ask, "What's the sit-rep on... ?")

The news wasn't good. It appeared that the fuel shortage was getting worse and there had been several shootings at petrol stations and large crowds gathering at the local council offices, which was also the place most meetings were held for coordination with INGOs and others.

Having asked for safe-route information, it turned out that, as we were accommodated on the edge of town, we didn't need to go through it to get 'home'. "Might leave going to the office for a few hours so I can assess the situation myself," I thought.

There was also an attack on the American coalition forces in town. Grenades were thrown and there was sporadic automatic gunfire. I didn't know of any casualties at this point, but it was obvious that things were starting to heat up. INGOs, on the other hand, were still reporting that the local population were waving and engaging with them and being friendly and helpful. While this was a particularly good sign, I did wonder how long it would, or could, last.

With the fuel issue being top of my agenda, I now had to really consider how to have it delivered. With anti-military feelings running high, the last thing I needed was to have a military convoy turn up at our bakery. The fuel tanker (a military vehicle) would no doubt be escorted by two or three armoured Humvee vehicles with machine gun turrets, and that just would not look good at all.

We had to be incredibly careful about local perception of our intent and affiliations. We had to be seen as totally independent;

having a load of soldiers milling around our project would not sit well and could (wrongly) put us in a dangerous position where we could be targeted. I needed a new plan.

On arriving back at our compound, our locally hired guard opened the heavy metal gate for us and gave us a huge smile and a wave as we drove into the open courtyard. We switched off, emptied the vehicle of the rubbish we had built up on the journey, fuelled it up fully again, turned it to face the gates and put the keys in the hiding place within the car, that only Nasir and I would know. We would change the hiding place after every trip, just to be sure.

I sat with Nasir for a few hours, trying to work out a plan to safely get the fuel to the bakery. I had an idea in my head, but I didn't think it was achievable as we needed external resources to do it. We had almost exhausted our thought processes and had not found a safe way to get the fuel in. We were resigned to use the cover of darkness to get the Military to deliver and leave as quickly as possible. But that was not any guarantee that we wouldn't be observed doing this. There were always eyes watching.

Exasperated, I said to Nasir, "If only we had a spare tanker."

I said this not really expecting any response, as you never just have a spare fuel tanker vehicle sitting around, let alone an empty and working one.

"My uncle has a tanker. It's at his house." Nasir said this as if it was the most natural and obvious thing to say.

"What?" I was shocked, surprised and almost lost for words.

"Yes. Let me call him. I am sure it will be okay."

I smiled and leaned back in my chair, just totally amazed that something I'd thought was going to be almost impossible was actually going to happen. Nasir turned up trumps, again.

We talked with Nasir's uncle, and I outlined my plan and stressed the risk that we would be taking and the risk his uncle would need to accept if he was going to help. His caveat was that only *he* was to drive his tanker. Everything was agreed. I called my New Yorker contact at Camp Whitehorse and told him of our plan. He agreed, and we set a time and location to meet up.

We couldn't drive our tanker to the camp and we couldn't let the military deliver to our bakery, so on a quiet road in the desert, just outside of the city, we would meet, cross-deck the fuel from the military tanker into our tanker, then return from whence we came. A decent enough plan; it had its risks but was the best we could do in the situation. We had to ensure our bakery could produce, as many people, mainly children, were relying on it.

The plan was simple: Nasir's uncle, with his tanker, would meet us at the bakery at an agreed time. Nasir and I would lead in our vehicle to the RV (rendezvous) point, where we would meet the military convoy with their tanker.

As I had thought, the military convoy consisted of four vehicles in total: a lead-scout vehicle (a Humvee) that would ensure the route was clear (this would travel ahead of the main body just far enough to allow a change of route by the tanker if the scout vehicle was attacked), a close-support escort leading the tanker (another 'Hummer,' slang for Humvee), the tanker itself, and a 'Hummer' as tail-end-Charlie. (Tail-end-Charlie is the name usually given to the last man or last vehicle in a group, who would be responsible for observing any potential attack from the rear.)

When we reached the last hundred metres, all lights on the vehicles would be turned off, signalled by my vehicle going dark. I had coordinated my plan with the military, and all was set.

We met up as planned in the bakery. I got Nasir to go over the plan again with his uncle, and we set out our ERV locations. (Emergency rendezvous points for when things go wrong. When you have to run, often in confusion, you need a place to meet up and account for each other. I used three for the route in, three to go to if we got bumped (compromised and attacked) while on task and three for the route home. Staying no longer than five minutes in each.) It would be radio silence and phone silence for the entire process. I had a trusted friend, who was with another organisation, to sit and monitor the radio at his accommodation. He would alert the world if something went wrong, but keeping the plan to just those involved plus my radio monitor was crucial to preventing us from being compromised. Anyone snatching our tanker when it was full would be in a great position to either sell it on (due to the shortages they would make a huge amount of money for themselves), or any militia taking it could fuel their vehicles for further attacks; they were suffering from the same fuel shortages as everyone else. We, as the custodians, would just be killed; simple.

We set off from the bakery, keeping the distance between us and the tanker at around 25 and 50 metres, depending on the road and line of sight. Sometimes, such as going through town, it had to be much closer but once we got onto the main roads at the edge of town, we could spread out a bit. It was dark; there was no street lighting, only the dim lights of dwellings scattered here and there. We were passed by only a small number of cars, all without incident.

With my window rolled fully down, I could hear the almost ever-present sound of intermittent gunfire across the city. Now and again, the little red lights of the tracer bullets could be seen arcing across the inky black night sky. The gunfire was punctuated now and again with a bright flash and a second or two later, a dull 'BOOM'. It sounded like hand-held rocket launchers firing, possibly RPGs. (The Russian RPG7 being the most widely used shoulder-fired anti-tank rocket launcher, used by militia and old Iraqi military units).

Around us it was quiet. A few stray dogs barked as we passed but nothing much else as we turned off the main road and onto the desert track. Two minutes later, I switched off my vehicle lights, looking in the rear-view mirror for the tanker to do the same; he did.

Up ahead, I could make out the silhouette of another tanker, then I saw the first 'Hummer' off to a flank facing outwards. We slowed down and drew to a stop. I got out and walked to the military tanker. "Hey, fella. You got here then," said a face blacked out with camouflage make-up. The strong New York accent immediately gave away his identity, and I teased him, asking if he was scared. He laughed and said, "I don't scare that easy, buddy."

After a short wait in silence to determine if we had been followed, I suggested we draw our tanker to his and begin the process to transfer the fuel. It was agreed, and was conducted in almost silence; there was not a sound, apart from the handling of the hoses and muffled orders to 'switch on', 'switch off', 'mount up' and 'let's go'.

I thanked him for this huge favour and told him I would return it some time. He laughed and said he couldn't wait.

His convoy remained static until we had completely moved out of sight and out of hearing range. I just caught a glimpse of his tail-end Charlie turning on his rear convoy light as they hit the main road again. It went off as quickly as it came on.

With our now-full tanker following us, I picked up speed to get back behind the walls of the bakery compound, get the fuel transferred and set Nasir's uncle safely home. Another favour I now owed.

With the static tank at the bakery now full, signs of daylight were just starting to show. We opened the main gates to get Nasir's uncle and his tanker off home. Nasir and I opened the door to the bakery, went inside, found a couple of chairs and went to sleep. Tomorrow, or rather the daylight, would bring another day; it was already tomorrow!

I woke up just as the bright sunshine burst through the door that Nasir was opening. I asked if he was going out. Holding out a small paper bag to me, he said he had been out already and bought breakfast. The bag contained a small, almost stale, bread roll and a small carton of orange juice with the straw glued to its side. I thanked Nasir, but he sensed I was disappointed with his offering. He smiled and reminded me, "This is why we are building a bakery." We both laughed, ate our bread and drank our juice.

A few days had passed, and we were ready to try out the procedure of making bread. We had bought a sack of flour on the black market, some salt and other ingredients, and our newly hired baker, who incidentally had never seen this type of automated machinery before, under the guidance of our Lebanese technical engineer, made up the dough, mixed it well with the industrial-sized mixer, then tipped it out ready for it to begin its journey to be transformed into flatbreads.

The oven was fired up (it sounded like a jet engine) and the machinery, with its various conveyor belts and racks, kicked seamlessly into life. The test worked. We had a little celebration with the locally hired team consisting of a technician, who was trained in basic running repairs (should the thing break down) by our Lebanese engineer, a site manager, a head baker and four packers.

Unknown to me, possibly to Nasir too (although I sensed he had something to do with it), the site manager went outside the building and returned with a goat... A GOAT!

There were smiles and little giggles all around as it was brought close to where Nasir and I stood.

The site manager, a man who was tough, big and strong (not the type you would like to get on the wrong side of), held the goat and addressed the gathering. He spoke mainly in Arabic, but he did have a good understanding of English. Nasir translated:

"Friends," he began, "what we have here is something that our people will benefit from for a long time. Our children will grow strong, and our families will be able to supplement their poor meals with the vitamins from this bread. You are all going to make this possible. Our people will see you as heroes, and they will thank you."

"Wow, that's a good speech," I thought; quite inspiring.

"Now to Nasir," he began again, taking me a bit by surprise. "Nasir, you brought this organisation here to help your people."

Not entirely correct, but I let Nasir have his moment of deserved praise.

"You," he continued, as Nasir's smile grew bigger, "are a special man to us all, and we wish you and your family a long and happy life. May Allah always smile upon you."

As I thought that was the end, and that he had possibly just taken his pet goat out for a walk, he turned to Nasir and handed him the rope that held the goat. Nasir took it without hesitation. The site manager then nodded to Nasir who began a speech of his own, but it was clearly aimed at me. I knew this because: one, he was looking directly at me as he spoke, and two, he spoke in English.

"Mr Philip (my official title when Nasir was being formal and serious), I have told all of these people about the work you have done since arriving in Nasiriyah. I've told them that you are a good man. I have been requested to ask you to perform a very important ceremony to bless the bakery and to bring good fortune to the building, the equipment and the people who will work here."

I said it would be a pleasure, and thanked everyone for the privilege. I really didn't want to make any long speech or to offend anyone, so I whispered to Nasir to get on with it and tell me what I had to do.

As I spoke, a large metal container was brought and placed in front of the goat. I had a feeling I knew what was coming next.

Nasir handed me the goat, and the site manager handed me a large and extremely sharp knife. Some of the workers were whispering to each other, and little smiles were passed between them; no doubt, in anticipation of what I would or wouldn't do next.

I looked at Nasir and asked quietly, "Am I expected to sacrifice this goat?"

"Yes, Mr Philip," he replied. "You must cut its throat and allow the blood to fall into the container."

"OH, SHIT!" was the first thought in my head. "Really?" I asked Nasir.

"Yes," replied Nasir. "It is a great honour to do this."

I thought to myself, "Best get on with it. The longer I hesitate, the worse it will be."

I straddled the goat, holding it as firmly as I could between my legs, put one hand under its chin and flexed its head backwards, and with a firm but quick motion, I ran the sharp blade across its throat, going as deep as I could so death would happen as quickly and humanely as possible. The loud splattering as the blood fell into the container took me by surprise. The goat twitched as it died. It only took seconds, but I didn't enjoy it one bit. The team cheered. One of the packers took the carcass from me, laid it out on a white cloth and expertly butchered it for the joints of meat.

The site manager shook my hand, said something complimentary then told me the fresh meat would be taken to families living close by, those who could not afford to buy meat, and it would be a gift from us to them.

A least there was some benefit from the sacrifice. A local imam was called to bless the bakery, and as he did, he dipped his hand in the fresh goat blood and left a bloody handprint on the doors, walls and on each piece of bakery equipment. Nasir later explained that this was a tradition to bring good fortune. A day I won't forget in a hurry. "It's so much easier cutting a ribbon with oversized scissors, like opening a new Tesco," I thought.

Early the next morning, I called my important friend in Kuwait. I told him we were ready to go and we now needed the flour he had promised. He was pleased to hear the news, and arranged to visit us in two days' time, informing us that the first flour would arrive tomorrow 'Insha Allah'.

With the one sack of flour we had bought, we made lots of flatbreads, like a large, round pitta bread type of thing. This tested the equipment and helped get our team into the swing of things for when we started to scale up on production (if we ever did!).

We sent each of the guys home with a bag of twelve for their families. We opened a table at the gates of the bakery, and under Nasir and the site manager we gave away bags of four breads to the locals. We still had quite a lot left. I wanted to take some back for our accommodation, for my friend and his organisation and the team next door too.

I had an idea. I asked Nasir to go to the market and buy some onions, some peppers and some tomatoes. I had a tube of tomato puree, which was always in my emergency ration pack in my backpack, that went everywhere with me, along with the little bottle of tabasco sauce.

On Nasir's return, we chopped the vegetables, fired up the oven, took the leftover round flatbreads, spread the puree thinly on each, sprinkled the chopped vegetables and tomatoes on them and ran them through the oven. As they came out the other side, we took them off and folded them in half and sent them back through the oven a second time. Hey presto! A veggie pizza calzone, or as close as we were ever going to get at this point in time.

We made about 15 of these and put them in a box. I got Nasir to drive me to Camp Whitehorse, where I met up with my diesel-providing New Yorker friend. He was surprised but still pleased to see me.

"Here you go, matey. Favour returned as promised," I said as I handed him the still-warm box.

"What you giving me here?" he asked, being quite suspicious.

"The best pizza in the whole of Nasiriyah for you and your team," I told him.

"No way," he laughed as he opened the box.

"Enjoy," I said as we got back in the vehicle. We drove off as the smell of the freshly baked food drew the attention of those standing around. My last look in the mirror as we drove out was a happy New Yorker stuffing The Child-Focused INGO pizza into his mouth while fighting off others trying to snatch one.

I said to Nasir, "No matter what it is you give, you should always seek to repay those who do good for you, even if they are not expecting anything in return. It's the right thing to do and keeps them onside should we ever need a favour again. Take two bags to your uncle and tell him I say thank you for his help."

Nasir smiled and laughed a little. I asked what he was laughing at.

"If what you say is correct, can I have a pay rise?"

Nasir was truly learning what a Scouse sense of humour was, and he was now using it against me. We both laughed.

I was driving back to our home accommodation, which was a small compound within a larger compound, all fenced and walled off. The main compound had about 15 small residential dwellings, one of which housed Nasir and his family. Other buildings were larger and were used for the manufacturing of cloth, carpets and curtains, etc.

My 'home' was a single-storey building, with its own walled compound with a kitchen, a bathroom, a toilet, a shower and a small sink with a mirror. I had divided up the large, open main with aluminium- framed, prefabricated, temporary walls to make four different bedrooms, each with its own door for some level of privacy. I'd left a large area open with some soft seating, a couch and some chairs. Later on, we got a TV and a satellite system (not that there was a lot to watch in those early days). Outside, and in our walled courtyard, we had a medium-sized, built-in swimming pool. It was in a state of disrepair, with no filtration equipment (looked like it had been stolen out of the pumping shed). It was quite a large set-up.

The pool had about two feet of water in the 'deep end'. Over a period of time, it had gathered foliage from trees, dust, muck and litter which had settled into a thick layer of mud with dark brown water covering it. It smelt bad too.

Next to the pool, there was space for three or four vehicles to park and a small seating area. To enhance our standard of living, I had found an old oil barrel in the scrapyard, which is on the road into town. I had it cut in half lengthways, hinged it as a lid and mounted and welded it horizontally on a frame. A piece of scrap steel mesh sat on the lower half and... hey presto, a home-made barbeque.

Behind the main building was a garden of sorts, with a looping figure-of-eight pathway running through it. This I used as a running circuit, around the garden, up the side of the building, around the pool and parked vehicles and back to the loop again. All in all, it was a loop of about 300 metres. It helped with my fitness when I found time, but the summer weather was coming in and the temperature was climbing into the high thirties and was set to get warmer, much warmer.

I had toyed with the idea of trying to get the pool functioning but it proved to be way too expensive, and the equipment and know-how wasn't available anyway.

I had a conversation with Nasir about the pool, and he very nonchalantly said that I should not touch it as he had been told that there were a few landmines and some unexploded grenades in the mud at the bottom.

"WHAT?" I yelled.

Nasir told me that this whole compound had been taken over during the war by the Iraqi army and used for a time as an ammunition storage dump. Immediately prior to the war ending, most of the ammunition had been taken away, but they'd left live landmines for the advancing Americans to face; some had been cleared by locals and thrown in the pool, left unattended and then forgotten about.

With the war being still very recent, there were lots of unexploded munitions left all across the city and in the residential areas too. I was often woken in the night by the muffled explosion of grenades going off. I had asked for the American de-miners to visit some of the residential compounds to remove or destroy munitions that residents had found in their gardens or to deal with items that children had picked up and taken home. Some children after picking up what they thought were attractive items sadly never made it home.

Even with my extensive experience of landmines, there was absolutely no way I was going anywhere near these things. If they happened to be anti-tank mines, they could cause considerable damage. Time to get the American military de-miners in.

To cut short what turned out to be a drawn-out process, the outcome was that we had to drain the water out of the pool. The de-miners came, waded through the two feet of mud and crap that was left, used their detection equipment... and found nothing. As they were starting to extract themselves from the mud, one soldier stood stock still. The look on his face showed absolute fear. He shouted to his commander that his foot was resting on 'something'. It was hard and felt round. Everyone froze. Eyes all went to the commander, waiting for his next instruction.

If this was an anti-tank mine and it was pressure triggered, there would be little chance of this guy escaping alive. Having said that, on a standard fuse, it would take a lot of weight to set it off, but we had no idea what it was or what type of fuse it had. Some are more sensitive than others. It could be an antipersonnel mine, designed mainly to seriously injure, although they do often kill; the idea was that one wounded soldier needs two others on average to help him, therefore reducing the fighting strength more so than if he was killed outright. War is horrible. I know.

The commander took control and showed courage and bravery. He took a 'prodder' and told the remainder of his troops and me to move back and get behind cover.

He took off all but his essential equipment and slowly approached the lone soldier in the pool, who was now sweating and looking very scared. The commander told his soldier to stay very still and he would 'prod' around the area of the mine to see if there were any more and try to identify what type of mine it might be. He crouched low and began to prod. He was talking to his soldier all the time, trying to keep him calm.

"Okay," he said. "There is another one to your left and possibly two just behind you. I am going to remove all the other mines and then we will disable the one you have your foot on."

Agreement made, he began the very dangerous task. Best result: both come out unscathed. Worst case scenario: both are blown to bits and maybe further injuries to us observers, even though we were at what was deemed to be a safe distance. (Shrapnel can fly far from the point of explosion; it throws sharp jagged metal for some distance, moving exceptionally fast and being red hot too. Not pleasant.)

After about 10 to 12 minutes, the commander spoke. "I have the first mine isolated, and I am ready to remove it. Stay calm," he told his soldier. "Don't move. It will be okay."

It took about another five minutes before the 'mine' was carefully and very slowly lifted from the mud. It was a strange shape, with an amount of mud on the top of it. The commander placed it on the side of the pool, and with a careful movement started to clean off the mud so he could identify the item and then work out how to disarm the others. It was tense.

The commander started to smile, then laugh. The soldier, who still had a foot on the item under the mud, shouted almost hysterically to his commander, wanting to know, in-between profanities, what was so funny.

"It's a turtle shell," he shouted.

It was here that I saw the best and worst of soldiering professionalism. The commander shouted to his soldier that it was okay to come out, it was just turtles. The soldier slowly and carefully moved his foot off the hard item he had been standing on for over 30 minutes, then stormed out of the pool to a rousing cheer from his comrades. The commander picked up the other 'mines', all but one found to be turtle shells; the last was an upturned dinner plate. He threw them all on the poolside and declared the pool clear.

After they had gone, I thought, "What a fool. He risked his and the soldier's life by assuming all the other items were non-explosive. It could have been very different. If that was me, I would have paid very careful attention to each item in turn and assumed they were mines until I could physically identify otherwise. The process this de-mining team applied, right up to identifying the first item, was professional and courageous, but what followed was unnecessarily dangerous and reckless.

The pool was declared clear of all objects. After they had left, I decided to take my own 'prod' and carefully confirm that this was so before I took the next step of emptying the mud and cleaning the pool so it could be used for exercise. It had a steep slope which would be good for running up and down for fitness. After nearly an hour of crawling through the smelly, rancid, sticky mud, I deemed the pool was indeed free from any further objects. After Nasir hosed me down, I asked him to hire some locals to shovel the stuff out and clean the empty pool. Over a few days it was done, and it became a mini football pitch, a volleyball court and a ramp to run up and down on. Turtle shells: I mean... Ha!

There was a loud banging on the door to my small make-shift bedroom.

"Mr Philip, Mr Philip. There is someone at the gates who wishes to speak with you. You must come." It was Mustapha, one of our gate guards.

I opened my eyes, and it was still dark. I looked at my watch. It was 4.30am. I climbed out of bed, put on my tracksuit bottoms and a t-shirt, opened the door to the ever-smiling Mustapha and followed him out of the main building and past the vehicles to the main gate.

I could hear an engine running. It sounded like it was a rather large vehicle but I couldn't see it just yet. I wasn't sure if this was because of the dark or the fact that I hadn't woken properly yet; probably the latter.

I got to the gate and was met by a small-framed man, probably in his late forties, who was quite scruffy in appearance and looked like he, too, could use another few hours of sleep.

"Al Salamu Alayakum," he greeted me as I appeared.

"Wa 'alaykum al-salam," I responded as I tried to sound at least half awake.

He then started talking very quickly and was pointing behind him at something I guess I needed to see. It wasn't at all unusual to have residents coming to our compound at all hours if they had found something suspicious in their gardens or close by. I was always the first call for any unexploded munitions, I thought this was one of those times.

As the guy spoke, he took a sheet of crumpled paper from his trouser pocket and handed it to me. It was written in Arabic. I was just about to ask Mustapha to walk around to Nasir's house, which was only two minutes away, when I noticed the logo of the Kuwaiti charitable organisation. I smiled and then walked the short distance to where I could hear the engine noise, the same location that this little guy has been pointing to earlier. It was a 40-foot sea container, as promised from my important friend. I got Mustapha to give the driver directions to the bakery and told him to drive there, enter the compound, park up, get some sleep and we would be with him in an hour or two. With a smile and a fast conversation with Mustapha, he climbed back into his cab and drove off.

Going back to bed now wasn't an option. If I did, I was likely to fall into a deep sleep, and when woken, I would feel worse than I do now. So I decided to get some breakfast and catch up on some report writing and accounting for the sums of money I had spent.

We had a 'secret' safe at the house. There was great difficulty in accessing cash in Iraq, so on the 'admin' runs back to Kuwait, we would access the bank and draw out often very large amounts in US dollars (American dollars were at that time the universal currency that most people accepted). The dollars had to be new and unmarked notes, any with ink, writing or that just looked old would not be accepted, as the level of counterfeit was very high, so if there was any doubt, your money was refused.

On the odd occasion, we had no choice but to buy some items in Iraq with Iraqi dinars. It had been devalued so much that you needed a sackful just for the simplest of purchases. At one point, I wanted to buy a simple uniform of printed t-shirts for the bakery team and for Nasir and myself, three t-shirts each and a few in reserve. We also needed to buy a few items for the bakery; all of which added up to piles of Iraqi dinar notes stacked up waist high and covering most of the living room floor. Looked like a bank heist.

In the safe, I had split the US dollars into two distinct amounts. One was three quarters of the total amount for programme expenditure and the final quarter was put into three envelopes of equal amounts. This was to be sealed, with the seal signed by me.

It was the emergency escape money. If everything went really crazy, this would be the cash reserve and would help me buy my way, if required, out of Iraq into either Kuwait or Jordan. We had already, in the first few days, driven these routes and mapped them. All were now committed to my memory. But money would be needed for bribes, sustenance (if I needed to lay-up for a few days) and basically anything else needed to get me, and any other team members, out to safety. Best to have it and not need it, rather than need it and not have it.

After a few cups of coffee, the sun was well and truly up. The day was warming up nicely. It was 7am. I heard the metallic clank as the viewport in the compound gate was slid back, followed by the metal on metal squeak as the heavy metal gate was partially opened. Minutes later, Nasir was standing in front of me. He already knew that I'd had a visitor and that there was a truck at the bakery. I offered him a cup of coffee; he declined and took a box of orange juice from the fridge instead.

As I was finishing up a mix of paperwork and the last dregs of lukewarm coffee, Nasir went outside to start the vehicle up and get the morning radio checks done.

We soon arrived at the bakery. The gate guard swung the gates open for us to drive in and we parked next to the large container on the back of the articulated lorry.

After greeting each other, the driver went full throttle into a conversation with Nasir; at the time it appeared to be quite animated but as no punches were thrown I guessed all would be okay and Nasir would tell me all I needed to know. Nasir left the driver of the lorry to finish his breakfast, wash himself and do whatever he needed to do.

It appeared from the conversation that the driver had been told in Kuwait that as soon as he arrived an unloading team would unload his vehicle and he would be on the road back to Kuwait within a couple of hours. All news to me!

Nasir had told the driver that we'd received no notification that he was coming. He also told him that we had to hire a local workforce but could only do so once the consignment had arrived. He finished by promising that we would work fast to get a locally hired team and unload so that he could leave. The driver shrugged his shoulders and said he wasn't leaving until after nightfall anyway.

In Nasiriyah, there was always gatherings of men looking for work. 'Cash in hand' was the way it was done; it was a day-to-day existence for the majority of people whose livelihoods had completely vanished due to the war.

It was pandemonium once it was announced that work was available, and fights often broke out in the race to be selected. We only wanted five strong guys to unload the container which was filled from top to bottom with large sacks of flour. It would be a tedious and back-breaking job.

It turned out much later that the still-pro-Saddam groups used this clamour for work as a weapon.

The tactic was to drive a van or minibus to the crowds awaiting work, which could number in the hundreds, use a hand-held tannoy to announce that they needed 20 to 40 men for work. The crowd would then surge over to the guy in the van with the loudspeaker, and when a sufficient amount of people crowded his vehicle, he would detonate the explosives in it, killing himself and many more. Such was the divide in the country and the hatred some had for others.

Nasir safely navigated the job market and brought back five eager young men ready to start work.

We didn't have a forklift truck, nor did we have an unloading bay for the truck to reverse up to, so we would walk in and out of the container on a level platform. This was going to be hard work.

Luckily, to one side of the newly constructed building was a large mound of construction rubble and some wooden planks. I guessed that with a bit of careful driving and reversing we could get the container doors close to the mound and position two planks as a walk up into the body of the truck; this would be much better than passing sacks of flour down about five feet to someone else who would then carry it in. That would be backbreaking. This way, we could walk up the planks, grab a sack, shoulder it and walk down into the bakery. Still backbreaking but a little bit easier.

I had sent Nasir into town to buy as many soft drinks as he could: Coke-a-Cola, Fanta, juice boxes and whatever else he could find. The carrying of hundreds of 60-pound sacks of flour was not only going to take time but it would also be exhausting, particularly as the day was getting warmer by the minute. A long day lay ahead of us.

For payment, we offered very little, although it was always at the top end of what we, as a charitable INGO, could afford. I was half expecting our new workforce to tire and walk off, leaving the job, as the day got hotter and they grew increasingly exhausted. I had arranged breaks for drinks, and we would supply lunch and take a break(s) for prayer so I was hoping that we would keep our workforce on track and working hard. I left Nasir to run a few errands and check on the school/education programmes we were running. I opted to stay at the bakery and help the workforce unload the container. The bakery site manager and our Lebanese technical engineer were also on site; both could speak some English, much more than my broken mispronounced Arabic, so I thought I could manage without Nasir for a few hours.

Within 20 minutes, our workforce (me included) looked like ghosts. We were covered from head to toe in fine flour dust from the sacks we had carried into the bakery. It felt good to be grafting alongside our locally hired group. We shared laughter with each other and had mini competitions, such as who could carry the most sacks at once without falling over, who was the quickest, who was the slowest, who had the most flour in their hair; all silly but it boosted our morale and made the time go much quicker. It took nearly four hours, with breaks, to empty the container. All the guys stuck at the task and were extremely grateful for the food, drinks and humour we shared.

We got the flour inside the bakery and stacked it up. The driver, who'd sat in his cab the whole time, was now closing the container doors and preparing to leave. Nasir had returned just in time to help me pay the team. I shook the hand of each of our departing temporary workforce and thanked them for their effort. Nasir took the time to translate my gratitude and conversed further with one or two of the guys.

After they had all disappeared home, we began the process of getting the bakery to its start point for tomorrow's visit which would hopefully secure more donated flour. Once done, Nasir and I climbed into our vehicle and set off back 'home'.

I asked Nasir about the conversation he'd had with some of the guys when they were leaving. He told me they were very surprised that I'd decided to help them, considering it was very heavy work. One of them said they'd wanted to leave as they were very tired but stayed because I was doing the same as them. They thought people like me were (and I quote...) "too important to do such work".

I laughed surprisingly loud, which, by the look on his face, startled and confused Nasir. "Important? Me, a nobody, important? No, my friend I am not important, far from it. I am no different to the guys we hired today and no different to you my friend".

Nasir smiled and looked at me, still covered from head to toe in flour. He must have thought I was mad. Maybe I was, but I didn't know any other way other than to get stuck in and get the job done. 'Lead from the front, and don't ask others to do tasks you wouldn't do yourself.' I had learnt that from my very early years in the army. During the first nine years, I'd learnt by watching a large number of very good soldiers who led by example: no fuss, encouragement for those who were slower or weaker but solid personalities who commanded respect because they were fair and approachable while getting the job done. As my career progressed, I also saw the flip side of this where some hid behind their ranks, were very autocratic and full of self-importance and behaved like high-ranking bullies; to me, it was a sure sign of being insecure in their own abilities. I knew quite a few people like this, and I disliked them with a passion. They probably felt the same about me when I challenged them, often.

Just being a soldier doesn't mean you are automatically cast into a stereotypical role: shiny boots, loud mouth and always looking for a fight. Many people, in my early days in the humanitarian sector, did pigeonhole me as a stereotypical soldier, but only once they knew I had served in the forces. Not once did I receive any comments about being a soldier or being overtly militaristic until I mentioned I had served previously. This just went to show how pre-programmed some people can be to particular situations or prejudices.

I remember sharing some safety information with a lady who was the country director of a well-known INGO charity. Over a period of weeks, I had helped her out with information, safe routes and some low-level security training. We got on well, so I thought. After a meeting held by the American military liaison officer at the Nasiriyah council offices, we stood for a while in a group of people and just chatted.

She was French, working for a UK-based charity. I asked her what she had been doing before she got into the humanitarian work?

She told me had been a teacher, primary school level, and had enjoyed it very much. She said she'd decided to work in the humanitarian sector for a challenge and to help people in a very different environment.

She then asked me the same question. I told her of my short-term printing and design business, and she seemed very interested in the artistic side of the design stuff. Then when I then told her that I'd had a full 22-year career in the British Army, it was almost like a light switch went off. Her seemingly very friendly personality went cold, bordering on hostile. She turned away, got in her vehicle and left. We never spoke again.

She avoided me at meetings, even when I tried to talk to her. So I gave up trying. I met her years later in the Congo. She came over to me and said she recognised my face but couldn't remember from where. I reminded her of Nasiriyah. She remembered, and the conversation ended again. I usually don't tell people that I was in the army, only because it's not usually relevant in general conversation; what is relevant is that I can do the job I am employed to do and do it to the very best of my ability. If I can assist others along the way, I am very happy to do so. That's it.

I had telephoned and sent Suleiman emails to the Kuwaiti charitable organisation, all without reply. The visit was supposed to be the following day, and, as I had no communication, I wondered if they would turn up. The flour had so I hoped they would too.

I planned for a light lunch and a tour of the bakery, introducing all the staff and finalising with a short presentation on the programme and its aims, etc. I briefed Nasir, and in turn he would brief the team at the bakery. Our technical engineer would lead the production line and guide the staff through what would only be their second production run, but this would be on a much larger scale.

I sent specific instructions and timings in my emails and hoped they would be adhered to, but I had sensed that some flexibility would be needed.

As we arrived back at the accommodation, my thoughts turned to Rasha and the hospital in Basra.

Three days had passed since we came back, leaving Rasha and her chaperone in the care of the doctors. Nasir had phoned each day to check on her progress. He then informed the orphanage manageress and me on Rasha's progress. It was hoped that she would be completing her medical tests and be ready to return to Nasiriyah in about two days' time. With everything else that was happening, I was still trying to establish my next steps for Rasha's treatment in the longer term. Everything hinged on what the doctors and tests had found. Fingers crossed.

First things first: bakery visit and securing the flour donation.

As planned, we were up, washed and ready at 6.30am. As normal, Nasir was getting the vehicle ready. He would then come into the kitchen and refuse the offer of coffee, taking a juice carton out of the fridge instead; this was now his morning ritual.

We arrived at the bakery just as the first batch of dough was being mixed. It was 7.30am. The pre-prepared lunch was put into the large fridge-freezer that we had bought, with the drinks and a few small cartons of UHT milk I'd brought back from one of the trips into Kuwait just in case any of our guests wanted tea or coffee with or without milk! We were ready.

I asked Nasir to take our vehicle and sit at the road junction about 400 metres away, and to radio me when our visitors arrived. A bit of warning is always a good thing.

In the meantime, we got the bakery into full swing. It was amazing watching the process. The new, shiny equipment was rumbling to life and the oven was noisily firing up to create a tunnel of heat as the dough went in one end on the metal conveyor as flattened circles of dough and emerged at the other side as cooked, warm flatbread. The smell was now in the air. The smell of warm, fresh bread was comforting and reassuring. It took me back to my childhood, when I could smell the baking from the Sayers factory near Broadway, Norris Green, in Liverpool. When shopping, you could smell the ovens baking bread and cakes if the wind blew in the right direction. The smell was fantastic.

The packers were soon loading the warm breads into the bags, tying them closed and carefully placing them in the large wheeled tubs ready for delivery. We had spent a lot of time assessing our beneficiary groups to get a close estimate as to how many breads would be required for schools, hospitals and vulnerable groups across the city. We took local advice, and for the hospitals we would be providing two breads per person per day. The same would be for the schools.

The vulnerable groups would be assessed on family or group size, with families of up to six members getting one bag a day and those with seven to twelve members getting two bags. It was easier to operate on a full-bag basis at the beginning for ease of packing and distribution. We found, as anticipated, that once we started production, the numbers climbed. Vulnerable groups and families suddenly got bigger. Even some schools and hospitals increased their numbers from one day to the next; sometimes numbers increased not by just one or two, or even five or ten, but there was a climb of between twenty and fifty! We couldn't sustain that level of increase, so we changed our assessments and our distribution plans. Funny that the numbers increased but never decreased, ever!

"Whiskey Charlie One, this is Whiskey Charlie Two. Over," Nasir's voice crackled into life on the radio.

"Send. Over," was my short reply.

"Visitors at my location. I will bring them to you now. Over."

"Roger. Out," I concluded the radio call.

Nasir's voice procedure was really improving. He was no longer using the VHF handset like a telephone, often waffling for a long time before pausing. He was now concise and was remembering his 'overs' and his 'outs' in the right places.

I informed the team that our guests were on the way. There was a little bit of tension in the atmosphere but the production line continued. New batches of dough were measured and mixed, and the roar of the oven was filling the air alongside the wonderful smell.

Nasir's vehicle was now at the gate. To my surprise, it was followed by four blacked-out 4x4 Land Cruisers. As they entered the bakery compound, I directed the vehicles to the parking area. I felt a little uneasy at the number of vehicles that had arrived; this was compounded when I saw that the first to emerge from the vehicles was a camera crew and a photographer.

Once they were out and set up, the doors to the other vehicles opened and nine other people emerged from the air-conditioned comfort. It appeared very well choreographed, almost rehearsed.

Out of all those who were walking over to the bakery entrance, I recognised only one: my very important friend. I walked out and shook his hand. As we walked the short distance into the building, I engaged him in small talk, asking about his health, his family, his organisation and his journey.

I gathered everyone, and using Nasir to translate, I began by welcoming everyone and quickly showed them around the equipment, which was now in full swing. I gave everyone a piece of the warm bread to taste and asked for any questions. This all took about 20 minutes. I finished by thanking them for the donation of flour and stating that I looked forward to more in the very near future.

I noticed that during the time I'd been speaking and Nasir had been interpreting, the film crew had stopped filming. A few still photographs were taken but not many.

My important friend then took centre stage. He began by thanking me in English. He said he appreciated my help with this project and was sure it would be a fantastic success. He then switched to Arabic. The film crew now started filming.

At the end of the speech, I was asked to have a photograph shaking hands with my important friend. I agreed. I served up our light lunch with drinks and fresh bread. Within another 20 minutes, it was over. Goodbyes were said, pleasantries were exchanged and off they went to their vehicles, the camera crew hanging back to catch it all on film.

I walked over to the passenger window of the lead car, where my important friend was sitting.

As the window came down, he smiled and thanked me for hosting him and the members of his organisation. I said it was a pleasure. I followed up by asking when I could expect the next delivery of flour. He smiled and said he would be in touch. I told him we were logging all the usage and would hopefully, in a few days, have some figures showing how many breads per sack of flour we were producing. We would share our figures each month to give a guide as to how much flour we would need and be able to forecast how long the current amount would last. With a smile and a handshake, his window went up and they moved off. The visit was over.

I then sat with Nasir and interrogated him on what was said during the speech by my important friend. Nasir looked puzzled and said he didn't understand the entire talk as it hadn't made sense and there was some confusion in the things he had said. I asked Nasir to summarise if he could and to highlight the areas that were obviously causing him some concern.

He thought for a while. Nasir then began to tell me that it appeared he (my important friend) was telling everyone that the bakery project was owned by the Kuwaiti charitable organisation and we, or rather I, was project managing it for them. He finished by confirming that he was really unsure about the message that was being given, as it was, in several places, contradictory, but that that was his understanding of what had been said.

If what Nasir said was correct, it would explain the careful use of the camera team and their attendance in the first place. Were they going to take full credit for The Child-Focused INGO Bakery? I thought about it and tried to make sense of it.

What did my important friend have to gain from this? Credibility for himself? A fundraising project to draw attention and show involvement in the Iraq intervention? I was baffled. I hoped Nasir was wrong but I had an uneasy feeling he was right.

I heard the buzzing of my satellite phone ringing. I answered it and after a second or two I heard that soft Southern-Irish accent.

"How's it going, Phil? Was the visit a good one?" Paul was keen to find out.

"It went well, I think, but there may be some issues to be resolved about programme ownership." I then started to tell Paul about what Nasir had said and about my observations.

Paul asked me what I thought this could mean and how it would impact the bakery project. I said I was unsure, but at the same time, I was asking myself questions and answering them: "Is this going to stop us producing breads as planned? No," I thought. "If they continue to supply flour, our plans will go ahead. Have any demands been made on us to publicise the Kuwaiti charitable organisation? No. So any publicity would be largely internal to their organisation or to Kuwaiti newspapers; maybe.

Is The Child-Focused INGO concerned about a possible question mark over ownership? This is a difficult one, as the donors who funded The Child-Focused INGO may possibly think we are not using their funding for its intended purpose. Is there a possibility that we could be seen as falsely taking funds and not using them for the original and intended use? Now that would be serious. However, we could clearly account for the expenditure and for the donated funds, as this is a process that is fundamental for donor reporting; accounting for every donated penny is crucial, and the management of every project is scrutinised by donors demanding accurate accounting. So it could be a minor hiccup and a slight perception of a blemish that could be easily and quickly disproven."

There was no evidence that would suggest there were any underhand motives. This was all based on Nasir's confused understanding of the speech given by the Kuwaiti charitable organisation and my observations and 'feeling' that something was 'not quite right'.

Paul agreed that it was good to bring this to his attention. The main concern would be from donors but as there was nothing concrete to suggest any foul play, it would be unwise to raise an alarm before there was solid evidence to support any wrongdoing.

We were still walking a tightrope on the sustainability-of-flour issue. UNWFP were still holding off on any agreement to supply. Our verbal agreement with my important friend had produced enough flour for about 90 days, maybe more, given that we were still fathoming out our production figures. The 90 days was at best a SWAG (scientific wild-arsed guess).

75

Paul suggested that we continue as planned and review any actions if and when the situation changed. I agreed, and we quickly moved on.

Over the following few days and weeks, the bakery took care of itself. We had ironed out our distribution and had put a system in place to authenticate numbers with the vulnerable groups. It was a success. The next issue for the bakery was the exit strategy and who to hand the project over to, so it would have long-term sustainability after the INGO population departed. All of this was in the planning and was to be given detailed thought over the few weeks that followed.

For the remainder of the day Nasir and I took on the role of distribution and delivery to the identified vulnerable groups across the city. The temperature was climbing into the forties; it was very hot and sticky. Outside of any shade or the air-conditioned comfort of our car, it was instant sweat city; it just poured off me. The one major benefit that came from this hot weather was that almost everyone remained inside their homes. It was way too hot to be working outside in the oppressive heat. You would have to be crazy; and that's exactly what Nasir thought I was.

My thinking was simple: there was a clear trend showing that most attacks took place either in the mornings or in the late afternoon, when the heat of the day was not so oppressive, so, as most of the roads were empty, it was far easier to navigate around what is usually a very busy city. During the hottest part of the day, it was almost like a ghost town. This trend didn't last for long, but then, it was the best time to get out and about.

I enjoyed the deliveries, as it brought me face to face with the beneficiaries. Many of the vulnerable groups were displaced people. (People who are displaced from their homes, or from different districts or regions, but are still within their home country borders are referred to as internally displaced people, abbreviated to and often referred to as IDPs. This is not to be confused with those who are forced to move across international borders to flee their homeland for whatever reasons; they are referred to as refugees.)

Meeting with families and listening to their issues, and sometimes their harrowing stories, was very humbling. Many of these groups were living in what we at home would call condemned or semi-condemned buildings. There was no mains electricity, no running water and the buildings were badly damaged, showing very obvious signs of war damage; bomb blasts and bullet holes were everywhere.

I met with one group that was a very large extended family. They were two brothers in their thirties; one had a wife and the other had lost his wife while trying to flee Baghdad during the fighting. She had been caught in crossfire and killed. Between the two families, there were fourteen children, all between five and sixteen years of age. The children consisted of nine boys and five girls; they all got very excited when we turned up. They would come rushing out of their derelict, temporary home, which looked very dark and dilapidated compared to the very bright and hot open compound. They bounced around our vehicle, waiting for us to hand out the bags of bread.

One particular visit stands out in my memory. Two of the girls, who were aged nine and eleven, always led the race out to our waiting vehicle. Previously during our education assessments, we had highlighted the vulnerable groups and made strides with the local authorities to include the IDP children in their school reopening plans. As part of the agreement, we gave 'school packs' to those of school age in preparation for them eventually attending the schools when they opened again.

Each pack contained pens, pencils, crayons, coloured pencils, drawing and writing pads, and books, along with other useful items. It was with drawings and colourings in hand, created using the packs we'd delivered, that these two girls in particular came running to present their pictures to us.

Arriving at their location on the outer edge of town, we pulled into the damaged compound that held the dwellings. We drove in through a hole that had been blasted in the compound wall, as the gateway was obstructed by rubble from a destroyed and collapsed building.

Nasir was already out of our vehicle and had climbed into the rear to the covered loadspace. He carefully untied the rope lashing holding the tarpaulin, to reveal the neatly segregated packs of breads, each clearly labelled and showing the location and amount for each delivery.

The two brothers came to meet us, as it was to them that we delivered the bread for their group, which, by the way, contained four more large families living in the same crumbling compound, Nasir and I greeted the brothers, took their registration card (we had issued cards to all beneficiaries, with the information of their group and their bread entitlement), rechecked it against our records and started to count out their delivery.

As Nasir was counting it out with the brothers, the kids suddenly surrounded me. They always wanted me to take their photograph and show them their picture on the small digital screen. It can get a bit hectic with every child pulling at your arms and clothing to get your attention.

The two girls, who always led the race out, showed me the drawings they had done. One showed a few trees with people walking among them, with red, yellow, and black explosions happening. In the sky there was an aeroplane. It had lots of windows, so I took it to be a passenger plane and not one dropping bombs. This was the drawing of the older girl.

As I looked at it, understanding that the explosions were a picture window into what she had experienced, she took my left hand, pointed to my wedding ring then to me. Then she pointed to herself and, finally, to the passenger plane in her drawing, finishing with a gesture: the wave of her hand, pointing with her finger to the sky. She repeated the entire gesture several times, as she saw the obvious confusion on my face.

One of the brothers shouted to all of the children. They went to him, picked up the bags of bread and ran back to their dwellings. I waved to this particular girl, motioning for her to wait. I asked Nasir to ask her about the picture and the gesture she was making. Nasir stooped down to the girl and spoke softly to her. She replied and pointed at the picture, then to me, then to the sky. Nasir smiled, spoke softly again and told her to go inside.

We tied up the tarpaulin again, shook hands with the brothers, got back into the vehicle and headed off to our next drop off.

I asked Nasir about the girl.

He said that she was explaining that she wanted to go with me and my wife (wedding ring gesture) to England, and to live with us where there was no war. At that moment, if I could have taken all those kids to England and guaranteed a better life, I would have. But I couldn't. I felt sad, but consoled myself, knowing that we were helping them, albeit in a small way. It *was* help, and for the moments during the delivery when the kids jumped, shouted and ran about, they had a small but welcome break from the boredom and monotony. I met many more children like these. The scale of the hardship was huge.

We had completed the day's deliveries. I was very hot and sweaty, and starting to smell a bit too. I decided to turn off the air-conditioning and keep my windows open. There were two reasons for this: firstly, and most importantly, was to hear what was happening outside (if there was gunfire or explosions, I wanted to, as best I could, get a direction so we could avoid that area) and secondly, I was never going to acclimatise to the very hot weather if I stayed in an air-conditioned 'bubble'. Nasir told me later, with a smile, that he had lived in Iraq all his life and had never got used to the summer heat.

As we were getting close to our office, the satellite phone buzzed, and as I was driving I told Nasir to answer it. A conversation in Arabic ensued. On conclusion, and with a huge smile, Nasir told me that Rasha would be returning home the next day.

*

Chapter 4:

Rasha's Return – Now What?

I spent most of the evening trying to get as much information as possible on the ever-changing situation with regards to attacks, route clearances and any patterns that were forming from it all. For some reason, Nasiriyah seemed to be a lot less active in terms of attacks. Many locations around the country were having around five to eight attacks a day, ranging from random long-distance shooting or sniping to public disorder, such as rioting, to car bombing and kidnapping.

Ambush attacks were becoming more frequent, largely on the main highways. They usually looked for 4x4 vehicles. In and around Nasiriyah, vehicle-jacking was increasing, whereas further north, the carjacking was increasingly being targeted at INGOs or any foreigners, who would then be killed or kidnapped. The risk factor was escalating, but escalating slower in Nasiriyah than most other locations across the country.

Many of the public-disorder issues, such as riots, looting and attacks on government buildings was a growing frustration against the 'stand-in' government. The Coalition Provisional Authority (CPA) was an American-appointed-and-run government which was widely unpopular. The reported or alleged mismanagement of funds, the awarding of construction contracts to favoured American companies and the hiring of private security companies at huge expense all added to the alienation of the Iraqi population.

Added to the political unrest were the false promises given to the Iraqi military on their agreement to disband, disarm and regroup as a new force. Many of the top-ranking soldiers had made 'deals' in return for their cooperation to ensure a smooth transition from war into peace and the restructure of Iraq.

Many of the Iraqi forces of lower rank had not been paid by the old regime, some for months. An agreement was reportedly made in conjunction with (or driven by?) the CPA to pay what was owed to the army and to bring the 'old Iraqi army' on side, and they would, so it was reported, be pivotal to the management of the overall rebuilding of the country, politically, physically and in terms of security. The Iraqi Police Force at this time was not an effective body; what did exist was corrupt, disinterested and, to be fair, ill-equipped to be an authoritative body with any real credibility.

I had witnessed what was an honour killing in an open street in Nasiriyah. A brother repeatedly stabbed his pregnant sister in full view of two police officers who just stood and watched. The story I got from Nasir several days later was that the sister lost her husband during the war. She had only recently discovered that she was pregnant, and her family apparently didn't know. Now she was a widow and pregnant. She didn't want to invite any shame, so she started a relationship with another man.

As she was now obviously showing she was pregnant, her family had formed the opinion that she had been unfaithful to her (now deceased) husband, and the brother was 'tasked' to perform the honour killing. It was brutal, sickening, barbaric and very, very, sad. It was over in seconds. She lay dying in the middle of the road. Her injuries were such that it was obvious that the baby could not have survived, and from the blood loss, I reckoned she died very soon after the attacker ran off.

The traffic that had come to a halt as the attack happened remained still. Even at a time when death was not a stranger to most families in Iraq, those that witnessed this dreadful attack still looked on in shock and horror.

I remember talking to a very high-ranking Iraqi army officer, who was a pleasant guy. We discussed in English the situation with the disbandment of the army. He told me clearly, and without hesitation, that the old regime was wrong; it was oppressive and brutal. He told me stories of the Ba'athists and the secret police who would spy on the local population and would order 'disappearances' or 'executions' of whole families who had been heard talking badly of the government.

This soldier was clearly no fan of Saddam Hussein and what he stood for (even though he, too, was a Ba'ath party member). He continued to tell me how angry his soldiers had become at the inactivity of the CPA, who had promised to meet the wage bill for the Iraqi army as a sweetener to keep them on side. Several times, a date would be set for payment but for various reasons very few were paid or it didn't happen at all.

The original idea was to make payments at particular dates and in rank order. Sometimes the pay was delayed and anger ensued; it was a perception (I was told) that the higher ranks were paid only a fraction of what had reportedly been promised. This confusion was really loading the tipping point at which control and favour was lost from the disbanded army. A huge mistake by the CPA.

Another issue which (in my opinion, and many, many others) destroyed Iraqi confidence was the process of de-Ba'athification. This was based on the theory that the ruling party (Saddam Hussein's party), the Ba'ath Party, was staffed by bad people who were perceived to (still) be Saddam loyalists. Driven by the warped idea that 'if you are a member, you are a bad person', a group of influential people (questionable in this case), through the CPA, decided to gather the members, get them to denounce Ba'athism (whatever that is) and recommit to the new Iraqi (CPA-led) government. Properties and offices around the country that were linked to the Ba'ath party were destroyed, as were some residential dwellings too, by association.

The truth of the matter, as I had it explained to me by Ba'athists and none Ba'athists alike, was that it was just not the case. The truth was, apart from those very close to the leadership, most others who joined the party had to do so to hold certain positions. Those who aspired to key positions in management couldn't hold a post at a high level unless they were members. It didn't at all mean that they were involved in the underhand and brutal dictatorship. The decision-makers for de-Ba'athification scored a real own goal by alienating people and bringing unwanted and sometimes aggressive attention to those who had previously not declared membership and were members just for job-specific reasons.

Many of the experienced soldiers who were sitting on the fence with regards to who to align with were now falling off on the opposite side to the coalition and the CPA. History has shown that the immediate poor governance went a long way to alienate the Iraqi ex-military and wider population. A huge backlash was already in the planning: not being paid, or at least being short changed, on what was promised combined with what many Iraqis saw as the rape of their oil industries and the longer-than-anticipated occupation by the coalition forces (many of whom had not stepped down from the war-fighting stance and had remained aggressive to all Iraqi citizens).

One hope was to use the defunct Iraqi military to take on the main infrastructure roles in order to get the country off its knees, but by alienating the people, who they hoped would be a key resource, it was always going to lead to disaster.

One other major issue that tipped Iraq over the edge was the tribal conflict based on religious differences. Saddam Hussein had kept the Shias and Sunnis apart, largely by supressing the Shia population, as Saddam himself was Sunni. The suppression was publicly expressed to the wider world as tolerant cohabitation; while in some areas this may have been true, in others, the Shia was brutally controlled and kept suppressed. In fact, the regime of Saddam Hussein brutally controlled and manipulated the entire country by fear, aided by his two sons Uday and Qusay Hussein.

I spent yet another uneasy night trying to sleep. I had been thinking about what I would be told about Rasha when I eventually arrived at the hospital in Basra. What would be my next step if presented with worst or best case scenario? I went through many different possible situations, trying to find a 'next step' for each one.

My thoughts were also based on the journey to Basra. Finding the right time, picking the right route, particularly when we'd get closer to the city, keeping Nasir and I safe when entering the city and keeping us all safe on the way out. Speed and time were going to be critical; that was for sure.

The next morning, I sat at the breakfast table with my first cup of tea. It was still dark outside. The familiar metallic squeak of a bolt sliding and the hinges of the metal gates grinding as they opened broke the silence. A minute or two later Nasir walked into the kitchen.

"Juice is here on the table mate," I said without looking up.

Nasir raised his eyebrows and smiled. "You are learning, my friend," he said, almost mocking my forethought.

"I try boss," I said grinning, mocking him back and finishing with a lazy salute.

We smiled at each other and admired our early morning humour, which I ended by rising from my chair with stating that sitting there being a pair of comedians wasn't going to bring Rasha home.

I had taken emergency envelopes from the safe; I gave one to Nasir and I took the other. We kept these on our bodies, not in bags, as they could easily have been taken by opportune thieves or snatched out of vehicles.

We finalised our vehicle kit check. Radios, the HF vehicle-fitted Codan, the smaller VHF set and the VHF handheld sets. Nasir had a hand-held radio, I had one and we took a spare. We had freshly charged batteries for the hand-held and two spare batteries per radio, including the additional radio.

In the rear loadspace of the twin cab, we had two spare wheels inflated to the correct pressure, a vehicle toolkit, eight two-litre bottles of water and two spare jerrycans. We covered it all with the tarpaulin, lashed it tight and conducted a visual check of the outside of our vehicle. We didn't want to be setting off with a slow puncture or leak. All was good.

In my backpack, I carried a small but very well-equipped first-aid kit, although it was more like a trauma kit, which is quite a few steps above just plasters and eyewash! I could deal with gunshot wounds, blast injuries, critical bleeds, broken bones and both simple and complicated fractures.

Coupled with this was a few American ration meals called MREs (meals ready to eat). They were high fat, high protein compact meals which could be eaten hot or cold. They looked awful, and the taste wasn't great, but they served a purpose.

Doing joint exercises in my past life with the Americans, I knew that they were always eager to swap their MREs (nicknamed 'meals rejected by Ethiopians' by the Americans we trained with, relating to the famine between 1983 and 1985 in Ethiopia; even hungry people wouldn't eat them! Soldiers' dark humour) for the British rations, containing tinned meats, such as bacon grill and luncheon meat which, for some reason, the American troops seemed to love. Strange.

We conducted our pre-arranged radio checks, called in and confirmed our journey; not by detail over the radio but in a manner that was partially coded, only so as not to give times, routes or destinations, as the radio signals were often listened to by militias and criminals. With final checks complete, we were ready to go.

We left our compound in the silence of the very early morning. There were no vehicles on the road as we hit the highway on our way south to Basra.

As I was driving, I took to the reasoning that if we were to drive into an ambush at any point it would best to be going as fast as the vehicle would allow. So with that in mind, we went flat out all the way. The vehicle was only capable of 120km/h (roughly 75mph), so we didn't break any land-speed records. But it was still fast enough to keep Nasir awake and gripping the door handle all the way to Basra. Nasir still sometimes drove like a nervous learner even though he'd had his licence for many years.

I had learnt rather quickly that it's best to keep the air-conditioning off in the car as much as possible if you are trying to acclimatise. Constantly going from a cold environment into the hot sun isn't the best thing to do. Your body just doesn't adjust; you continue to sweat like a loony as soon as you step out.

When driving fast, it's best to keep the windows up; it's better for wind resistance and, therefore, fuel consumption. When reducing your speed, particularly when entering built-up areas, it's best to lower your window so you can hear what is going on in the outside world. The music within the vehicle is always turned off at these times.

We made good time to Basra. No scary moments and no assessed potential attacks, so no reason to slow down. Now we were entering the outskirts of Basra. On approach, you can see the oil refinery towers, the large industrial chimney stacks and buildings. Seeing these across the flat semi-desert is an indicator we had just under an hour to go before arriving at the hospital.

It was early morning. The sun was up and getting hotter by the hour. People were moving around the streets, some pushing wooden handcarts loaded with fruit and vegetables; "Going to market," I thought. The traffic was building up, with vehicles in an almost-chaotic dash to get somewhere in a hurry, although the hurry was a stop-start type of hurry.

I pulled into a side street where it was quiet and swapped with Nasir, so he could drive the last short distance to the hospital. While we were static, I made a phone call to my contact at the hospital to inform them that we would be there for Rasha in a few minutes. I also phoned the Lebanese doctor. He answered quite quickly, which surprised me. He told me to come to his office before we collected Rasha, to discuss further her condition and suggest next levels of treatment. I agreed and sat comfortably in the passenger seat. I nodded at Nasir, and we set off to join the madness of early morning Basra traffic.

Arriving at the hospital, we parked our vehicle between two ambulances that looked to be in disrepair so wouldn't be moving any time soon. This put our vehicle out of sight, hidden all but for the large CODAN radio antenna that could be seen over the top of the ambulance. I removed it and placed it under the tarpaulin. There! Invisible!

We made our way into the main hospital building. It was quiet but busy; the quiet being broken now and again by a shout or two but it was quickly over, with the quiet buzz of people returning.

Nasir asked a passing hospital porter how we could find the doctor's office. We were directed up two floors and told which door to enter. A few minutes later, we were sat down waiting for the Lebanese doctor to finish whatever he was writing and look up.

He did look up but just to say he was waiting for the other two doctors to join us. As he spoke, the door opened and in they came. Great!

One of the two doctors was holding a file which held what looked like lots of paperwork and two x-ray photographs (radiographs). After we stood and shook hands, gave greetings and took our seats again, we got down to business: Rasha.

The file was handed to the Lebanese doctor who opened it, glanced at the x-ray images then thumbed through the sheets of paperwork, nodding his head as he went through it all. Once he was satisfied, he closed the file and looked up.

He began by telling me that Rasha's medical situation was indeed serious. He then paused before telling me that with the correct treatment her life expectancy could be dramatically extended. But the problem was that now she had been correctly diagnosed, he could do no more for her, as the hospital in Basra was not equipped to treat her condition. In short, he was saying that he was at his limit with this case and I would now need to expand my original referral system (which didn't exist anywhere but in my head) to the next stage.

The doctor's parting comment held a glimmer of hope and was something I would never have known if he hadn't shared it with us. "When you start your referral," he said, " I have included a personal and professional letter within the file."

I moved forward onto the edge of my seat, concentrating hard on every word he was saying.

"I understand," he continued, "the Americans have installed a new radiotherapy and cancer care unit in the main hospital in Baghdad. If your referral process can end at this hospital, it will give this young girl the best of chances to improve her life beyond the year I predict without treatment."

He ended the conversation by handing me a transparent, plastic, resealable bag containing three bottles of tablets and a tube of ointment. There was a folded piece of paper which he told me was the instructions regarding how to administer the medications.

My heart swelled and burst in quick succession. I was being told that there was some hope, but the realisation that it was a terminal condition and that a twelve-month estimate had been put on her life was hard to take.

It took me a few seconds to absorb the information. I stood up, took the bag, shook the hands of all those present, took possession of the file and expressed my gratitude for all they had done for Rasha before leaving the room with Nasir in hot pursuit behind my speedy exit.

I was telling myself to be calm and to control my emotions. It was difficult, and I needed some time to sort out just what to do next.

We arrived at the ward on which Rasha had been accommodated. As I looked down to the bottom of the room, I could see her sitting on her bed talking with her chaperone. Next to her on the bed was her bag, packed and ready to go. I wondered what her mindset was going to be. Would she be deflated after all the tests and just want to go home or would she have some hope?

Nasir was already in conversation with someone whom I understood to be a nurse on the ward. He pointed several times at Rasha, nodding his head as the nurse answered his questions. Nasir then approached me and told me that Rasha had seen the doctor this morning and was free to leave. There was something else. I could tell. When Nasir has bad news to give, his whole demeanour changes and he 'huffs' and 'puffs' a lot.

"Nasir, what else was said?" I asked him.

Nasir looked up very slowly, and with another huge sigh, he said, "Rasha has not been told the whole story; the doctors thought she was too young. So they decided it would be better if *you* explained it to her."

"ME?" I said with a mixture of shock and confusion. My head buzzed, like I'd had an electric shock; I felt a surge of emotions from sadness to helplessness, and finally anger.

"I can't do that. I can't tell that little girl that she may only live a year if I fail to get her referred." I felt sick. "Surely," I rambled, "the doctors should have explained that."

As I was talking, the realisation began to dawn on me: I was the one who'd initiated this visit, brought Rasha to Basra and was driving the whole process, and I was, at this point (in the absence of the orphanage manageress), probably Rasha's guardian. I didn't think I could do it. Certainly, it would need to be done in her own language so there was no misunderstanding, but this was also outside of Nasir's responsibility too.

"I'll think about this on the way back," I told Nasir. He smiled, took my arm and led me to Rasha's bedside.

Rasha's chaperone leaned in to Rasha's ear and whispered something. As she did, Rasha looked up and saw Nasir and me approaching. I then got a huge shock. Rasha climbed off the bed and ran to us. She threw her arms around me with such force I nearly fell backwards. Once she let go, she took Nasir's hand and mine, then walked us to the bed, where her chaperone and her bag were waiting. It was a shock, but such a pleasant one.

After checking that we had everything and paying a food bill for Rasha and her chaperone, we headed out of the ward, out of the hospital and, finally, to the car park, slipping between the defunct ambulances to our waiting vehicle. I refitted the thick, tall CODAN antenna to the tuning base on the front of our vehicle and tested the radios, then Nasir started the engine.

Once we were all in and seat-belted, we gave our new passengers a juice box and straw each and some biscuits. We then set off for 'home'.

We swapped positions again at the edge of the city. Nasir became the front passenger and I took the wheel. It was just past mid-afternoon, with the sun at its highest in the sky and the air hot and oppressive. I gave in to my acclimatisation plan once we were on the highway; it was windows up and air-conditioning on, just for the comfort of our two passengers, you understand!

We had a delay on the route back. It appeared that an American convoy had been attacked, a hit-and-run type ambush, and several vehicles had been disabled and destroyed (hit with RPGs was my guess). There were some small-arms bullet holes in the sides of some of the trucks they were escorting. They looked like 7.62mm in size; possibly AK47 assault rifles or RPK machine guns.

The attack must have been a good few hours before we arrived, as the troops had opened up the opposite side of the highway and had a comprehensive cordon placed around the incident. We waited in a small line of traffic for about 30 minutes before our vehicle was checked by a soldier controlling the traffic flow. We were questioned by him, and identification was asked for and shown.

The time spent sitting static was tense. We were a sitting duck among a partly destroyed military convoy. The attackers could return at any moment to conduct a second attack upon their wounded target.

My eyeballs were on stalks. The air-conditioning was off and the windows down from the moment we stopped. I was going through all the 'what ifs' in my head. What if we were attacked from the left? What if we were attacked from the right? Looking at escape routes off the road (I couldn't reverse, as someone had stopped directly behind us, so I could move out forwards but only go to the left or right; the direct route ahead was blocked by damaged vehicles), I saw that both routes would take me across a narrow ditch-cum-drain, which I was confident the vehicle could cross. But after that, it was open desert and a mad dash away from any fighting. This was the best we could do in the hope that we wouldn't be pursued. The chance of that was low, I thought, as the attackers would be focused on their military target and we would be insignificant, I hoped.

We managed to pass the now-static and battered convoy. I kept our windows open for about an hour after, just in case anything else had been planned up ahead. I radioed the incident back to the radio room and suggested that the route not be travelled for the remainder of the day.

We cracked on at best speed without further incident.

The route into Nasiriyah from the main highway took us down a long, empty, desert road; nothing more than just a track but well used, as it was very prominent. This bumped out onto a dual carriageway which took us to the main intersection of roads at the south of the city. We were about ten minutes away from getting Rasha home.

As we finally drove into the compound of the orphanage, the manageress was waiting. Nasir had called to let her know we were coming.

Smiles and waves from the back of our car to the manageress, and waves back from her, continued frantically until we stopped and got out of the vehicle. It was almost a fight to see if the manageress could get into the back of the car before Rasha and her chaperone could get out to greet her. It was a moment of excitement and pure joy. Nasir and I just sat for a moment to watch, as we waited for the excitement to calm down a little bit.

The manageress came over to the vehicle window and spoke to Nasir. Nasir spoke to her, apparently giving her some instruction. She took Rasha and the chaperone into the building. Once they had gone, Nasir said we should wait in her office and explain everything we had learnt.

We could hear the shouts of children and the banging of doors as we sat in the manageress's office, waiting for her to return. Some ten minutes later, she appeared with a huge smile and offered us both some tea.

As she made a small glass of too-sweet tea for us both, I talked with Nasir and took his advice on how to break the news of Rasha's diagnosis and what her future might be. We agreed on the way the news should be delivered: bit by bit and slowly, using no medical terminology but putting everything in layman's terms, ensuring clarity.

I again asked Nasir to trust in what I had to say and asked for no embellishment unless it was really needed. He agreed.

I started by telling the manageress of all the tests that Rasha had had during her time in hospital. I produced the file that I had been given and told her that we now had a complete diagnosis of Rasha's condition. I explained how kind the doctors had been and the change in Rasha, who appeared to be much happier than the first time I'd met with her.

The manageress smiled then spoke. Nasir translated. She said, "It is the first time I have seen Rasha smile and wave and be so happy." A tear appeared in her eye, which she immediately wiped away.

I looked at Nasir and said, "Now for the difficult news." I told Nasir that we needed to explain the bad news and then discuss what to do next. "Nasir, please translate," I said, looking the manageress directly in the eyes.

"Rasha is very sick. There is a chance that she may never improve. Her sickness may be with her until she dies." I paused as the manageress leant forward onto her desk. I then continued. "We thought that she may survive another four months without further treatment. Happily that may not be the case. The doctor thinks that Rasha could survive up to a year without any further medical help, which is more than we originally thought."

I was really hurting inside. I tried hard to stick to the facts and not mislead, holding back the emotions I was feeling, and seeing the pained expression on the manageress's face, it was clear that she, too, was trying to hold back.

"Nasir and I are going to try to get further treatment for Rasha, but that treatment is in Baghdad. We will have to communicate with them and hope they will see Rasha as a patient. At this point, we have no idea if the hospital will accept her but we will try; we will try our very best."

I concluded there before I started some emotional babble.

Nasir interpreted. There was lots of headshaking in agreement, a few '*Insha Allah*' comments were made and several '*Shukraans*' were said in a low almost-whisper. The manageress agreed to talk with Rasha and let her know what she considered to be appropriate.

We drank some of our tea and then told the manageress that we were leaving but would be back in a day or two to deliver some items for the orphanage, but most importantly, we hoped to have more news.

While driving back to our compound, I thought aloud, looking for answers and next steps. I mumbled to myself and to Nasir, running through different ideas and thinking how we could make things work. All this was done in an 'I might be talking to myself but I hope you are listening too, type of way.'

I thought that if we were looking at a transfer or referral, we would need the cooperation of the local hospital in Nasiriyah, and we would need transport on a regular basis to ensure Rasha could get to and from Baghdad for ongoing treatment; all this was said as if I was reading from a puzzle book, frowning and scratching my head as I went.

Nasir suddenly sparked up! "I think I can arrange that! My uncle (one of what seemed like hundreds that Nasir appeared to have) is the administrator for Nasiriyah Hospital. I am sure he can help.

"What?" I spluttered. "Nasir, is there anyone in this city you are not related to?" I laughed.

Nasir tried to explain who he wasn't related to, missing the joke completely. I laughed, and after some careful thought, he laughed too.

My plan for the next day was starting to take shape.

I slept quite well that night. It was a little bit of encouraging news, and the next morning I planned to rise early and start to establish communications with the Baghdad Hospital. I was hoping that Nasir could get his uncle to assist us in how to get Rasha to and from Baghdad.

In theory, it was looking better than it had done previously; in practice, I was sure we would have some significant obstacles to navigate.

I made myself a cheese and onion toastie with the bread from the bakery and got a hot cup of real tea (you know, from those little fellas who make teabags that make tea); it was brown, hot and not sweet. The Iraqis (and most middle-eastern countries) serve tea black in small glass cups, and they almost always have a thick layer of sugar undissolved at the bottom of the glass. It makes my teeth hurt just looking at it.

I spent the last part of that evening making telephone calls, sorting out issues for all the projects we had within the country programme and, finally, calling a couple of contacts in Baghdad. Just before I dragged myself off to bed, I obtained a satellite number for a guy at the hospital who could be of assistance. I would ring in the morning. Fingers crossed.

A crash and the sound of breaking glass woke me from what was a very deep sleep. I jumped up, grabbed my shorts and t-shirt and ran into the living area. I was looking at all the windows when I spotted slivers of glass poking out from under the layers of net and heavy crushed-velvet curtains. I put on my shoes and pulled back the curtains. A huge rock lay just inside the broken window frame. It had obviously been thrown over the compound wall... by kids? I had no idea.

Our compound guard was quickly on the scene. He'd heard the window smash and had run around the outside of the compound to see if he could catch the culprit. Mustapha lived with his family in one of the houses close to the spot from where the rock had been thrown.

He gestured to me that it was just kids and that they'd gone now. He told me that he would get the window fixed in the morning and

I should go sleep. At least that was my interpretation of all the hand gestures, smiles and 'okay, okays' in his broken English.

There had been other incidents in the past when rocks and stones were thrown into the compound. This usually followed the joint fitness sessions we had with the organisation across the road. They had no space to exercise so I offered my friend, their country director, access to my place to run around or play volleyball in the now-clean, empty swimming pool.

Even though we were behind a high wall and anyone wanting to peek in would have to climb onto their roof, it appeared that what we were doing was frowned upon by some. I would ask Nasir and Mustapha to investigate this. If needed, we would have to stop the fitness sessions. Getting on the wrong side of this community would be a bad idea, as several of our staff (including Nasir) were part of it.

It was Friday; usually a day off for all the local staff, as it was the start of the weekend in the Middle East. Friday was the holy day and Saturday was also a day of rest. Sunday was a normal working day. For me, Friday was an administrative and planning day: ringing London, getting on top of accounts, reports and the coming week's programme activities; not to mention organising the meetings that I was expected to attend as well.

To my pleasant surprise, Nasir, Mustapha and Alem, who was Mustapha's relief for the gate guard, had arrived to clean up the broken glass, and had a new piece ready to put in. I joined them and invited them all to have breakfast with me. They all smiled and very politely declined. I gave them all a drink of cold juice anyway.

Once the window was repaired, I asked Nasir if he and Mustapha would mind staying a few minutes to discuss the increase in stone throwing and the broken window. They agreed.

The issue appeared to be the staff from the other organisation, which consisted mainly of young ladies aged between about 25 and 32. There were about six of them and three guys, plus their country director. Fitness for them was largely done while I was away out on projects. It transpired that some of the girls got a bit loud and giggly when playing volleyball with the guys. When they were running the compound circuit, they would often shout and joke with each other. This caused some of the close neighbours to climb up onto their flat roof to see what was going on. While it was just curiosity at first, to see why there was such a noise, it turned into anger for some of those who disagreed with men and women dressing in very provocative and disrespectful clothing and openly mixing together. (The clothing, just shorts and vest tops, which we would consider normal dress for conducting exercise, was probably not appropriate for outside. But within the walls of our compound, I thought it would have been okay.)

Mustapha and Nasir said they would call a meeting of the heads of families and discuss this issue. Mustapha was particularly influential within this residential area, and was seen as a community leader.

I told Nasir that I would speak to the guys next door and postpone all fitness in our compound until we got some feedback and understanding from the residents. I offered to attend the meeting, but Nasir said it would be wise for just Mustapha and him to do so, as people would probably speak more freely. I agreed.

I sat at the kitchen table with my laptop, my BGAN satellite modem (a portable satellite modem receiver which looked like a laptop; when opened, the lid became the receiver and a small compass gave the right direction to point it (it was portable and reliable but very expensive to run)) and my Thuraya satellite telephone. I called London.

I spoke to Paul, asking if there was any news on recruitment as I was being stretched very thin and I couldn't advance the plans for the drop-in centres or the safe play areas until I got some help. He told me they were still looking but had some candidates they were trying to arrange an interview with. He reassured me that someone would be out soon.

I wondered if I should mention Rasha?

I decided against it for now, but I knew I would have to come clean sooner or later. I was using my own money to fund all the added expenses: the additional fuel, the hotel, the food and the hospital expenses.

I gave Paul the sit-rep for the last two weeks; the education programme and the school bags, the printed exam papers, the orphanage progression, including an inventory of all the equipment we had supplied to each orphanage, the bakery progression and the ongoing efforts to make it sustainable. I told him I would email my plans for an exit strategy for the bakery sometime in the next two weeks, and I gave a security update, in detail for Nasiriyah and in general for the Dhi-Qar province, and an overall assessment on the whole country. I finalised by speaking briefly on the broken-window issue as a point to watch.

As usual, he was full of praise for the amount of work I had completed while on my own. Partially, I thought, to keep me sweet, but praise isn't what drives me. I don't really feel comfortable with it. I was employed to do a job and it didn't matter if I was part of a team or on my own; I would like to think I would put in the same type of shift, regardless. After all, outside of work, there really isn't anything else to do.

I was really tired, though. Every day was a long day. The heat sapped your strength and really tested your will to go out and get things done. But it all had to be, so that's the way it was.

Nasir really didn't like our bread-distribution timings. Distribution was always done at the hottest time of day, when the roads were mostly empty, markets were closed and the population were indoors. I loved the freedom of being able to get around the city unhindered. (I was often thinking that 'mad dogs and Englishmen go out in the noonday sun' from Noel Coward was very relevant). Nasir often told me I was mad. Mad maybe, but it was for sure the safest time of day to travel in a city that had a slowly escalating terrorist attack rate. Mad and safe was okay in my book.

Paul finished by telling me it could be another two to three weeks before he could get some staff out to help me. I asked if he could make a senior country director a priority. I needed someone with more experience than I currently had, to handle some of the more complex meetings with the likes of the Department for International Development (DFID) and other key donors. I had very little experience other than short inputs to London's reports and some financial accounting. All of those high-level meetings I had tried to avoid until someone else came out were now meetings I had to attend. I found them tedious and boring; real bean-counter types of affair. While important in their own right, they were not for me.

With the call completed, I got stuck into the mountains of paperwork. I became so engrossed in sorting receipts, getting the books to balance and counting and recounting the Iraqi bank notes which had so many zeros on them it was untrue. The currency had devalued so much that a new currency was being printed; mainly to take Saddam's face off it but also to cancel a few of the zeros so you no longer needed a sackful of money just for a loaf of bread!

I was startled by a tapping on the door, I looked up, and there was Nasir. Five hours had passed since he left earlier but it felt like just half an hour, such was the level of concentration I had on the paperwork; I hated it.

As Nasir pulled up a chair, he said he had come to tell me of the meeting with the residents.

As I thought, it was the male/female mix. This was considered very bad practice, and the news of what had been going on had spread to other families. Some of the teenagers, hearing their parents frowning upon and discussing the terrible activities that had taken place inside our compound, took the opportunity to show their anger at our fitness exercise sessions.

Nasir explained to me that Mustapha had spoken on our behalf and reassured them that the activities would cease. He told them that we must exercise to stay healthy but that it would be done in separate groups, the men then the women, rather than mixed.

Nasir had taken the opportunity to tell them of the work we were doing around the city and how we were helping the poorest and assisting the schools and hospitals. This, he told me, appeased the gathering, but it was still a fine line and we needed to be careful. Attitudes can change very quickly, and stones could easily be changed for petrol bombs, bullets and grenades; there were plenty about.

I went over to my friend, who was the country director of the other INGO, and explained the situation. I told him that for this week there would be no exercise and could he ask his ladies to keep a lid on the noise. All was agreed.

We decided that Thursday evenings would be a barbeque night, and we would have a quiet meal with a few quiet beers. This turned out to be a bit of a sing-song night with 'In my Liverpool Home' being prominent. A few of the lads from the other organisation were Irish, so many Irish songs were sung too. A great way to decompress from what was always a long, busy and, at times, stressful week.

Saturday morning arrived with the usual bright sunshine and sticky, dry heat that made me sweat from morning till night. I was now habitually waking before the alarm clock sounded; as usual, it went off just as I was putting the kettle on.

I felt quite sick; not the throw-up type of sick but the feeling you get from a mixture of dehydration and exhaustion. I was routinely working on average sixteen hours or more a day. The stresses and strain were building up. I was starting to notice that it was becoming difficult to concentrate; what was usually a simple decision, had become harder to think through. While I was always ensuring Nasir was drinking enough water throughout the day and eating regularly, I was neglecting my own advice. I needed to change my routine or I would burn out in a spectacular way.

I called Nasir and told him not to come to work until 10am. He usually arrived between 7am and 7.30am, even though his official start time was 8am. Always eager. I had allowed that routine to continue, when I should have stopped it at the beginning. I always tried to get Nasir finished and home at a reasonable hour so he could spend time with his young family. This wasn't always the case, but, again, it was something I needed to make happen.

When Nasir went home at the end of each day, I still had several hours' worth of paperwork to do, calls to make and plans for the following day to go over. Due to overstretch, my plans often changed, so everything had a huge amount of flexibility built in. My working aims switched from what I wanted or needed to achieve each day, to ensuring that the weekly aims were met. It was easier to manage that way and gave a greater level of flexibility.

I made a cup of tea and sat alone in the living area of the house. I sipped the hot tea, put on the TV and listened to BBC World. It was all news, mostly bad, but news was about all I could get in English. I put my still-very-hot tea down on the table and relaxed. As I half watched the news, I thought, "I have to change my work pattern."

"Mr Phil... Phil." It was Nasir's voice.

I slowly woke up, my first thought being it must be about 10am, maybe 9.45, as Nasir is always early. I must have dozed off for a short while.

I greeted Nasir, reached for my mug of tea, which was absolutely stone cold, then cleared my eyes and looked at my watch. I looked again, looked at Nasir, looked around the room and back at my watch. It was one o'clock! I couldn't believe my 'little' nap had lasted nearly six hours. I couldn't believe I'd just lapsed into such a deep sleep. It wasn't like me at all. Usually I was up by 6.30am and ready to go by 7 or 7.30, depending on the day's schedule.

Nasir, the diamond that he was, explained that he'd come to the house at 10am to find me asleep in the chair. He quietly called my name and got no response. He took one of the vehicles and went out to visit all of our projects and attended a local INGO coordination meeting and had just returned to find me still in the same position in the chair.

I apologised to Nasir several times and thanked him for 'holding the fort' (which I then had to explain the meaning of). Nasir smiled and said he had been worried about me and the long hours and lack of sleep. He said, "One day without Philip in the world is okay but two is not good."

I laughed. He'd cheered me up, but it did confirm that I was closer to burnout than I had thought. I decided to rest for the remainder of that day; to sleep, to eat properly, taking time in doing so, and to relax with no work.

Nasir assured me that there was nothing that was so urgent that it couldn't wait just another day. Reluctantly, I agreed.

Before Nasir left, he told me that the next day, he would be meeting with his uncle, the administrator for the hospital in

Nasiriyah. This was so I could outline what I needed from them in order get Rasha the treatment she needed in Baghdad.

Nasir told me quite sternly to rest and he would return in the morning as usual. I corrected him and said his time to come in was 8am, so I would see him then. He smiled, nodded and left.

I stood looking out of the floor-to-ceiling windows, which formed two of the four walls in the room, and watched as Nasir walked out of the compound. He spent some time talking to Mustapha, the guard, before he left. They both looked back at my building, unable to see me behind the thick net and heavy curtains. They nodded at each other, then Nasir left.

I spent the rest of that day trying not to work, but a mix of boredom and a never-reducing mountain of paperwork got the better of me. Suddenly Mustapha appeared at the door. He had a paper bag in his hand and a mug of steaming hot tea.

"Mr Philip," Mustapha began, "Mr Nasir said I should prepare lunch for you."

I walked over to him in the doorway. Mustapha handed me the warm paper bag and the smell made me salivate. I called him into the room, and he cautiously followed me in. I thanked him and asked if he would join me and share the lunch he had so thoughtfully and kindly brought to me.

With his hand over his heart and his head slightly bowed, he most politely and with a smile, declined. I offered him the money that he must have spent on the lunch, but he said Nasir had already paid him for it. I thanked him again as he set the hot mug of tea down and left the room to continue his shift guarding me in my compound.

I opened the bag to find eight falafel balls, made from vegetables with chickpeas and fried until golden brown. They tasted great.

I thought to myself, "Just what do the guards, Nasir and other Iraqi people I have met think of people like me? I have been shown nothing but kindness and great courtesy from everyone I have met, apart from the stone throwing and broken window issue." It was quite... no, it was *very* humbling.

It was very hard for me to have the perception of being elevated in importance; it was a false status. I was no more important than or different to those I worked with or managed. I had met so many good people; people who, due to the years of sanctions and the devastating recent war, had very little, yet they were always willing to share and were kind.

As a soldier in the first Gulf War, prior to the start of battle, I had a preconceived idea of what an Iraqi was like. I was, however, quickly educated during the war. The prisoners that were taken were often conscripts who didn't want to fight and had been abandoned by their commanders, often left without food or water and many times without weapons or ammunition. The so-called elites of the National Guard (who were not as elite as they were perceived to be) had left the normal army conscripts to their fate in the desert.

Now, many years later and after a second war, I was getting another perspective from the ex-soldiers and the people of Iraq straight from the horse's mouth. It was different to most western perceptions at the time. To me, it opened up the almost-total suppression of a nation's people, who feared speaking out and were indoctrinated with propaganda and deliberate misinformation. It was a brutal regime that led to a nation being, in many cases, wrongly pigeon-holed.

The flipside was, of course, those who were driven by hatred and an extremist viewpoint that all foreigners were enemies and took action to inflict violence, barbaric violence, against them. This became more of a feature as time went on across the Middle East.

The terrible 9/11 attack on America sparked a war and a wave of terrorism across the Middle East into Europe and America. The rise of Al-Qaeda (AQ) to a wider and more active platform, from its beginnings around 1988 followed by its spawning of other terror groups, such as Islamic State in Iraq and the Levant (ISIL), more commonly referred to across multiple factions as ISIS, led to a perception that those with Middle Eastern origins were all terrorists and this, in turn, led to an isolation of particular communities and alienated huge swathes of people at home and overseas, eventually aiding the recruitment for such groups.

There are more good, kind and friendly Iraqis than there are terrorists. There is good and bad in people wherever you are from, whatever religion you care to follow. Having been the subject of stereotyping myself, I can understand the confusion, the fear of those wrongly accused and, sometimes, the hatred that can be easily derived from it, from both sides.

After my unexpected but delicious lunch and my hot cup of tea, I relaxed for a while. I typed an email to my wife to let her know that all was well and I would be home in just a few more weeks. We sometimes skyped for very short periods; it was expensive to do on the BGAN but it was part of the agreed welfare package (I was allowed two skype communications home a week). Each call had to be no longer than five minutes, so while very welcome, they had to be planned and well thought out. It worked, and I was grateful for it.

The next morning, I woke just before the alarm on my travel clock sounded. I remembered to switch off the alarm when I got out of bed this time rather than running back from the kitchen as my toast burnt to cancel it.

It was 6.45am, and the sun was in the sky already, as it was almost every day. I put the kettle on, headed to the bathroom for a shower and a shave, dried off and got dressed ready for breakfast.

It was 7.15am when I poured the UHT milk on my Rice Crispies to go with my habitual cup of tea.

I heard (over the obvious noise of my snap, crackle and pop) voices outside. It just sounded like normal Arabic conversation. I wondered if there was anyone at the gate?

I placed my now-empty breakfast bowl in the sink and took my tea and walked out into the open compound. There was Nasir talking to Alem. It was 7.30am and Nasir wasn't due to be at work until 8am. I slowly walked over to them; their conversation stopped, probably as they heard me slurp my hot tea.

"Good morning, guys!" I exclaimed as I got closer to the pair.

They both smiled and nodded at me. I asked Nasir why he had arrived so early. His reply was that he'd arrived at 7am but decided not to come into the house until 8am as I had instructed. I smiled at him and told him he should be here for 8am, not 7am then wait until 8am to announce his arrival. "You should take the extra time in the morning to be with you family a little longer and maybe have breakfast with them instead of coming in early and drinking all my juice," I joked.

With a shrug of his shoulders, he set about his normal routine of preparing the vehicle for the day's business.

I had a security meeting hosted by the American military and attended by all INGO groups in the city (that was at 8.30am) followed by a trip to Nasiriyah hospital to meet with Nasir's uncle, then a round of programme visits to the schools, the bakery for distribution and then, hopefully, to take some good news and some bread to the orphanages.

The security meetings were often a very rigid affair. Even though the majority of the audience was civilian, many had no real concept of military briefings; they always remained a very formal and militaristic occasion. In all honesty, while there was some good information, it was generally the same briefing the soldiers got prior to their patrols, leaving out the critical and mission-orientated stuff, so the useful information was limited for INGOs. There was no forum for questions either; when even the simplest questions were asked, the response was almost always uninformative, such as "that information is classified at this moment", or "I am afraid we can't divulge that level of information to civilians".

Some of these guys delivering the briefings were less than six years into their service, and for many, this was their first operational tour. I owned socks that had longer military service and had been on more operational tours, but that's the way it was.

I arrived at the meeting in the Nasiriyah council offices in good time. We parked in the barbwire-surrounded car park and, using The Child-Focused INGO ID cards, we gained access and stood around with a coffee chatting to other like-minded folk.

I was ushered into the meeting room, which at its centre had a long line of tables pushed together to give an overall table length of about 20 feet (nearly seven metres). The chairs were packed in around both sides of it, and at the top end of the table, stood three US Marines talking quietly, no doubt discussing what to deliver at the briefing.

The walls of the room, once painted white, were now faded; the paint was in places peeling back. Two of the walls had maps on them; notably, one set of maps had a curtain over them so you couldn't see what was marked on them. The other set of two maps, one of Iraq in general and one of Nasiriyah city, were totally unmarked.

After a few minutes, the briefing started. Notepads were out, and pens were at the ready, with no one really taking notes at this point. The briefing started with an overview of Iraq in general and a brief mention of any major incidents across the country. There were no specifics, no pin-point locations and no analysis of events looking for patterns of attacks. I knew only too well that the Marines would have produced all of that information and analysed it to establish the growing threats, to calculate the risks and to identify their vulnerabilities to them, but this was never discussed, even when the threat and risk extended to us civilians.

The process bored and angered me. Apart from one or two very small pieces of sketchy information, it could be seen as a waste of time.

As the meeting ended, I stood up and asked all members of the INGOs to wait behind for a few minutes once the military and the councillors had left. They all sat down again. As the military and all the non-INGO people left, I closed the door and addressed the group.

"Okay, guys. Most of you know me, and for those who don't, my name is Phil and I am the acting country director for The Child-Focused INGO." All eyes were on me and no one spoke. This was all done on the spur of the moment and fuelled by the time these meetings wasted and the little information that was offered.

"I suspect that many of you have the same opinion as I do, that the meetings we attend here, particularly for security, are not as fruitful as we would hope."

"Fucking waste of time," was the answer in a French accent at the back of the room.

I continued: "I propose that we form our own INGO safety and security meetings each week and we discuss the issues that we deem important so we can swap ideas on how best to safely operate. After all, we operate closer to the population and we employ local staff, so I guess our sources of information are much more reliable and focused than the military's."

There were nods of agreement around the room, but I sensed it needed a bit more in the way of commitment, so I put myself (again) in the firing line. I guessed no one else in the room would lead at this time. I went on: "I will agree to chair the meeting and hold the first one at The Child-Focused INGO office next Monday at 9am. I would ask you to bring with you any information relating to any attacks, any activities that have caused you to stop the delivery of your programmes, any threats you may have received and any information related to the safety of us all doing our jobs."

The nods were now more pronounced and whispers were emanating from the gathering, so I thought just to finish off...

"Please involve your trusted national staff, your team leaders, your guards, your cleaners and your cooks too. These are the guys who know what is going on out there, as they live with it every day. Please try to use suggestive questions or gently approach any issues; don't ask direct questions such as 'do you know who is trying to kill us?' or 'when do you think the next attack will be?'. That will just cause suspicion, and they won't volunteer any info. Remember, they've lived in fear for years, being afraid to talk about things like this, as they could be locked up, or worse. So go gentle and let's see how this works. It's for all our benefits. Questions?"

There were a few questions, but in all, we were in agreement that we should be looking after our own safety and security, as our needs, approach and aims were radically different to the military's. A threat to our lives would be one we possibly couldn't fight; we don't have tanks, guns and hundreds of soldiers to guard us. Our plans, our methodology, would have to be more considered, and a really 'smart' approach would need to be applied.

Immediately after the meeting, several people approached me on the way out to express their gratitude that something more INGO-focused was being done. As one guy said, "It's been a long time coming and it's much needed."

I smiled and shook his outstretched hand, but couldn't help wondering if anyone else would have taken control had I not proposed and taken the lead in implementing the idea. Anyway, things to do people to see.

I came out from the meeting and met up again with Nasir. (No INGO national staff were allowed to attend the security meetings. The only Iraqi nationals present were senior councillors who usually just sat at the back and had no input at all.) He smiled and asked how the meeting had gone. I told him it went as expected: lots of talking but not much being said. I filled him in on the fact that I had opened a security forum for just INGOs, and we were scheduled to host the first one the following week. Nasir looked at me as if to say "more work?" I smiled, winked at him and set off to the car park.

The journey to the hospital only took a few minutes, and soon we were parking up and heading for the main door.

There was a large queue outside the main entrance. At the entranceway there was a small window with metal bars on it, the type you would imagine would be on a prison cell. It had a small cut-out were people in the queue pushed in pieces of paper then went away. Nasir explained that it was a pharmacy, but that only about five per cent of prescriptions were ever given out. They just didn't have the medicines or drugs in stock.

Most of the faces in the long queue looked blank. There was little hope that they would get the medicines or tablets they needed; they knew that, I think, but they still went through the motions.

We pushed our way through the crowd and into the open corridors. Nasir knew where the office was and led the way.

We reached a dimly lit corridor which had a row of chairs and benches along one wall. Some people were sitting quietly, some even slept; or I hoped they were just asleep.

Nasir asked me to take a seat while he went to find his uncle. I sat down and started wondering what I would say to Nasir's uncle, or what my plan would be. Before I got totally lost in my thoughts, Nasir's head appeared from a doorway about halfway up the corridor. He beckoned for me to join him.

I walked into the small office. It was very dim. Even though the sun shone brightly outside, this room faced away from it. The drab net curtains also kept out some of the daylight. The room looked shabby, with paint peeling from the walls and ceiling. Of the four tubes in the ceiling light, only one was working, and that was flickering and about to fail too, I thought.

Nasir's uncle was sitting behind a desk that was overloaded with paperwork, books and files. It looked a lot more chaotic than my desk; mine looked tidy in comparison.

Two chairs had been set out for Nasir and me to sit on; old metal-framed chairs with red upholstered seats and a strip of upholstered cushioning on the backrest. The upholstery was, on both chairs, torn in places, showing the faded yellowish sponge underneath.

As I entered the room, Nasir's uncle rose from his chair (which, by the way, looked like a leather, high-backed, executive, office swivel chair, and looked a lot newer than everything else in the room) and greeted me with a wide smile and a strong handshake. He motioned for us to take a seat. As we did, he introduced himself to me as Mr Adnan. (Adnan was his first name (Christian name, but he wasn't a Christian; we get used to terminology that may not be correct in other cultures, but, yeah, that's his name.) The 'Mr' before his first name was a title used in many countries I had worked in, out of politeness, I think. I was often Mr Philip.)

Just as we sat down, the one flickering light went out. For a second or two, there was a loud buzzing noise, then it stopped. It was yet another electrical shut down, or rather power failure. During the war, a lot of the infrastructure was damaged, including the power stations. Power was often and deliberately shut down so repairs could be carried out. Other times, the system just failed, as it was so badly damaged. The 'buzzing' was the internal alarm which was usually followed by the hospital generators starting up; but they didn't, as they, too, were badly damaged and in need of repair.

We now sat in an even gloomier and almost-dark room. From his desk draw, Mr Adnan produced a battery-powered lamp, placed it on his desk and then asked how he could assist me.

I started from the beginning: the referral project, the assessment based on a single patient (Rasha), the trip to Basra for diagnosis and the referral now from Nasiriyah to Baghdad and what that would look like in terms of administrative support for the patient.

I had spoken to Nasir previously about the 'line' we should take with his uncle, understanding that this brought Nasir very much into the plot, dealing with his relations, who just happened to be in the right job at the right place and at the right time; fortunate and slightly unfortunate at the same time.

I produced a copy of the letter that the Lebanese doctor had written and showed Mr Adnan his point about treatment and potential referral. I decided to be bold. "In order to make this process work and for it to be the success we need, to base future referrals on, we need this hospital to support the patient in the following ways," I said confidently.

Mr Adnan looked at Nasir, who nodded. He then looked at me, waiting for the punchline, so I didn't hesitate. "We would like to have a nominated doctor who would be the link between Nasiriyah hospital, the patient and Baghdad Hospital." I paused just for a few seconds to try to gauge a response. There wasn't one, so I continued, "The patient would require several visits over an unknown period of time to Baghdad Hospital, and your hospital would need to facilitate this, in the latter treatment stages, by ambulance."

With that last statement, I thought I had gone a step too far. Ambulances were a precious resource, and not many of them had survived the war in working order. I stared back at Mr Adnan with my poker face. He met my gaze, and quietly and calmly explained his hospital's very limited resources, told of how overwhelmed all his departments were and that after thirteen years of UN sanctions, just as he had found a way of coping with very little, a new war started and compounded his problems.

He asked, "So, Mr Philip, what does my hospital gain from this referral system?"

That was the one question I had hoped he wouldn't ask, but I knew it was the one question he would ask. Luckily, I was prepared for it and was brutally honest.

"At this point, I can't make you any promises. There is no immediate gain, and further, it would be to the detriment of your resource management," I said calmly, hoping that my honesty would appeal to him. I continued, "The success or failure of the trial project would dictate which follow-on actions may or may not be taken. All hospital administrations involved in the trial would have to agree to fully support the process, and that would then need to be agreed between all major hospitals across the country."

I paused again, and this time, I got a small but noticeable reaction from Mr Adnan. He raised his eyebrows ever so slightly and his shoulders relaxed as he took a deep breath. "I need more," I thought...

"The process of assessment has to start somewhere, and it can only begin with those who are courageous and can see what the future could be if the project was successful, while at the same time be able and willing to accept the consequence if it fails, which is a possibility."

Mr Adnan smiled, stood up and walked to the door. He spoke to Nasir in Arabic, then to me in English, simply saying that he would be back soon. He smiled and walked out of the room, closing the door behind him.

Nasir, anticipating my question, said that his uncle was going to talk to some senior doctors and the management team of the hospital. We would have to wait.

There was a knock on the door and then it opened. A young woman stood in the doorway and spoke to us in Arabic. Nasir replied, and she left. Nasir then told me that she had been sent by her uncle to ask if we wanted tea or coffee; he had ordered tea for us both.

A few minutes later, our drinks arrived, and we took the time as we drank to mull over the conversation we'd just had and to discuss possible outcomes. Nasir was sure we could not achieve what we had asked for, and to be honest, I agreed. I thought I had asked too much and pushed, no matter how gently, too far.

Nearly two hours passed and I was fearing the worst, planning what I would do next. I was running short of ideas but I had a basic plan of how to proceed. It was going to be costly, though, and I would have to come clean with my organisation; not a thing I was looking forward to doing.

The door opened, and in walked Mr Adnan. He smiled and apologised for the wait. He sat behind his desk and leaned back in his chair. The room was silent. It seemed that in that moment, the whole of Nasiriyah was silent. I was fully and totally focused on Mr Adnan's face.

He leaned forward and spoke slowly, clearly and very deliberately. "Mr Philip," he began, "Nasir has told me of the work you have been doing over the two and a half months you have been in Nasiriyah. I would like to thank you for helping our people when you could be safely at home with your family."

There was a long pause.

"My cousin on the Nasiriyah Council has also spoken of you and your work for the children here. You are a good man, and Nasir is a very good man to have as your assistant. I thank you for all you have done."

Another pause.

I know what usually follows such praise; it's usually bad news, only wrapped up in nice words. An old military saying is: 'A pat on the back is often a recce for the knife.' Is that what was coming? I glanced quickly at Nasir, who now had his head down and was looking at the floor. I thought to myself, "Brace for this; it isn't going to be easy to accept, no matter how inevitable it may have been."

Mr Adnan took a deep breath and continued. "You understand that our resources at this hospital are few, and those resources we do have are always under pressure. We have given consideration to your request and our decision..."

I was right on the edge of my seat, trying hard to maintain my poker face and keep my emotions in check.

"... is that we will agree to transport the patient to Baghdad for the first three months of her treatment. We will take her by car to Baghdad and bring her back to Nasiriyah by ambulance. The hospital has appointed two of its senior doctors to oversee the patient's case and will act as liaison. This is the most we can do. We understand and accept that there is no promise that this project will succeed, but God willing, it will."

"*Insha'Allah*," Nasir said.

"*Insha'Allah*," Mr Adnan and I said, almost together.

It was hard, really hard, to control my emotion at this point. I was elated. I stood up and offered my hand to Mr Adnan, who, with a wide smile, shook it and thanked me for what I was doing. I thanked him, his colleagues, his hospital and anyone else I could think of. With emotions only just in check, I said we would be in touch very soon to make arrangements.

Nasir and I almost collided trying to get out of the door; a comedy moment in an exceptionally poignant situation.

We didn't speak all the way back to the car. Once we had driven off, I burst, telling Nasir what great news this was and what a diamond he was for having Uncle Adnan and what a star Uncle Adnan was for making this happen.

Suddenly, I had a flashback. It was to the time our window had been smashed and all that had followed. I'd totally forgotten to tell Nasir that I had made contact with the hospital in Baghdad and that they had agreed to see Rasha if we could independently arrange her transport. The window-smashing had caused me to completely forget to tell him the news of the phone calls I'd made and the success I'd had. It was all coming together.

After such a long day, I decided to go back to my office in town, pick up some documents and go home. I didn't have long left on my contract but I still had a lot of work to do.

As we drove into town, we heard lots of gunfire. It seemed to be distant but loud enough to be of concern. The gunfire was accompanied by the 'crump' sound of hand grenades exploding. I saw a rising plume of smoke from what appeared to be the northern side of the city. It sounded quite ferocious.

I turned the vehicle around and headed home, which was at the southern edge of town.

On arrival, I made several local calls. Nasir also checked with his contacts to try to piece together what was happening.

It appeared that a large militia group had attacked the American Camp Whitehorse. The camp was situated close to the old airstrip on the Tallil airbase (which later became a prisoner camp for captured Iraqi fighters). The resulting action involved the pursuit and battle in town between US forces and what was left of the militia.

Actions like this were getting much more frequent. We had, I thought, passed the 'honeymoon period', whereupon the locals first greeted the US/coalition liberating forces as heroes who deposed the old Saddam Hussein's regime. The locals were now becoming tired, due to the lack of improvement and the aggressive nature of what was being increasingly referred to as 'the new occupation'. Things were changing for the worse.

After arriving back at my home base, I parked up the vehicle, sorted it out ready for a quick evacuation if needed, got my grab bag and made sure I would be ready to move at a moment's notice if the situation got any worse. I was hoping it wouldn't, but the country was changing fast and while the north around Baghdad and Mosul were constantly witnessing ongoing attacks, Fallujah and Najaf were also heading into the chaotic mess of terrorism-guerrilla-type hit-and-run attacks.

It was time to call London.

I got myself organised, made my cup of tea, sorted out my laptop and called the office.

As the call got underway, I was pleasantly surprised by the news: Paul was sending out an experienced guy he'd recruited from another INGO. He would arrive in two days' time via Kuwait City Airport. I would need to be there to meet him, spend the day in Kuwait at the same hotel we'd used the last time, conduct briefings, etc., get his paperwork sorted and then, the following day, drive back to Nasiriyah.

This was great news; news I had waited a long time to hear.

I updated Paul on all the programme activity. The bakery was running really well. The exit-strategy paper I had sent to him a the week before was being reviewed and was looking good. (We would hand over the bakery to the council-run grain-storage company who would continue the production in conjunction with a selection of small corner-shop-type bakeries to ensure they wouldn't be put out of business. The proviso being that the council agree to continue to supply the orphanages, schools and hospitals we had already committed to. This would ensure the sustainability of production, as the new owners would also be the new suppliers of flour. That was the plan and it appeared to be a good one.)

I was struggling with the dilemma of whether to tell Paul about my escapades. Coming clean about what I had done and disclosing all the information about Rasha was becoming a heavy burden I really needed to share.

After all the financial information had been explained, the conversation started to draw to a close. Paul then asked if there was anything else to discuss.

I took a deep breath.

I was only a couple of weeks away from leaving Iraq at the end of my contract, so I thought that, with the new guy coming in and the promise of a new team almost finalised, this was the best time (if there ever was one) to confess.

I started by cautiously saying that there was something I needed to tell him...

I began. "Do you remember when you came out here to help me and we went to the orphanage?"

"Yes," Paul responded.

I continued to tell him about Rasha and how she had been abandoned by her family because she was a medical burden that they couldn't cope with. I continued to tell him what I had done, the meetings I had arranged and the stories I had told to get the cooperation and help needed to try to save this girl's life, or at best, to make her remaining time more bearable, giving her some hope.

Once I had finished talking, I waited in silence. I could hear Paul breathing, but he didn't speak straight away.

Finally, he did. "Oh, Phil. What have you done? This isn't good."

My heart sank. I had known the response would be bad. "Can I just add," I interrupted, "that I paid all costs out of my own pocket: fuel, hotels and meals. I covered Nasir's costs as well."

There was another pause, so I continued. "I worked a lot of extra hours to make up any lost programme time and I ensured that all deadlines for programme activity were met."

Paul sensed my unease and took over the conversation. His first words really hit home. The impact of hearing this from someone else, particularly Paul, who had so much trust and faith in me, really shook me.

"Phil, what you have done?" he began. "No matter how well meaning, it could be catastrophic for us as an organisation and more so for the team there."

I was dumbstruck. I just kept silent and listened as he continued.

"If word gets out that we, a non-medical INGO, have done all of this for one sick girl, we could possibly have every parent with their sick child knocking at our door. That would be thousands of kids across Nasiriyah, not to mention the wider regions, who may get to hear about this."

I wanted to talk, to defend my actions and to argue my point, but I knew he was right. I had known for some time, but I couldn't turn away from it. I kept quiet, as I sensed that there was more to come... and there was.

"Phil, the potential knock-on effect of all those people being disappointed that we can't or won't treat their children could, and probably would, turn into violence, not only directed at our organisation, but at Nasir and his family and other INGOs who would be tarnished with the same brush: making promises they can't keep. Many people think that all INGOs are the same, so when one makes a mistake, we all get accused, and the trust, which is critical to our success, is lost."

There was silence again. I sensed that the message that I was wrong, badly wrong, was finished. I expected my services to go the same way; finished.

After the pause, Paul asked in a very calm manner, "So how do you feel about it all?"

His question took me by surprise.

"Honestly," I replied, "if met with the same situation, knowing what the possible outcomes could be..."

I hesitated for a moment.

"... I would do the same again. Sorry, but I just couldn't walk away from her and the situation she was in."

I thought that would be the final nail in the coffin for me and my career.

"Look," Paul began again. "You must keep this quiet and hope we can get through it without creating any institutional damage. For what it's worth, I understand. We are all human and have feelings and emotions, but sometimes we must learn to override them for a greater cause: to help the many were we can, not just the one. There are other medical organisations who would be better placed to care for children like Rasha."

Paul ended the conversation by saying that between him and me, he thought I had done a fantastic job getting Rasha through all the obstacles that existed. He wished me well in getting her to Baghdad for treatment. I was to keep him updated with Rasha's progress: informally, of course.

*

Chapter 5:

The End of the Beginning and the Start of a New Journey

I had made the mad dash down to Safwan and the Kuwaiti border to meet the new country director.

Malik was due to land in two hours' time after a trip, which over a couple of days took him from France, were he was working, to Morocco, his home, to collect the possessions he would need for his new job in Nasiriyah, then onward to London for his pre-deployment Iraq programme briefing and finally to Kuwait. His last few days would have been very tiring, and I expected he would sleep most of the night and all the way back to Nasiriyah.

The area around Safwan was fast becoming a mini bandit town. Often, when vehicles queued on the Iraqi side of the border waiting to enter Kuwait, they would be looted by various criminal groups, ranging from teenagers to armed men. Usually it was the large lorries that were targeted, but all normal cars and pick-up trucks would be taken around Safwan. Vehicles entering Iraq from the Kuwaiti side would usually be stopped a bit further north of the border crossing then attacked and looted or hijacked and stolen, vehicle, goods and all.

Policing on the Iraqi – Safwan side was almost non-existent. What police presence did exist, was ineffective; they usually just parked their police car, stayed in it and took turns sleeping their shift away.

On crossing the border into Kuwait, you were invited to park your vehicle, have it searched then walk across the road to a portacabin where you presented your paperwork, along with your passport, and received a stamped temporary visa costing just a few US dollars. Then it was back to your vehicle, and off you went.

Some days, the crossing and paperwork checks were quick, while at other times, they were frustratingly slow. Today it was the former, and in no time at all, I was driving away from the crossing and into Kuwait.

Leaving Iraq and entering Kuwait was always for me a calming experience. While remaining alert, it was easier to relax a little. The scenery when getting closer to Kuwait City always appeared brighter. It could have been the watered grass verges between the highways or the immaculate, almost-sterile streets or the modern and well-maintained houses and the tall buildings that all looked amazingly clean and bright. It may have been the familiar shops, colourful, organised and well stocked. Even the cars in Kuwait were mostly new, well maintained and sparkling clean. Porsche, Ferrari, Lamborghini; all expensive top-end cars announcing the country's wealth. It was such a sharp contrast to the immediate post-war, damaged and dull Iraq, with the familiar dirty brown-beige desert that rolled on for miles, devoid of colour. There were small towns with open street markets rather than shops, selling almost everything you could think of; most things, apart from fresh food, were second hand or just old. The bigger cities were not much better off. They had bigger buildings and more cafés, but they still, even in bright sunlight, appeared drab and dull. Cars were old and full of dents; many painted by hand with a household paint and brush after accident damage. This was the effect of many years of UN sanctions, a dictator who wouldn't spread the country's oil wealth to anyone outside his own trusted circle and neglect of large areas of the country to the point of total poverty. Yep, it was easier to relax in Kuwait.

I arrived at the airport in what I thought was good time. I parked up and went inside to get a cup of coffee and something to eat. I sat with my sandwich, slowly sipping my hot coffee, when I looked up at the arrivals board. I checked my notebook for the flight number and rechecked the noticeboard again. The flight had already landed: two hours ago.

I grabbed my sandwich, left my coffee and ran to the arrivals hall. I had a picture of Malik from his passport scan sent to me from the London office. "He should be easy to spot," I thought, "as he has a huge head of hair. An 'afro' of epic proportion." True enough, I spotted him sipping from a bottle of water and reading a book. I walked over to him.

"Malik?" I said as got close to him.

He stood and smiled. "You must be Phil. I have heard a lot of good things about you from Paul. It's good to meet you." He spoke with a slight French accent. (I found out later that he was also fluent in Arabic and English). He told me that he mostly spoke French, as he had lived in France for many years and had only very recently returned to Morocco, but that his English was very good.

We gathered his suitcases and bags and headed to the car park. Once in the car, I started to tell him our plan for the next two days. He nodded and made himself comfortable for the short journey to the hotel.

We had paid for a room in advance, on the understanding that it would always be reserved for us at this very small hotel, just in case we needed to leave Iraq in a hurry. It also gave us a base in Kuwait to either remotely manage the programme from, or to be our sleepover if we needed to visit Kuwait for the purchase of logistical kit and equipment for the projects; equipment that was not available in Iraq. We would also do our major food shopping every time we visited.

As we entered our small suite, I showed Malik to his room and told him to get a couple of hours' sleep. I had some supplies to buy and some equipment for the orphanages and the education programmes to collect, so I told him I would be back in a few hours and that I would bring back some lunch for us both, then I would brief him on his new job.

He agreed, headed to the shower then went to bed.

I completed all my errands and took several trips from the car to the room, carrying all the bits and pieces I had bought. I thought that after three hours I would have found Malik awake, but no. I had bought in a pizza for lunch and a couple of bottles of Coke. I thought it best to let Malik sleep a bit longer and I would reheat the pizza when he woke.

I sorted out my briefing, completed the accounting for all the purchases I had made and, finally, sat down with a cup of tea. A few moments later, Malik entered the room. I laughed.

His previously well-combed and styled hair now looked like a burst mattress. It looked hilarious. Malik was lazily trying to drag an afro comb through it, but still being half asleep, he wasn't having too much success.

I prepared what was now dinner, and we sat down together. I started to familiarise Malik with the programme activity. We started with the bakery project which was, by far, the largest project we had at the time. I showed him the exit-strategy plan and talked him through the process, once it was agreed, of how to get the handover underway. I would introduce him to the personalities involved once we got to Nasiriyah.

Next we discussed the orphanages. I deliberately left out the Rasha 'bit', as I thought I would discuss all of that on the journey back. It would give us something to talk about.

We then covered the education projects, the schools, the academic and administrative support, the youth drop-in centres and the planning and ideas for a major play area in the centre of Nasiriyah. There was a defunct play area that I had identified close to the centre of the city. It was ideal. It was fenced off and had a giant teddy bear above the gateway. It just needed some TLC and new play equipment, such as swings, slides and see-saws and the like. I had also found a supplier in Kuwait who could supply everything we needed; he was also open to negotiation on price.

I don't know if Malik was still suffering from his journey but at the time, he appeared really disinterested. I decided to put it down to tiredness and ended the briefing.

We finished up what was left of the pizza and sat watching the TV. Malik asked questions about the security situation. He was very interested in the war, what went on and what the attacks were like across Iraq. His questions appeared a little more than just curiosity or based on safety; it seemed almost like a morbid obsession, or maybe a fascination more than an obsession. The tone caught me off guard a little bit. I thought that being an 'experienced' country director (CD) he would have worked in similar environments before. If so, why did he appear almost excited by it all? Maybe it was my inexperience in this sector that was the problem. Maybe all humanitarian workers were like this? (I found out later they definitely are not!)

After fending off questions about my past life, I decided that it was time for me to get some sleep. We would be setting off early, so I had a good excuse. I left Malik sitting at the table, snacking on biscuits and crisps.

I was up early the next morning to load the car. After loading everything and tying the tarpaulin down, I went back to the room for a quick breakfast and to gather Malik and his bags, hoping to set off to Nasiriyah in good time.

Malik wasn't ready. His bags weren't packed. He looked like shite! He was already starting to annoy me slightly. I told Malik we would be leaving in about 20 minutes, so he should bring his bags down to the car then we could get on the road. Malik nodded and went to the cupboards looking for breakfast. Toast was about the limit.

Fifteen minutes later, Malik made it to the car, put his bags on the back seat of the twin cab and climbed in. I drove to the front of the hotel, ran inside, checked the room to ensure we had left nothing behind, locked the door and returned the key to the manager at reception, along with an envelope containing pre-payment, in new unused American dollars, to secure the next two months' accommodation costs.

The trip back to Nasiriyah, once we had negotiated the border crossing, was uneventful. I had started to tell Malik about Rasha, her connection to the orphanage, her medical condition and her assessed lifespan, culminating with the procedure now in place via Nasiriyah hospital. I told him, quite proudly, that in two days' time, Rasha would be going for her first visit to Baghdad.

Malik looked at me quizzically. "Does Paul know what you have been doing?" he asked.

"Yes, I told him the whole story a few days ago," I said, deliberately keeping my response short.

Malik stared at me with a look of almost disbelief. After a short pause, he said he was very surprised that Paul had allowed this to happen.

I just shrugged my shoulders and told him that it was a steep learning curve for me and now that all the legwork had been done, it would only take the minimum of input to get Rasha the treatment she needed.

Malik turned to stare out of the windscreen and sat in silence until we got back to Nasiriyah. I was quickly forming a dislike for the new CD, and we hadn't even started our handover yet.

We arrived back at our home base in Nasiriyah. I spent what was left of the day familiarising Malik with the home layout. The vehicles always parked facing towards the gate so we could drive out quickly if needed. I showed him the fuel stash, which was half buried in the soft earth under a tree in the shade and covered with a tarpaulin to keep the sun off.

I talked about the radios in the vehicles, the HF Codan and the VHF Motorola. He wasn't familiar with HF, which I thought was strange. I printed off the radio call signs that were used by other organisations and ran through the emergency communications 'tree', which was an effective way of informing many organisations that something was happening. Each INGO had just one call to make, and in turn the message would be passed in a chain of calls, with the final INGO calling the initiating organisation, therefore, closing the loop of calls. This could be achieved using telephones or radios.

I spent the rest of the early evening going through all the safety and security protocols, which I had invested a great deal of time and planning into putting in place. I told Malik that Nasir, whom he would meet in the morning, would take him on a drive over the next few days to show him the emergency routes out of Nasiriyah, avoiding the jams and bottlenecks.

I sensed an air of arrogance from Malik. While he appeared to be listening to what I was saying, he seemed preoccupied. With what? I have no idea. But it was starting to annoy me.

"Days to do are getting few," I thought to myself. I mustn't spoil the good reputation I had established, by knocking seven bells out this arrogant shit, experienced or not (and I was seriously questioning what his experience really was and where it was gained).

I just continued to run through the briefing sheet I had prepared, to ensure I didn't leave anything out. I added a signature block to it later that day, with the statement saying that the new CD had been briefed on all the subjects listed and understood the role and responsibilities. I just felt, from his attitude, that I would need to cover my back, as my confidence in him was ebbing fast.

To finish off the evening, I took him across to the other organisation that shared our compound to meet Tim, the CD who had become a good and reliable friend over the previous three months.

Malik shook hands with Tim, and they engaged in a very short conversation, followed by Tim introducing his team to Malik. His body language was obvious, and it was instantly apparent were his focus was. He quickly shook hands with the male team members without speaking, but took a long time shaking or holding, I couldn't really tell, the hands of the female members of the team. I knew he was a single guy, but this was a bit obvious, and it was getting a little inappropriate.

I made the excuse that we had more to talk about, and said we should leave. As I walked to the compound gate with Tim and Malik, Tim asked if I had a minute to discuss the compound security plan before I left. I told Malik he should go on ahead and that I would be over in a few minutes. He left, and I sat in the courtyard with Tim.

I guessed that Tim really wanted to discuss Malik, and the security plan was just an excuse to get me on my own. I was right.

"Bloody hell, mate," Tim began. "He's a weird one. I think he may cause a few issues with the girls. He really comes across a bit strong, doesn't he?"

I told Tim that I had my doubts about him. His experience seemed questionable, but who was I to talk?

Tim and I had worked very closely together. We had supported each other's programmes at times. It was a good, mutually beneficial set-up between our two organisations.

I had confided in Tim about Rasha. His advice had been much the same as Paul's, but by the time I had confided in him, I had almost completed the plan.

Tim asked me what Malik thought about the 'Rasha situation'. I told him how disinterested he was and how surprised he was that Paul knew about it.

I told Tim that everything was set up now, and Malik would have very little to do other than to ensure that Rasha got to the Nasiriyah hospital on time for her transport and collected her for return to the orphanage when the ambulance brought her back from Baghdad. So minimum input.

We cracked a few jokes about Malik's hair, then I left.

As I walked the very short distance across the compound to my house, I could hear sporadic gunfire in the distance. It was a normal soundtrack to the Nasiriyah night; so familiar that I had found myself asking, "Why no gunfire tonight?" On those rare occasions, it was quiet.

The following day was spent familiarising Malik with the many meetings, visiting the project sites, meeting key personalities and just generally getting him familiarised with the city, the INGO community and their associated programmes.

I introduced Malik to the INGO security forum. The information that it spawned was good. It was real time and gave a very clear picture of what was happening across the entire region. The information was direct human-intelligence. ('Hum-int' in military jargon. The term intelligence, in a setting such as this, is often misused; it is raw information obtained from multi-sources, which is analysed, looking for similarities or patterns, and then classed as intelligence for assessments to be calculated.)

Malik had no input into the meeting, not even a hello when I introduced him. I also didn't think he grasped the level of information that was being shared. After the meeting, he spoke only to the females in the group, and from what I heard, it was all self-praise. He told anyone who would listen, how he had led programmes in Bosnia and Kosovo and of his work in Kenya; little did he know that many of the people in the room had also been there, seen it, read the book and bought the T-shirt. He was impressing no one.

I decided to finish the programme familiarisation with the reporting formats and the financial reporting. This would be done back at the house.

I called Nasir and asked him to meet us at there.

As we arrived, Mustapha opened the gate. He came to my window and told me that Nasir was already inside waiting for me.

I parked the vehicle, took out my grab bag, talked Malik through the vehicle preparation for the next day and then went inside.

Nasir was sitting in the living area, and had made tea for me and coffee for Malik, while he had a juice box with a straw. He had also put some biscuits that I had brought back from Kuwait onto a plate. I made a mental note to leave Nasir behind more often if this is what I got on return. I smiled to myself and thanked Nasir for his efforts.

For me, this was the boring but important part of any handover; the paperwork.

I printed off the reporting templates and all the reports I had completed during my time in Iraq. (I was amazed at how many different reports I had written: country programme overview reports, individual project reports, security reports, financial reports (I hated those the most) and a host of weekly progress reports.)

I gave Malik a bunch of files filled with paperwork and told him to familiarise himself with the content, as his first report would be needed at the end of the week. He reluctantly took them from me and agreed to read them all.

I decided to leave him there, and I took Nasir with me to see Rasha and to ensure she would be ready for her big trip to Baghdad tomorrow.

On the short drive across town, Nasir quizzed me about Malik. What was he like? What did I think of him? Would he be good for the programme?

I decided not to badmouth him, so I made all my answers very neutral, finishing by telling Nasir that he could make his own mind up after he'd got to know him a bit better. Nasir agreed.

As we approached the gates of the orphanage, I remembered the first time I had noticed Rasha; a sad, lonely girl, sitting on her own with probably little hope. It was a desperate scene. Knowing what I know now, it must have been a horrendous situation for someone so young to have been in, and to have no hope; it was hard to understand.

We drove in through the gates and into the compound. We walked up the three concrete steps and through the doors into the corridor. The noise of children laughing and playing rang in my ears as I looked along the corridor to the place I had seen Rasha sitting alone on several of my visits. The place where she normally sat was empty. I turned to follow Nasir, who was heading to the manageress's office. I wondered where Rasha was. I turned to have one last look up the corridor, when I was almost knocked off my feet.

Unknown to me, as I walked to the office, Rasha had come out of one of the rooms behind me and was running to greet me just as I turned around to look. She threw herself at me and hugged me, with the largest smile on her face I had ever seen. I put my hands on her shoulders and moved her back a little so I could see her face. It was a fantastic, emotional feeling. It was a moment I will never forget.

She was a changed girl. She had been playing with the other kids. She was enjoying herself, just being a child. Wow!

The manageress was sitting at her desk as we entered her office. She smiled and stood to greet us. Nasir spoke to her and pointed at Rasha. The manageress beamed back and spoke to Nasir. The conversation, after the usual greetings, started with Nasir saying how surprised he was to see Rasha laughing and playing. He mentioned how Rasha had greeted me.

The manageress, in sharp contrast to previous meetings, was happy, smiling and almost exuberant when telling Nasir about how much Rasha had changed since returning from Basra. She asked several times a day, every day, when we were coming back. Her outlook on life had changed dramatically. She had hope, I thought. She was enjoying being Rasha, the child among children, and being happy.

I confirmed with the manageress that Rasha and her chaperone would be ready for tomorrow's trip. After agreeing to take Rasha to the Nasiriyah hospital and arranging the time, Nasir and I started to unload our vehicle and bring in the new kitchen utensils and equipment I had brought back from Kuwait.

Finally, before we departed, I took Nasir back inside to speak with the manageress. I told her that I would be leaving Iraq in a few days' time. I explained that a new man had arrived and I had already told him about Rasha. She would meet him in a day or two. I asked if I could speak to Rasha. While I would see her tomorrow, this would be my chance, via Nasir, to say goodbye.

She agreed and left the office, returning holding Rasha's hand. She spoke softly to Rasha, telling her that 'Mr Phil' wanted to talk with her.

I think Rasha sensed that I was about to tell her something she might not like. Her smile now softened and she looked at me, waiting for me to speak.

I asked her if she was happy and if she was looking forward to her adventure in Baghdad.

She smiled and said softly that she was happy; she was happy that I was helping her and the orphanage. She went on to say that she was excited to be going to Baghdad.

I then told her that I was leaving Iraq in a few days' time to go home to be with my family. I told her of my wife, my daughter and my son, who I hadn't seen in three months. While I was happy to be going home, I was sad that I couldn't see Rasha through this whole process, but that is the nature of working on contract and being away from home.

I told Rasha that I would collect her tomorrow, and reassured her that Nasir would keep me informed of her progress. I told her to go and play with her friends and enjoy herself; I would see her tomorrow. Rasha smiled then looked at the manageress, who signalled that it was okay for her to leave. Rasha smiled at me again, then left the room to join the girls who had waited for her.

I thanked the manageress and then left the office.

Knowing that I would not get to fully follow through the entire process and see Rasha benefit from it was a really bitter-sweet feeling. It had been emotional, very emotional.

I asked Nasir to drive to the bakery. I wanted to get some fresh bread for tomorrow. I would make some lunch for Rasha and her chaperone. I arrived at the bakery just in time to find the last shift finishing for the night. The smell of fresh bread was still in the air as I walked through the doors.

I was met by the site manager who shook my hand and greeted me in Arabic and English. I smiled and responded in the same manner.

I asked how the bakery was running, and he responded by saying that all was well.

I took two bags of bread and put them in the vehicle. I would get a chance to say goodbye to all the staff across all the projects in the next few days, so I departed and headed back home to see how Malik was doing.

Entering the living area, I saw Malik still sitting were I'd left him, with lots of paperwork spread around him. I asked him how it was going, and he grunted and said he was about three quarters of the way through it all. He looked really naffed off; that made me smile.

"Got to be done, mate," I said.

"Yes," he responded, without looking up.

I prepared some food: chicken laced with tabasco sauce and rice. I reheated the bread, got two bottles of water and went to the living area where Malik was sitting.

I held out the plate of food for him and placed his water on the table. He never looked up. I went back to the kitchen to get my food and water, went back into the living area, cleared a space on the table and sat down.

Malik ate his food, again without looking up. He drank his water and continued reading. There was no conversation, not even a thank you. I remember thinking that this guy was arrogant, rude and a bit of a 'dick'. I had only a short time left with him, so I thought I would remain professional, give him the best handover I possibly could, and leave, never to think of him again; or so I thought.

After finishing my meal, I sat for a further hour, organising the activities for the next day. I finally stood up and told Malik that as I had made dinner, he should wash-up. Now he decided to look up.

"Wash up?" he repeated. "I have to wash up?" He was shocked that I had asked him to do such a menial task.

As I left the room, I shouted back, "Yep, and wipe all the surfaces down so we don't get infested by cockroaches." I smiled to myself and shouted goodnight as I shut the door to my room.

I slept a normal, very broken and very sweaty, sleep. I was thinking of so many things all at once. I thought of going home, being so happy to be back with my family and experiencing normality of life in the UK.

I thought of the contrast with Rasha, between my first meeting and my last. The transformation of a child from being in abject despondency, to being a happy, bright and hopeful girl who, rather than sit all day lonely and sad, now played, laughing and smiling was nothing short of amazing.

I thought of the situation in Iraq; how it had changed and continued to change. When I'd first arrived, it was very early post-war. The coalition forces and INGOs were welcomed as liberators and helpers. Due to many bad political decisions by the CPA, and military strategies that were too aggressive and appeared to have no end in sight, the population became frustrated with it all. Compounded by the very slow process of rebuilding infrastructure, the constant and prolonged power outages and fuel shortages, it was a lot to accept for those who had an expectation that all would be put right and the country would quickly prosper. Militia groups were coming more to the fore, mostly based along religious and tribal lines. The groups were previously and brutally suppressed by Saddam Hussein. Now, in the potential power vacuum, everyone was violently vying for power. In some locations the creep to violence and guerrilla warfare was slower than others, but it was happening right across the country. Attacks on the coalition were becoming more frequent and the targeting of INGOs was also emerging as a terrible tactic, spreading fear and, in some locations, a restriction on programme activity.

Humanitarian interventions had for many years (bar a few exceptions) been mostly untouchable, and an unwritten rule that they could operate freely in conflict situations, as long as they were impartial and gave the same level of support or service or medical assistance, or food, or shelter or... I could go on, but the situation was that their interventions were seen as being neutral and not tied to politics or religion.[5]

---

[5] There are several faith-based INGOs but they are bound by the humanitarian imperative to be neutral and transparent, bringing relief and support to all those who need it. Some terror groups and militias failed to understand this and often accused them of trying to convert the populations they were assisting. This added a greater risk to their humanitarian interventions.

It never really mattered from what country an INGO was founded in or the nationalities of those it employed. The follow on from the 9/11 attacks on the US, the war on terror and the Iraq war all changing that perspective forever.

Foreigners, regardless of nationality, were being targeted. Those of European and American origin topped the list due to their country's participation in the coalition forces' ongoing occupation. Later, it became less defined, and almost anyone could and would be targeted with many of the victims being beheaded for added terror effect. The barbaric action would be filmed and placed on the internet. Absolute terror at its gruesome worst. It wasn't going to get better any time soon, I thought.

I thought of what I would do next after all this. During my time here, I had mixed with several organisations and had helped a few out with their emergency planning. Several of them had offered me jobs, but it wasn't the right time to commit. It gave me hope that there could be more job opportunities in the humanitarian sector if I wanted to pursue it.

My final thoughts before I drifted off, were of Malik. I was thinking that he was a bluffer; always feeling the need to impress, particularly the ladies, of which there were many in this sector. I had often found that those who shout loudly about who they are and what they have (supposedly) done are pretty insecure about themselves and want to be popular. My other thoughts were about his arrogance. He had a tendency to look down his nose at people as though we were all below him. He really wasn't a pleasant person.

I woke early the next morning, leaving Malik to sleep. I got breakfast and sorted out the vehicle for the day ahead, all before Nasir arrived. He was surprised as I gave him his morning juice box outside next to the vehicles.

"Mr Phil, you are ready very early this morning. Is everything okay?" he asked.

"Nasir, my friend, everything is fantastic. How are you?" I responded in a surprisingly upbeat way.

Nasir just looked at me then laughed. "I will miss you, Mr Phil, when you leave," Nasir said with some sincerity.

I joked with him and said I wouldn't miss *him* at all. We laughed again, got in the car and set off to pick Rasha up and take her to Nasiriyah Hospital.

Rasha, her chaperone and the manageress were waiting on the steps at the entrance to the orphanage as we drove in. I took their bags and placed them in the truck bed, covering it all tightly with the tarpaulin. I asked Nasir to tell the manageress that I would be returning later that day with the new CD, to introduce him and show him the project.

Nasir invited our two passengers to get into the rear seats of the twin cab. Once they were in, he gave each of them a brown paper bag with sandwiches, biscuits and two juice boxes. They both quietly thanked Nasir, who then told them that I had made their lunches especially for their journey. This caused some surprise and a whole lot of repeated thank-yous. Nasir told me they were very grateful for the lunch and hoped Allah would bless me for such kindness.

"It was only lunch," I said quietly to Nasir.

"It was the kindness that they are thanking you for, Mr Phil," Nasir quietly responded with a smile.

It was very quiet on the journey to Nasiriyah Hospital. I kept looking in my mirror at the expression on Rasha's face. She watched the world go by outside of her window. I would have loved to have known what she was thinking at that time.

Nasir had phoned his uncle, Mr Adnan, in advance to ensure we were still on track to get Rasha to Baghdad.

We arrived as planned. We sat in our vehicle as instructed, until Mr Adnan finally appeared across the car park. We exchanged greetings, and we all got out of our vehicle to get into the car that was just pulling up next to us.

I took the bags and placed them in the boot of the car. The chaperone got into the rear of the car first. Just before Rasha got in, I gently tapped her arm. She smiled and looked at me as I got Nasir to translate. "Rasha, I won't see you again once you leave here. I will be going home very soon."

Rasha looked at me, and a small smile appeared on her face, but her demeanour was subdued.

I continued. "I am sure that all will be well and you will have a great adventure over the next few months. I will be asking about you when I talk to Nasir. I want you to be safe, and hope that all will be well with you soon. You will always be my special friend."

While in Kuwait, I had picked up a little present. I had it behind my back as I was talking to Rasha. As she got in the car and before I closed the door, I produced the gift from behind my back and gave it to her. It was a soft, cuddly toy rabbit.

Rasha almost reluctantly took it from me, looking at her chaperone then at Nasir then back at me. For a moment, I thought she would cry. The moment passed, and she produced the smile I'd grown to love. She hugged it as she thanked me.

The driver of the car had finished speaking to Mr Adnan and was now starting the engine. I closed the door, stood back and waved to Rasha. She waved, and kept waving, until the car pulled out of sight.

Before I could speak, Nasir quietly and calmly told me that everything would be good. He would ensure that Malik kept Rasha's treatment and trips on track.

Nasir was such a good man and a great friend.

We drove back to the house. We were both subdued. I was hoping that all would go well and that Rasha would get the treatment as planned for however long it took. She would have a better quality of life and a longer life than we had all previously thought.

I got back to the house and spent some time updating the security situation. I had called several of my information sources from around the country and a couple of 'in-the-know' guys back in the UK. They had all told me the same thing, albeit in different levels of detail. From Baghdad to the north, to Mosul, the attacks and opposition to the coalition forces were becoming more intense and, more importantly, more coordinated. Some small towns and villages were becoming militia strongholds, causing determined opposition to the coalition forces.

The continued rise of umbrella groups, such as Al-Qaeda (who spawned an extremist ideology which generated a level of terror across Iraq from its beginnings, years before in Afghanistan), hoping to exploit the power vacuum, were calling on anyone who would listen to fight the jihad against the infidel, calling for attacks of all types plus the kidnap and killing of all those who are 'unbelievers'.[6]

---

[6] AQ and its leadership insisted that anyone who failed to accept their understanding and extreme viewpoints were 'unbelievers'. This stretched to moderate Muslims and anyone else who opposed their (AQ) viewpoint.

Baghdad was having a particularly difficult time with vehicle-borne improvised explosive devices (car bombs or VBIEDs), shootings, multiple attacks using missiles, RPG and mortar attacks. The 'Green Zone', which was the main military base in Baghdad, based around the airport, was continually attacked. The levels of success varied, but it was a nuisance nonetheless; at worst, it was a fatal nuisance.

There had been a few attacks on the white UN vehicles too. Their HQ was often a target for snipers; sometimes, this involved just a couple of shots fired at the building as a reminder that there was still resistance to them being in Iraq.

There were some beginnings of rumours from more than one or two sources that there was about to be a major attack or incident in Baghdad. There was no indication as to what it would be or when it would be initiated, but several good sources were giving it credence.

I was compiling the reported incidents on my Iraq map, using different coloured map pins for different types of attacks. It was always a good visual method to see what was happening and to help identify any patterns of attacks that took place. Great for analysis purposes. Plotting the new attacks, it became clear that Baghdad was getting the worst, but a significant growth in the attacks in Basra was also noticeable.

As I sat trying to make sense of the map, I was disturbed by Malik, who came into the small room off the kitchen that I used as a very small office, mainly because it was the only place in the entire house that I could get a direct, unobstructed satellite signal for the BGAN, which gave good internet connection.

"Phil, I have to go to Baghdad tomorrow," Malik declared very enthusiastically.

"What?" I replied.

"There is a UN coordinating meeting at their HQ. It's a UNOCHA[7] meeting, and I should go," he concluded.

I sensed a real excitement in his voice. I also knew that the UNOCHA meetings were held regularly and, having attended one of them before Malik arrived, I found it devoid of any information that was not already widely known. They just asked questions of NGOs, mainly, I thought, to update themselves on information they couldn't be arsed to find out themselves. My opinion.

As a coordinating body, UNOCHA do have some value once you get past the bureaucratic niff-naff and trivia they seem to have in place. If you get a good head of office, it can be worthwhile attending, or at least have a one-to-one meeting; these always appeared to me to be much more beneficial. Unfortunately, nothing had hooked me to make me want to go back for a second meeting. Their emails were enough to go on.

I cast my eyes over my map again and told Malik I would need to get further security information to assess if it would be safe to take the travel risk. I showed him the attack map and the increasing level of attacks, not just in Baghdad but around all UN and coalition bases. My initial instinct was to say no straight away, but I decided to get more information first to see if it was viable or not.

Malik didn't appear very happy with what I had said. In fact, he looked really miffed.

I spent the next three hours making calls, sending emails and collating information from lots of sources. I went across to talk to Tim in his compound. Tim attended most of the meetings, several more than I attended, so he would be a good person to ask.

---

[7] United Nations Office (for the) Coordination of Humanitarian Affairs (UNOCHA)

"Shit, no," was Tim's response when I told him of Malik's request. He expanded by telling me that he had attended several UN meetings in Baghdad, and that was because his organisational masters had stipulated that he should.

Tim continued, "I stopped going to Baghdad last week, purely because the level of attacks was escalating and the meetings weren't that important to warrant the risk."

I agreed with him and told him of my findings from all the calls I had made that morning. I didn't say anything further to Tim but my decision was made.

I got back to the house, took two cold bottles of Coke from the fridge and went into the living area of the house, where I found Malik reading through some of the paperwork he was still trawling through. I offered him the drink, and I sat down.

I started to tell him that the risk was too high for any travel to Baghdad just now. I told him of the frequency of the UNOCHA meetings and that he should wait a few days or a week to see if the attack intensity changed.

Malik was clearly not happy. He tried to justify the need to go, and became quite animated and angry.

"I am the country director and I can decide when and where I go. I need to be at that meeting tomorrow."

Malik's teddy was not only thrown out of his pram, but was beaten, ripped open and lashed across the room; such was the ferocity of his rant. I was surprised by his reaction. This guy, I thought, was really unstable.

I'd just about had enough of his attitude and was becoming really pissed off with him. I'd held back almost since the day he arrived, but no more.

I cut him dead mid-rant.

"Malik," I said, raising my voice just a notch above his. I continued staring directly into his eyes. "Officially and contractually you are not the country director for two more days yet. You are still undergoing in-country training and familiarity."

I continued in a calm but forceful manner. As I spoke, he broke off eye contact and looked past me. I just continued to look at his face. I hadn't finished yet.

"As the CD, I have the authority to restrict any travel that I deem as too high risk and to assess what meetings are important to attend for the good of the programme and the organisation. For the reasons I have already outlined, there will be no travel to Baghdad until the situation becomes more manageable and a lesser risk. This is for your safety and the safety of the programme. You understand me?"

I had managed, regardless of my internal feelings of wanting to treat him like a computer (by punching the information in) to remain calm, while being obviously assertive.

He walked away from me while still ranting quite loudly in French, and sometimes English, punctuated with bits of Arabic. I guessed that the Arabic was used when calling me some very bad names.

I wondered if I should call London and tell Paul my thoughts on this guy that he was putting in charge? I decided not to; not yet. I thought that the issue had been dealt with, the message received and, apart from some childish behaviour, it was done.

I told Malik to go on a drive with Nasir to better familiarise himself with the town, the programme locations and the various routes in and out of the city.

While Malik sorted himself out and got ready to go, I left our compound, walked the short distance across the main compound to the residential buildings where Nasir and his family lived. I would usually ring him or send one of the guards to his house but I needed the walk to clear my head and think about the instructions I should give Nasir.

I got to his house and knocked on door. Nasir greeted me with his usual welcoming smile. I explained the situation, telling him that I needed him to drive Malik on a familiarisation tour of the project sites, the emergency routes and a general look around to point out the locations of all the other INGOs, the council buildings and the coalition military and police bases.

I made it clear that Malik was not to drive. I told Nasir that if any incident occurred, he must drive back using the safest route. I reiterated the code words that we had for attacks on the house on the close routes in and the code words if they were under attack. Breakdowns and accidents were sent over the radio in clear, with no codes.

Nasir walked back with me to our home base. We set the radios in the vehicle, and he and Malik left for what would be the remainder of the day. I sat in the small office and listened in to the radio babble on the HF and VHF sets.

As I sat looking at the map and reading the reports that had come in regarding the security across Iraq, I was starting to realise that over a period of two weeks, there had been a marked increase in attacks; these were mainly in Baghdad, but there had also been an increase in Najaf and Fallujah. Basra was becoming more insecure as well but it was a slower increase; but it was rising nonetheless.

There had been an increase in kidnapping and vehicle hijacking too. Some of the kidnapping was for ransom, but more alarming was the emerging trend of criminal gangs kidnapping then trading their victims on to the more extreme militia and terror groups who had no intention of seeking ransom. These victims were for public execution; shot, hanged or, as was becoming the main horrific trend, beheading.

In Nasiriyah, INGOs were still tolerated by the local population. We were generally greeted with smiles and waves. If I gave a thumbs-up to a group of people, I would generally get a wave or a reciprocated thumbs-up back. Amid all of this there was a growing undertone that it wouldn't last.

I was already thinking about lowering our profile. We generally use two white, twin cab, pick-up trucks that have our logos on. We had an old Land Rover Defender kitted out as an expedition vehicle with a snorkel exhaust, a large roof rack and additional spotlights; it looked great but was a pig to maintain and it drove like a top-heavy tank. We also had a black Pajero 4x4. It was the fastest car in our fleet but stood out like a bulldog's bollocks.

I made a decision to remove the logos from all our vehicles. I put in a request to London to ship out some magnetic logos that can be put on and taken off as needed, rather than the sticky plastic type we had now.

I made the decision that tomorrow I would ensure all our logos were taken down while taking Malik to meet the teams at the project sites. I thought that a bit of precaution now might be beneficial in the future if the situation goes to crap. At the very least, it could give us a little bit of extra time to organise and make our dash to the border. If our signage disappeared, people might forget we were there and we would become less obvious. Also, our locations would be harder to find. Well, that was the idea anyway.

I made a quick phone call to the London office. The purpose was to give a quick verbal update and to explain my actions. I would follow up with a security report in the regular manner in a day's time.

Nessa, Paul's deputy, answered the phone. I had spoken to Nessa several times over the last few months, and I liked her manner. A bit more business-like than Paul: very direct, no nonsense and called a spade a spade. She also had a very sharp but dark sense of humour. I always enjoyed our conversations.

I told her in brief, about the escalation of activity and my countermeasures, the logo issues and the restricted movement. She said I was the man on the ground so the decision was mine and I would be supported by both Paul and her at the London end. That was all I needed to know.

I thanked her for the support. She told me to crack on and to try hard not to get killed; the paperwork for her would be a real pain if that happened. I laughed and promised I would try. I just love that type of humour, said, no doubt, without cracking a smile.

I busied myself with outstanding paperwork, ensuring everything was up to date for my final handover. I had prepared the documents to sign over the cash sums we held in our safe; mainly US dollars, a good amount of Iraqi dinars and a small amount in British pounds.

All the totals were correct and they balanced with the receipts from the last few days. The emergency-money envelopes would also need to be checked but I would wait so that I could open the seal in front of Malik, count it then replace it, resealing the new envelopes.

I prepared three copies of each document that accounted for the finances. One would be kept on site, one would be delivered by hand to the London office and the final copy would be for me to keep just in case there was any discrepancy in the future. All copies were to be signed by Malik and me, with Nasir as a witness.

A good few hours had passed. I had received sit-reps over the radio from Nasir telling me all was well. He also gave very quick and simple information on the routes, which was always useful. Everything appeared normal and quiet: possibly too quiet.

Nasir and Malik drove through our gates, into the compound. The vehicle was parked in the correct position, and both driver and passenger got out. I went out to meet them and ask how the tour had been.

There were a few, almost tense, glances between Malik and Nasir before Nasir announced that all was good and they had driven to each of the sites as I had directed.

Sensing a little bit of anxiety from Nasir, I thanked him for being the chauffeur for the day and told him to go home. Nasir thanked me and left. Strange, I thought, no smile. Nasir always smiled when I told him to go home early. Something had happened. I guessed that Malik had said something or asked Nasir to do something he shouldn't while they were out.

Just as Nasir was about to exit through the gates, I shouted for him to wait. I caught up with him and told him to be ready to go at 8am tomorrow, as we would take Malik to the council building and do the formal introductions with the town council, the military and the UN rep, then we would visit all the projects and introduce Malik to everyone. Nasir said that was fine. I was just about to ask him what had happened, when I sensed Malik hovering just behind me in clear earshot of our conversation. I told Nasir that I would see him in the morning. He turned away, again no smile, and left the compound.

I looked at Malik and asked if had wanted anything? He shrugged his shoulders, turned around, walked back towards the main building and went inside.

"Something's definitely wrong," I thought. "I'll let everyone sleep on it and I'll tackle it in the morning. We must have a team that is together and supportive, particularly in an environment such as this, with an increasing threat to all our safety."

The rest of the evening passed without any further incident. There was just the odd burst of gunfire and an explosion here and there; all was, within the Iraqi context, normal.

I sat outside in the dark. I had a couple of biscuits and a steaming hot cup of tea. I was just relaxing, looking at the dark sky punctured by diamond-bright stars, trying to identify the constellations. I once knew many and could roughly navigate by them but it appeared I had forgotten quite a lot from my former life. If you don't use some skills, you tend to lose the knowledge, or at least doubt, as I did, if you're right. It helped pass the time.

I sat there in the very quiet and still night, thinking about going home. I would be heading off to Kuwait in two days' time for an overnight stay in our reserved hotel room then a flight home. I thought of my wife, Val, who had held the fort at home, looking after the kids, holding down her own job and just generally coping with everything. I thought how lucky I was to have such a strong and reliable wife, who I had relied upon to keep everything together while I was away, and I hoped she could keep things together when bad news about explosions, shootings and kidnappings in Iraq dominated the TV coverage on the news channels. She was always thinking about the possibilities if I had been or would be involved. Would I be the next one to be taken or shot or blown up?

She kept her things together in a remarkable way, shielding the kids from the situation I was in and keeping a sense of total normality. This would be truly tested in the years ahead.

It was very early morning. I woke up and looked at my alarm clock. It was 4.15am. I was still half asleep, wondering why I had woken?

I didn't need the loo, no one was smashing my windows, no one was shouting my name and the place wasn't on fire. I thought, amidst my drowsiness, that I had heard the gate opening. Could be a guard changing over? I fell back to sleep.

Before I knew what was happening, I was woken by my alarm clock. It was the first time in a long time that the alarm had woken me; most days, I woke up before it sounded.

I sat up, hot and sweaty, had a scratch, pulled on my shorts and t-shirt and wandered off to the kitchen to put the kettle on. I then staggered to the bathroom for a shower, if there was enough water pressure; otherwise it would be a bucket-and-jug job.

After emerging from the bathroom, I made a cup of tea and pondered over the first major decision of the day: cereal, beans on toast or just toast? Major decisions! I took the cereal option. Got to 'snap, crackle and pop'; it starts the day off on the right foot.

"Bollocks!" The box was empty. I'd thought there were at least two breakfasts left in that box.

Toast it was.

I took my tea and toast outside into the bright sunshine and sat at the small table we had put out by the barbecue stand. I sat down and sipped my tea. It was 19 August 2003, and I was two days away from going home. As my eyes focused and I looked around, I noticed the Pajero had gone. There was a gap in the parking order of the vehicles; it was most definitely absent.

I ran inside the building and banged on Malik's bedroom door. I knocked so hard that the walls and door shook. I shouted his name again and again but got no response. I opened the door; his room was a real mess, but it was obvious he was as absent as the Pajero.

I ran out to the guard. It was Alem. I asked, using animated hand signals and repeating Malik's name over and over while pointing at the empty car parking space and shrugging my shoulders, where Malik had gone.

Alem smiled and said "Mr Malik car go. Go out."

I asked Alem to go and get Nasir. To my absolute shock, he said, "Mr Nasir go with Mr Malik."

"Shit!" I thought. "These pair of fucking clowns had better just gone to the Nasiriyah market to beat the crowds."

I had a horrible sinking feeling in my stomach. Things were starting to come together now, but I hoped I was wrong. The bad feeling I had sensed between Nasir and Malik the previous day was beginning to piece together; it had to be about whatever it was they were doing today. Today was the day of the meeting that Malik wanted to attend in Baghdad. The fucker had gone, and worse, he had taken Nasir with him.

I had no doubt that that was the problem I had sensed between the two yesterday. Bastard!

I ran to get my satellite phone and I called Nasir. No response.

I went to the CODAN radio-base station. I called Nasir's call sign several times. No response.

As a last resort, I tried the VHF, hoping the relay stations would carry the signal, but only if they were not too far away and still inside the relay tower's signal umbrella.

I took a deep breath and broadcast. "Hello, Whisky Charlie Two. This is Whisky Charlie Base. Over!" I waited for a few seconds. Nothing. I tried again. "Hello, Whisky Charlie Two. This is Whisky Charlie Base. Radio check. Over!"

I tried a few more times. Still nothing.

I went to our daily vehicle and travel logbook to see if they had signed out and put the journey details in. Nothing. I was seething. Shit! I was so angry I wanted to punch Malik until he stopped moving. What a complete fuckwit.

I found a satellite telephone number for the UNOCHA in Baghdad, but it was way too early for anyone to be in the office there.

I had no option but to wait. I would also have to call London. I couldn't hide this if something was to happen. I didn't want to contemplate the chances of anything bad happening, but the call would have to be made.

London was two hours behind us on the timeline, so it would still be snoring.

The journey to Baghdad is roughly about 200 miles. It is largely open highway for the entire journey but parts of the road are closed. There are often very slow convoys to either negotiate or travel behind (at a safe distance). Once you get to the outskirts of the city, there are numerous checkpoints, and they would be hitting the early morning rush; not so much the volume of traffic but the chaotic nature of it.

I anticipated that it would take about three and a half hours, if all went well, to get to the UN headquarters at the Canal Hotel site. That was if they didn't stop for any reason.

I anticipated that with Nasir driving (like *Driving Miss Daisy*) it may take a little longer, so my estimated time of arrival was somewhere between 11.30am and midday. I would keep trying Nasir's number around those times, when I knew he was less likely to be behind the wheel.

I started to wonder what had been said between the pair of them to create such a bad atmosphere yesterday. For Nasir not to have confided in me, it must have been serious, or maybe it had been a threat of some sort of action when I had departed. I had no idea at this point, but I knew I had to find out.

I called London. Paul answered, his usual cheerful voice being a calming influence at that particular time. "How's it going, Phil?" Paul asked.

"I have a problem that you need to be aware of," I replied.

Considering the last time I'd had a problem (my dealings with Rasha), I expected that he was now holding his breath waiting for me to tell him something related or similar to that.

"It's Malik," I began.

I went on to tell Paul about my risk assessment, and the restrictions and other actions I had taken. He confirmed to me that he had been told by Nessa about my call and he agreed with the travel restriction but was a little concerned about the logo issue. I went on to explain further about the targeting of INGOs and the escalation of kidnap, and he reluctantly agreed. I went on to say that if we got the magnetic logos then Malik could refit them if he felt it was safe to do so, but I would not feel safe being logoed up during this very tense time. He agreed.

After telling Paul the full story, he was both disappointed and angry at the same time. He told me he thought Malik and I would get along really well. He thought Malik was a good guy. I told him of the potential issue with Malik and Nasir, which could leave Nasir in a very difficult position once I left.

But the point here was that of dangerous flouting of the rules; rules designed to keep us all safe. Paul agreed and said he would speak to Malik when he got back from Baghdad. He finished by thanking me for all I had done (again) and then slipped in a cheeky request. "Look, Phil, before you leave, can I ask you to stay for a few more months? Two at the most."

I was shocked. Shocked and flattered at the same time.

"I'm sorry, Paul, no," I replied. "I am really thankful for the opportunity that you gave me and for the trust you had in me to get on with things, even when everyone else had left."

I was very careful with my next statement. It started well but...

"Paul," I said, hesitating slightly. "Firstly, I am totally exhausted, and I feel as though I am close to burnout—"

"What if we give you a week or two at home, then you come back out?" he interrupted.

I quickly countered, "Paul, I really appreciate your offer but I know Malik is on a six-month contract as country director which starts tomorrow."

I was fighting to restrain what was coming, and I didn't want what I was going to say to sound bad... but then again...

"I can't work with Malik. He is an arrogant, selfish prick. I would end up punching him, probably on a daily basis. I just don't like or trust the guy, so I'm very, very sorry but it's not an option. But thanks for the very generous offer."

I heard a loud sigh on the other end of the phone. I sensed this was a big disappointment, so I apologised again.

"No, Phil," Paul said. "If I am honest, I didn't think you would stay, and between me and you, Nessa thought there would be a problem with Malik but I ignored and overruled her in order to get him out there, as we were struggling for people."

I considered what Paul was telling me and was starting to understand his reasoning. He had tried to alleviate the pressure on me by sending someone out as quick as he could. He thought Malik was a decent guy (And who knows? He still could be, once he settled in a bit more) but we all make mistakes.

I told Paul that I would get Malik to ring when I'd made contact with him, but it that might be tomorrow. Paul finished by asking me to submit this incident in my security report: my final one due in tomorrow. I agreed, apologised again and hung up.

A few hours later, I managed to get through to Nasir.

He told me they were lost, somewhere close to the city centre. Malik had gone into a café to use the toilet, so he had time to speak with me.

I found out that Malik had told Nasir that he would be taking him to Baghdad and if he told me, he would make sure that Nasir lost his job. The two had then had a little bit of a physical fight. Punches were reportedly thrown, sounded more like 'handbags at twenty paces' rather than a fight, but nonetheless it was a threat followed by aggression; that was absolutely out of order. I felt my blood boil.

Nasir, almost in a panic, told me that Malik was coming back so he had to go, and then hung up.

I felt helpless, but this, I thought, would not be the end of it.

At least, and at the very least, I knew that for now they were safe. Luckily, they were in a vehicle that had no logo on it to draw unwanted attention, an Iraqi national was driving it and the passenger was someone who could, if he kept his gob shut, pass as an Iraqi, at a stretch.

I fired a quick email back to London just to say that they had been in touch and were safe for now. I couldn't say much more.

I waited for another few hours before I got a call from Nasir. It was hurried and not really clear, so I guessed Malik was out of the vehicle again for some reason. They had found their bearings and would now get to the UN headquarters, but they were at the opposite end of the city and would have to travel back through the centre to get to the meeting on time.

Before I could respond he hung up.

This whole situation was really getting to me.

I called the UNOCHA number and eventually spoke to a lady called Martha I think. From her accent, she sounded American. It took three calls to different numbers to find someone who I could leave a message with.

I mentioned that Malik was attending a meeting on behalf of The Child-Focused INGO and, if possible, could a message be given to him to call his office in Nasiriyah.

The lady said she would do her best. I thanked her and hung up.

The meeting was due to start at 2.30pm and finish at 3.30pm but knowing the level of waffle and questions etc., it would more realistically go on until between 4pm and 4.30pm. In an unusual step, I would instruct Nasir and Malik to power through, leave no later than 3.30 and drive at best possible speed back to Nasiriyah.

I had no further contact with Nasir or Malik.

I had been trying every 15 minutes to make contact with the guys, but to no avail. I looked at the time. It was 4.40pm, and I was hoping that the two would be on the road back.

There was a knocking on the front door. It seemed panicked. I hoped it would be the two errant idiots. It was Mustapha, with Alem and the manager of the whole compound, who was called Mohammad the Egyptian (this nickname identified which Mohammad he was, as there were many Mohammads working on the main compound).

Mohammad the Egyptian spoke very good English; it was because of his language skills that Mustapha brought him to my home.

Mustapha pushed passed me, closely followed by the other two, and went straight to the TV, selecting a news channel which showed a building with a huge plume of smoke emanating from it. The scrolling banner below it was in Arabic, but then to my horror the letters UN appeared. I looked at the TV. Mohammad the Egyptian then started to explain. It was the UN headquarters in Baghdad. It had been hit by a truck full of explosives. Much damage had been done and many were dead.

I felt sick. Where was Nasir? Had they left before the attack? Had they been caught in it? Were they both among the dead?

I phoned Nasir's number over and over again. Nothing.

This was going to hit the UK news very soon, if it hadn't already done so. I called London.

Paul answered.

"Have you seen the news?" I asked him.

He hadn't, so I explained the situation. I told him I couldn't get hold of either Nasir or Malik. Paul said he would make some calls from London and that I should keep trying to call Nasir.

I asked Mo the Egyptian if he knew Nasir's family. He did, very well. I asked what the probability was that his wife would see this on the news. He told me that Nasir's father lived with them, so he would go to their house and talk with them.

I told him to tell them that I was trying everything to find out where Nasir was. It was a terrible time: wanting to talk to Nasir's family but not being able to. I just hoped he was safe: and the prick he was with too.

Time was passing, and I still had not heard any news.

The BBC World News was now reporting from the scene, so I had a better understanding of what was going on. Pictures were being shown of the scene. A large part of the building had collapsed; it must have been a huge explosion. Deaths were being reported; there were no numbers yet but there were concerns about the top UN representative, Sergio Vieira De Mello, who was reported to be critically wounded. His office was directly above the exploding lorry.

Mo the Egyptian appeared back at my house some 30 minutes after setting off to speak to Nasir's family. They had already started to watch the situation on the news and were understandably shocked and deeply concerned. It was now 6pm.

My phone rang. It was Nasir. He told me he was about an hour away from Nasiriyah and asked me if it was okay to keep travelling or if he should find somewhere to stop, a guest house or similar, until the next morning.

I told him to push on and get back as soon as he could. He asked if all was okay with me, as I sounded stressed.

Fucking stressed! Damn right I was stressed.

I asked him what time he had left the UN. He told me they had got lost again and never made it to the meeting so Malik decided to come back.

I asked him if he knew what had happened? Neither of them had a clue about the devastation that they had just missed out on. I quickly told him of the bombing but said I would talk to him later.

All this time, Malik said nothing. I finished the conversation and hung up.

I dispatched Mo the Egyptian back to Nasir's house to pass on the good news.

My satellite phone chirped into life. It was Paul. I told him the short version and said that once I'd spoken to Nasir and Malik, I would complete the report and send it. Paul agreed that he wouldn't talk to Malik until he had read my report.

I had arranged to travel to Kuwait the following day with Tim in one of his vehicles. He had a trip planned, so it made sense to share the drive with him. I was on the verge of cancelling my trip and stopover in Kuwait; instead, I would drive myself on the day of my flight, taking the Land Rover and leaving it parked in the hotel car park for the incoming guys, whenever they arrived.

I went to see Tim to confirm his departure time. I told him the story of the day's activity, and he agreed that rather than a 7am start, he would delay up till 10.30, but no later. I agreed and thanked him and went back to my house to wait for Nasir and Malik to arrive back.

Sure enough, nearly two hours later, the vehicle rolled into our compound.

I stood silently and watched as they parked up and switched off. Nasir was first out of the vehicle. I went over and greeted him. He cried. He kept apologising, but I told him it was okay and I would see him in the morning at eight. I warned him that his father and wife were anxiously awaiting his return. With tears rolling down his face, he thanked me (for what, I didn't know) then he left.

As I was talking to Nasir, Malik sneaked off into the house.

I walked in and there was no sign of him. I called his name. He then appeared from his bedroom.

"What the fuck do you think you were doing?" I felt my temper rising along with the volume of my voice.

"It was a meeting I needed to go to, so I went. It's nothing," he said as he shrugged his shoulders

I could barely contain myself; the rage at his attitude caused me to almost reach boiling point but I kept a lid on it, just.

"You arrogant arsehole. You didn't only disobey my instruction and put yourself at risk but you put Nasir's life at risk too."

Malik summoned up a little bit of backbone and stood up to me. He came close, not quite nose to nose but close enough. His fists were clenched. Would he take a swing? I doubted it, so I challenged him directly.

"If you have something to say, then say it; if you want to do something, then do it," I said as I stared into his eyes.

He stepped back and then came out with a torrent of verbal shite. "We are here. We are safe. Nothing has changed. You go home tomorrow, so you have nothing to worry about. I will run the programme and you can sleep in your bed, safe at home."

It was then that I thought I should walk away, be the better man, but I just couldn't. I snapped.

"You are safe because you fucked up, not by your design or planning. You got lost and missed the meeting. If you had been on time, you most likely would have been killed, you arrogant arsehole. You're not fit to be a CD. You're a liability."

My inner common sense was screaming at me to walk away; I almost did, until he spoke again.

"What do you know? You are on your first job and don't know how things work yet."

Another arrogant shrug of the shoulders, and that blew the lid right off.

"Malik!" I called as he walked away.

He stopped and turned around to face me. His fists clenched again.

I walked up to him. "You arrogant twat. You think you know it all and are too good to do wrong? Bollocks!"

He was about to shrug his shoulders again, when I punched him right in the face. It wasn't the hardest of punches but enough to startle him and put him on his arrogant arse.

It was wrong. I shouldn't have done it. I should have just walked away. Did I regret it? Hell, no!

I stood ready for him to get up and possibly fight back. He didn't. He just cried like a baby and swore a lot in French.

I left him there and went to bed.

Malik thumped about for a bit, banging plates and cutlery and slamming doors; all immature tantrum stuff. I just ignored it, and sure enough, after about 15 minutes it stopped. I heard his bedroom door open and close, and he finally settled down to get some sleep.

The next day I was up earlier than usual. Up with the sun. My last day. I had my last breakfast and a hot brew. "Tea and toast, the breakfast of champions," I thought to myself and laughed.

I walked out into the compound, sat at the little table and enjoyed the early morning. Mustapha was on duty. I waved to him, and he smiled and waved back.

Before I knew it, Nasir entered the compound. He came over to me, and before he sat down, I gave him a juice box and straw.

"Morning, mate. How are you this morning?" I asked.

Before he answered me, he cautiously looked around; checking for Malik, I guessed.

"I am good, Mr Phil. Thank you," he quietly replied.

I sensed Nasir's unease, so I got straight to the point.

I told Nasir that he would drive me very quickly around the project sites so I could say a quick goodbye. It would then be quickly back to the compound to get my bags, which I had packed two nights ago, then to wait for Tim to collect me for my last run from Nasiriyah to Kuwait.

I watched as Nasir prepared the car for the morning's work, just as he had done for over three months. The same routine, well prepared and drilled.

I took my breakfast dishes back to the kitchen, washed them in the sink and left them to dry on the draining board. All was tidy;

everything was in its place, the floor was swept and the chairs were placed equally spaced under the kitchen table.

I went to my bedroom and collected my 'grab bag', checked I had my passport, The Child-Focused INGO ID and my emergency money, and off I went to climb into the vehicle, now devoid of all logos, and set off on our final tour.

Due to the time factor, the trip around the programme sites had to be fairly swift. I spent a little longer at the orphanage and bakery, though.

The orphanage manageress was very thankful for all we had done for the children, ensuring they had proper beds, utensils to cook with and a stove to cook on. She also thanked me for what we had done for Rasha. She thanked me over and over as she cried.

I left, telling her via Nasir that Rasha was now established for her treatment and she would get the best medical care in the whole of Iraq. Nasir, I told her, would be looking in on her while the orphanage was a project of The Child Focussed INGO.

I left the orphanage with very mixed feelings. Happy at what we had done to support all the children and make their lives easier with all the interventions we had put in place, but very sad and emotional at not seeing Rasha for a final time and not knowing what the final outcome of her treatments would be. But that was the way it was.

The bakery was my last stop. What a surprise I got. The site manager and all the workers were gathered and waiting for me. I sensed Nasir had had a hand in this.

We pulled up in the usual place, and when I got out of the vehicle, all the staff clapped. Embarrassed? Shit, yeah!

The site manager came over and shook my hand. He kept a firm grip on it, as he led me into the doorway of the bakery. The staff followed.

There was a table set out with drinks (non-alcoholic, I must add), and the table had laid upon it several of our breads, all with different types of pizza-like toppings. It looked like a feast fit for a king. It looked great.

The site manager spoke loudly in Arabic which quietened everyone, so I guess it was the equivalent of "shut up and listen in". They did, and I did too.

The site manager began his speech in very good English. "Mr Philip," he began, putting his right hand over his heart as he spoke. "I must tell you, when I first met you I didn't like you."

That was a shock to open with I thought.

He continued, "But once I understood how you worked and what you wanted to achieve, I liked you. Your work is very good, but different to the Iraqi way. *We* talk about what we want to do; sometimes we talk a long time. It's our way, our culture. *You*, Mr Philip, didn't speak much when you first came but you explained what you would do, explained what you wanted from us, and then your actions spoke for you. You made no promises but all that you said you would do, you did."

I noticed Nasir discreetly point to his watch, which was acknowledged by the site manager.

"Mr Philip," he continued, "we all have a special memory of you and it will stay with us all for ever: the day you helped us unload the flour and you looked like a ghost, covered in flour dust. I never thought that someone like you would help with the task of unloading so many bags of flour. You showed us that you are one of us, and we liked that very much."

There was a quick pause, and from the table, he picked up a box, opened it and pulled out three copper plates. The face of each was painted black, and etched into the paint, revealing the copper beneath, were pictures of ancient Iraq.

"Mr Philip, this is from us all. It is something for you to remember us by. Come back soon."

I was totally gobsmacked. It wasn't something I had expected. I had to quickly think of something to say. "This is such an unexpected and pleasant surprise. Thank you," I began, with Nasir interpreting.

After thanking the site manager for his very kind words, I started on my final speech. "This bakery has been a success, not because of me but because of you. You have helped feed children in schools, the sick and needy in hospital and groups of families spread across the province who would otherwise have gone hungry if you had not produced the wonderful bread in the large quantities that you have. In your name, we also delivered bread to many local households and to the small bakeries that produce breads in their small shops so they can continue to trade. This has all been possible due to your hard work. I thank each and every one of you for your contribution, and I hope you will all stay safe and continue with this work for many years to come. Thank you all."

With that truly heartfelt and emotional speech, I told Nasir that we really must go.

Nasir addressed the gathering in Arabic, and each worker, in turn, came forward and shook my hand. I got a really big bear hug from the site manager, who I swore had a tear in his eye; but I bet he would never admit it.

We still had about 15 minutes left until we needed to head back. Nasir decided to drive through the unusually quiet city as he spoke to me.

"Mr Phil." He paused, almost to compose himself. I felt that an awkward conversation was about to follow. "I have worked with you almost every day since you arrived in Nasiriyah, and I have learned many things from you. Having a plan 'A' is good but having a plan 'B' and 'C' is better; this is very good advice."

A small smile crept across his face but disappeared as he continued.

"I know you don't like being spoken about but you have done many good things here for the people of Nasiriyah; The town council even awarded you a certificate for helping the city and its people. The help with the education programme and the exams was very, very good, and the bakery would not be a success if you had not been involved; if someone else had been in charge, it would have failed."

Nasir was starting to get quite emotional now, which made me feel very uncomfortable. I was used to the lively, happy Nasir who had developed a decent sense of humour.

Nasir was in full flow now.

"You are a very special man, Mr Phil. You treat everyone as an equal, and you are thoughtful and kind; Rasha is the example of that. I don't want you to leave, Mr Phil."

Nasir was now weeping, wiping the tears away from his eyes. The floodgates truly opened now as he sobbed; it was getting uncontrollable. Luckily, we had entered the larger outer compound and were very close to our home base. Nasir's next sentence stunned and shocked me.

"Mr Phil," he said through the sobs, "I love you like a brother. You are the best man I have ever met. I don't want you to leave. Malik is not good for this programme. He is a bad man. I think I will fight with him."

At first, I didn't know what to say or think. No one, certainly no man, had ever said anything like that to me before. I felt embarrassed, humbled and a little proud to have made such a positive impact on someone's life. Observing Nasir's emotional state, I thought his words were quite profound.

I told him to drive into our compound and park the car, and I finished by telling him I wanted to talk to him in a personal capacity in the car, then he was to go home, have the rest of the day off and report to Malik at 8am ready for a new day's work.

As we parked and Nasir turned off the engine, I turned to him and looked at his tear-streaked face.

I began what would be my final conversation with Nasir.

"Nasir, mate, you have been the backbone of this programme. Even before the old team bailed out, it was you who people were relying on. You are intelligent, thoughtful and caring. Your advice to me has always been of great help. You adapted quickly to my work pattern, and even though you didn't like working in the heat of the day, you saw the benefits and went with it to support those vulnerable groups that needed our help. Not only have you been an outstanding manager for the organisation, but, to me, you have been an invaluable person to work alongside; but most of all, you have been a loyal and fantastic friend."

Nasir's emotions got the better of him. I had never seen him like this. He usually wore his heart on his sleeve, but this was way beyond anything I had seen from him before. I told him to go to my bathroom, wash his face and compose himself before he went home.

"I'll go and say my goodbyes to the guards now, then I'll wait by the gate until Tim comes with his vehicle. I will see you leave, so go and wash your face." I smiled and winked at Nasir, and he forced a smile as he turned and walked into the house.

I stood with Mustapha and Alem at the gate. We shook hands and used the touching of our own heart as a warm gesture. I said *"Shukraan Lakum"* several times.

Nasir eventually came out of the building, his eyes still tearfully bleary, but he had managed to control himself and kept his emotions in check.

I asked Nasir to formally thank our guards for the work they do and the friendship and kindness they had shown me. He did.

I quickly thanked everyone again and told Nasir I must go and get my case and say goodbye to Malik, who was now pottering about the house eating his lunch.

I shook hands with the guards and finally shook Nasir's hand. I could see the emotion welling up in him again, so I told him, in a slightly sterner manner, to go home. I smiled. Nasir turned and walked away.

As I walked into the living room where Malik was sitting, I said to him, "I am leaving now. I have given Nasir the rest of the day off. He will be here tomorrow at 8am, ready to go."

Malik didn't lift his head to look at me. Instead, he just nodded in agreement and continued eating.

I spoke again, just to confirm with him that the handover was as thorough as it could be. "I know you have signed the handover paperwork, agreeing all is in order, and you understand your role and responsibilities. Are there any final questions you want to ask?"

Malik shook his head to acknowledge what I had said and to confirm that he had no questions.

I walked over to him, wished him the best of luck and every success for the future and held out my hand for him to shake; he didn't take it.

My departing comment to him was short and sharp.

"Whatever you may think of me or whatever disagreements you may have had with Nasir, just remember why you are here and who it is you are serving. Give Nasir every assistance he may need and help him, if needed, to ensure that Rasha gets the support she needs."

He didn't look up, speak or show any sign that he had heard what I had just said. He just sat, eyes down, and continued eating.

I did, however, catch a glimpse of the two black eyes he was sporting; I smiled to myself as I walked out and thought what an absolute 'dick' Malik was.

Kuwait and the UK were now clearly on the horizon; just a final report to submit and that would be the end of this seriously testing adventure.

*

Rasha and me.

This appeared in *The Sun* newspaper.
The article was written by the
organisation I was working for, and
published without me knowing.

A friend of mine spotted it
and sent me a copy.

Fame at last?

The building of the bakery in Nasiriyah

Producing vitamin-enriched flatbread for the schools,
hospitals and other beneficiaries

The bakery team.

Me, standing centre rear.
To the right, is our
Lebanese engineer. To the
left is the site manager

Next to him is Nasir

173

North Darfur

The men as women,
and the women as men.
A de-stressing get-
together of INGOs.

I am on the left in the
fetching pink blouse.

North Darfur

The wreckage of the Land Rover after the mine strike, and
the crater from the explosion.

The Land Rover Defenders
with the CODAN antennae
fitted. Note the logos on the
tops of the vehicles so they
can be identified as INGO
from the air. We had to stop
regularly in Darfur to clean
off the sand and dust to
keep the logos visible.

Some of the kids from The
IDP camps in Darfur. One
has an injured
leg and uses a home-made
crutch.

Libya

A small collection of unexploded munitions and the inside of one
of the ammunitions storage hangers.

The munitions were ransacked by various groups but much reportedly
found its way into the hands of ISIS.

Misrata, Libya

A rebel soldier who was manning the
checkpoint on the main road into
Misrata. I spotted his Everton shirt
and, as an Evertonian, I had to stop
and take this photograph.

De-mining in Misrata, Libya.

A selection of my new best friends.

These kids had nothing but were always smiling and curious. I always had time for the children, no matter what else I had to do.

The Ghosts of Sierra Leone

Wearing full PPE, they would attend the sick and dying, remove the dead in ambulances and cleanse dwellings with a detergent spray.

The Ebola Medal

Given to all military and civilians who contributed to the Ebola crisis in West Africa.

Indonesia

Banda Aceh Tsunami. Boats and bodies smashed by the wave into
a bridge. A boat carried from the port onto land.

Ambon, Indonesia

Playing football with
the kids and trying to
show off.

Kabul, Afghanistan

Our unmarked vehicles
being checked for any
under-vehicle explosive
devices.

Kashmir

The Kashmir, Pakistan/ India, earthquake response. Living in tents, as the buildings were still unsafe from the massive quake.

Interviewed live on the BBC

Regarding the risks to INGOs working in hostile locations in light of several kidnappings.

Training sessions in Zimbabwe Going through the types of communication equipment and their correct use and radio voice procedure and the importance of field communications.

Tripoli, Libya

My near miss.

Top left: Bullet hole through the white UPVC window frame.

Top right: Through the bathroom door.

Bottom left: Ricochet mark on the wall in the bathroom.

Bottom right: The core of the bullet I picked up from the floor in my bathroom and photographed standing on my laptop.

Bolgatanga, Ghana

Delivery and presentation of books to a remote school and celebrations

Chapter 6:

The Return Journey, Departure and Hoping to Get Out Alive

It was great to be home. Being paid for my time away had given me some money in the bank and some slack time, so I didn't need to go away again just yet.

We enjoyed a holiday, driving down to the south of France. The drive itself was a great experience, with some lovely scenery and a hotel stopover at the halfway point. The kids thought it was a great adventure; we did too.

Being home again, it was easy to slip back into the normal routine. This time, however, was a little bit different. I kept myself busy by updating myself on world events (taking a great interest in Iraq, Afghanistan and other places), keeping abreast of any natural disasters, such as earthquakes and hurricanes, and, finally, taking a great interest in global poverty and famine.

I became absorbed in all aspects of humanitarian interventions and responses. I hit the internet with a vengeance; looking up the big humanitarian organisations and following their activities and searching their job vacancies, wondering if there was anything for me in the future.

I began sourcing information on terror groups, their locations and their recent activities, pairing this information with any humanitarian interventions in the same locations. I was really researching in detail, and would do so for many hours on a daily basis.

While Iraq was starting to emerge as a dangerous place for terrorism, Afghanistan was very problematic and had been simmering for years and Sudan was getting very busy, particularly a little-known place (at that time) called Darfur.

I still felt very close to Iraq. Apart from being the location of my first humanitarian-based role, I kept thinking of Nasir, the bakery team and, of course, Rasha. I tried hard to remain focused on my work and research, but these issues kept flooding back.

I had made a lot of contacts in Iraq, from many organisations. One American INGO, I noticed, was advertising for a security manager in Iraq, based in Al Kut. It also had offices in Al Diwaniyah, Amarah and Baghdad. I decided to apply.

I discussed the issues with my wife, Val. We talked about the risks and the issues she had regarding the kids and their schooling. We looked at what childcare was available if we needed it. The eldest, Vikki, was almost 14, then there was Ryan, who was nearly five. Everything was in place, and Val's work would not be hindered while I was away, so we agreed that if I wanted, I could apply and accept if I was offered the position.

A funny story:

When my previous life ended and we returned to civilian life, I had decided that I would be a stay-at-home dad and free up my wife to take up her career. She had studied to be an accountant and had home studied to further her qualifications. As she had been the mainstay of our family while I was engaged in operational tours of Northern Ireland, Cyprus (UN tour), the Gulf, Bosnia, Kosovo and other places, we had agreed that I could find a home-based job and she could 'crack on' with her career.

It didn't quite pan out that way…

(Note: my wife did go on to be very successful; first working in an international school supply company, followed by an international health insurance company, during which time we actually met at Heathrow airport; me coming back to UK and her going out to South America. We met at arrivals, had a coffee, handed over the kids and went our separate ways. Val finally set up her own business and continues to run it today, very successfully operating and exporting to many different countries worldwide.)

I applied for the job, underwent a series of phone calls and email correspondence. Eventually, I was offered the role of safety and security adviser for a large US-based INGO. The interview process was very different to that which I had experienced previously and was to be the 'norm' for the US-based organisations. It was very paperwork heavy, with lots of forms and questions, some of which I refused to answer, including what my previous earnings were. What that had to do with them was anyone's guess? They'd advertised the job and stated what the pay level was, so for me, it was take it or leave it. What I earn will always be between me, my paymaster, whoever I am employed by and the tax man. I remain of the same opinion now. I never disclose my previous earnings to new employers. They just don't need to know it if they are offering a fixed wage.

I very nearly refused the job, such was the level of application paperwork, but I took the job and took a flight into Jordan and then another one into Baghdad, which was a real experience in itself.

I can't for the life of me recall the name of the airline, but it operated a small twin turboprop plane, probably seating less than 20 people. It was, I am sure, apart from military aircraft, the only civilian airline at the time flying into Baghdad. The passenger list was a mix of contractors, INGOs from various organisations and one or two members of the CPA.

The pilot and co-pilot were New Zealanders who had a great sense of humour that didn't quite sit well with some of the more nervous passengers. I remember boarding the plane, and one of them announced it was the Baghdad flight, landing or crashing into Baghdad in about an hour and 40 minutes, depending on the conditions over Baghdad Airport. I smiled at them as I boarded, and listened to two blokes behind me complaining about their 'inappropriate' humour.

As we took our seats, the co-pilot gave a safety briefing, covering all the usual details you'd expect to hear on any flight you would take, worldwide; but then he finished by saying, "The engines will remain at full throttle when we land until we are sure no one is shooting at us. If they are, we may very quickly attempt to take off again." He concluded by telling us (with a smile) to relax and enjoy the flight.

"Brilliant," I thought.

The flight itself was unremarkable; that was, until we approached our destination. Usually, on approach to a destination airport, the plane starts its descent a good way out from the airport. We had stayed at the cruising altitude until we were directly over Baghdad Airport.

Then came the announcement: "Guys, we are now over Baghdad International Airport. Due to the ongoing hostile situation on the ground, our landing procedure will consist of a number of very tight turns as we spiral down within the confines of the airport boundary, losing height quickly, which will generate an amount of G-force that you will not be familiar with. Please relax, and we hope to get you on the ground as quickly and as safely as we can."

I just started to think that this was going to be a hell of a ride when we banked over sharply and descended. I was pinned to my seat. I couldn't lift my arms or legs at all. My head felt really heavy. It was an experience I have never forgotten, a really extreme ride; corkscrewing in tight turns and losing altitude rapidly. Those pilots were amazing; their skill and control of the aircraft and the way they handled the G-force while controlling the aircraft and landing was nothing short of outstanding.

As we taxied to the terminal, the passengers were silent. Most, I think, were in shock. One guy sitting across from me had a huge grin on his face. I smiled and looked back over my shoulder at the majority of the other passengers, who looked as if they just wanted to get their feet back on the ground.

As we left the aircraft and picked up our luggage, which had been unloaded from the rear of the plane and now stood on the runway, the two pilots were standing on the runway wishing us a safe onward journey. One of them looked at me and noticed me smiling as I left the plane. He asked if I enjoyed the ride. I told him I had, but the G-force had affected me badly. I joked that I was six-foot-six before the decent, and now I was only five-foot-eight. He laughed loudly and said I could book my return seat with them if I wanted to. It was a great experience, and not once did I feel unsafe. Great pilots.

Walking into the main terminal building, I noticed that the security inside was provided by a private security company (PSC). I wondered how professional they were? The way some were carrying their weapons was a sign that they were not too familiar with weapon handling in confined spaces or among the public. Some were holding their weapon very loosely and one was using it to point at people in the airport, including members of his team. Others, I observed, held the pistol grip with their right hand and had the weapon resting with the barrel over their shoulder, pointing at the ceiling; really poor weapon handling. Professionals who are well trained in weapon handling know not to point a weapon at anyone unless you intend to use it. Poor training can lead to accidental discharging, often resulting in killing or badly wounding innocent bystanders. I immediately thought that this bunch of security operatives were amateurs jumping at a chance to earn lots of money, carry a weapon (or weapons) and strut around like John Wayne.

I wouldn't want to be there if a close attack happened; these guys were more likely to kill each other and the public rather than any attackers.

I walked through the airport looking for someone holding a placard with my name on it. I stood back, moved against a wall and just observed what was in front of me. Watching those who had come to greet the passengers off this isolated flight, I noticed a placard with the organisation's logo on it.

I waited a little longer; just watching. The airport was emptying out and the logo placard was still there. I could now see the guy holding it. He could pass as Iraqi but I doubted he was. I approached him, and as I did, he asked me if I was Phil Jones. He held out his hand for me to shake. Before I shook his hand or confirmed my name, I asked him for his ID and questioned him on who he was meeting and why.

I had checked out the organisation's website before my departure, looking for names, job appointments and photographs. I recognised his face, and it tied in with his ID.

I confirmed my ID with him and then we walked out of the building and through to the car park.

The car was unmarked, with no logo identifying us as foreigners or INGOs. "That's a good sign," I thought.

We spent the rest of the day and night at the Baghdad office. The office manager, Amar, was a big guy. He spoke perfect English and was a very open and polite guy. I liked him a lot. We spent much of the early evening talking about football and sharing jokes. We had one or two conversations where I used leading questions to gauge his thoughts on the organisation and the situation in Iraq; on both accounts, I sensed he was not happy and was being protective and defensive.

The next morning, we left for Al Kut. I was now in possession of my new organisational ID card, and my 'in-country' copious documentation was now complete, I hoped.

Arriving in Al Kut, I quickly took in the set-up of the office and living space that this organisation had acquired, probably at a high cost. It was a street consisting of a few houses. One large building was the main office which also had some accommodation space. The CD and his deputy had a rather large house, and I had a temporary home in a house at the end of the street all to myself. But I would be moving around the different locations, to conduct my assessments and deliver training, so I wasn't about to get too comfy.

I had already planned my work in outline; understanding the aims in the job description, I had set out what the framework would be: starting at HQ in Al Kut, assessing their current security protocols, delivering appropriate training at the headquarter level, getting any changes or additions signed off then taking those new updated protocols out to the field offices. I would brief the teams and conduct the training, observe for compliance then repeat at the next location, until everyone had the same level of understanding about their emergency procedures and how they would link to the HQ elements for support, coordination and direction where required. That was the plan.

I intended on spending about four to six weeks at each location. This would be broken down into week-long periods, with a week for assessment of all aspects of operation set against the threat and risk; a week to put together a workable briefing and training package; a week to deliver the training done at two levels, the management, highlighting security planning and management, and training, aimed at the field teams (the management would be included in this training too.); and the final week or two would be to check on compliance and offer guidance on the new protocols, probably more accurately described as a mentoring period. Depending on the levels of understanding and application of the teams at each location, I could lengthen or shorten the total time spent with each team.

I had planned to write a report on conclusion at each location for HQ to mull over, then to write a final report on the overall findings of the entire organisational safety and security, which I hoped would be a reference document for those who followed when my contract ended. During the entire period of my contract, I would be helping the CD and his deputy to manage the day-to-day safety and security across the entire programme. That was the framework; it would be flexible, but it gave structure to my role.

I was corrected early on, that the CD was to be referred to as the 'head of mission'; apparently, the American-based organisations didn't like or use the 'country director' title. Some got quite anal about it, while others didn't care, but HoM, as it was abbreviated, was the way it was.

The first couple of days for me was basic familiarisation. I still, on day two, had not had a meeting with the HoM to discuss my role and the plans I had set out. But that would come, quickly I hoped.

The deputy HoM had informed me that each location had a team leader and a nominated safety and security focal point. The team leaders were international staff (non-Iraqi) and the focal points were national staff (Iraqi).

There was, at Al Kut, a national safety and security manager who, it was suggested, would eventually take the role in the longer term, to manage the entire programme and the international position would no longer be deemed necessary. I understood from this information that I should spend a good portion of my time with this guy, to mentor him and educate him on emergency security management. It would be good to have this guy who, as I was briefed, was new to the role in that he had no security background nor any military or police background: both of which would have been an added advantage.

I looked forward to having this guy alongside me, so he could see the entire process and learn as we went. It would be, I hoped, an invaluable but practical learning experience. His local information could be very valuable. "He could be the new Nasir," I thought, but that was a large ask at this early stage.

It took another two days before I finally got time with the HoM. I sat for just under an hour and was spoken at for most of that time. The majority of the one-way conversation was based on this guy telling me that he had been in Iraq for six months and knew all there was to know. He went to great lengths to tell me how he had a very good understanding of the security situation and was sure that all would be safe for the teams to continue to work in the field.

I sensed that this guy had already made his mind up about the situation and wasn't going to be swayed, whatever happened.

There was a pause in the conversation so I jumped in, as I thought I may not get another chance.

I explained my plans, justified the process and ended by highlighting the long-term benefits that could be achieved if the entire programme took ownership of safety and security on a personal, as well as a collective, level; ending with what became a bit of a mantra, 'working safer and smarter for longer'.

I may as well have been talking to myself. He smiled a very obviously forced smile and told me that I would be going to Al-Diwaniyah for two weeks, leaving tomorrow, then Amarah, then on to Baghdad then finally back to Al Kut, where I would assist the deputy HoM in updating the programme safety and security documents.

I interrupted and told him that two weeks in each location was not long enough to achieve what was stated on the job specification.

"Yes. Well, Phil, things change. We are pretty much on top of the situation here," he told me, maintaining his false smile.

"Okay," I replied. "Just understand that the results you may have been expecting will possibly not be achieved due to the restriction on the time factor you have set out. I would like to have this conversation recorded on my file for any future reference."

His forced smile disappeared.

"If there is nothing else, Phil, then that's all for now. I am sure you have a lot to do and plan. I won't see you tomorrow. Stay in touch and I will catch up with you again when you get back. Have a safe trip."

He made it clear that the conversation was finished by picking up his pen and focusing on the paperwork on his desk. The conversation was over. No discussion, no further reasoning; we were done.

I went back to my house and started to re-evaluate the tasks in hand. I already knew that it would be long hours but the time restrictions had made things much worse.

The next morning, a car arrived at my house. The driver, employed by the organisation, greeted me and told me he was ready to take me to Diwaniyah. He didn't speak much English but just enough to save me the embarrassment of trying to converse in my limited and poor Arabic.

Before we set off, I asked the driver if he'd had any driver training and what he should do if there was an emergency. The blank look and shrug of the shoulders told me he had no idea what he should do and I guessed he'd had no training.

I spent the next 20 minutes trying hard to explain the absolute basics about defensive driving and emergency procedures if under attack but this all went way above his head. He told me he was just hired as a driver. (Note to self: train the drivers)

The drive to Diwaniyah took me through some small villages and towns. In one small village, there was an open market stall, a butchers, with different cuts of meat hung up from the roof beam of the stall. The flies were having a fine old feast, but that wasn't the main spectacle. In the middle of the road (well, sand-and-dirt-covered track) was a dead cow, and standing over it was, I guessed, the butcher, with two very sharp and long knives. He was about five minutes into his job of turning this animal into various joints of meat to adorn his market stall. He was precise with his knives, and laid out his cuts of meat on the road, supposedly ready to hang up once he had finished.

Normally I am a lover of steak and cuts of beef, but right now, I considered becoming a vegetarian, if only for the level of hygiene I had just witnessed. I just hoped the potatoes had a better route to the dinner tables. (Ha!)

The situation regarding attacks on the coalition forces, the kidnapping of foreigners and tribal fighting had escalated since my time in Nasiriyah. There was a different atmosphere; people everywhere were tense.

The beheading of Nick Berg, an American businessman, and Ken Bigley, a contractor from the UK (living in Liverpool), two foreigners kidnapped, paraded for propaganda and brutally and publicly beheaded had been publicly televised. Incidents like these were escalating, and the terror they spawned was palpable. There was more to follow.

Tribal feuds were becoming more frequent. The previous animosity towards the CPA and their appointed councils had grown from a toxic dislike by portions of the population, into a true hatred by large swathes of the many communities across the country. Retribution attacks were being made against those who were, or perceived to be, connected to the old regime. Those who had money and lived in nice houses were all targets for the multitude of criminal gangs and emerging militias. Whether the wealth was legitimate or not, seemed to have little sway; everything was there for the taking.

I eventually arrived at the Diwaniyah office. It was situated on a main dual carriageway, where passing traffic was evident but not too busy. The organisation's logos were emblazoned on the building. There were smaller ones on the gates, and most surprising was a temporary road sign with the organisation's logo on it, clearly announcing "WE ARE HERE!", which, at that point in time, was the last thing you wanted to do.

We drove into the courtyard as the gate guard opened up the double gates to allow entry and parked up next to the main building as the large gates closed behind us. I took my bag and walked into the office, following a guy who didn't introduce himself but shook my hand and asked me to follow him.

The building, obviously converted from a very large house over three very spacious floors, was a hive of activity. In many of the rooms, meetings and gatherings were underway; people moving from room to room with papers, files and maps. Everyone whose eye I caught, smiled as I was whisked past them to the office of the team leader (TL) or field office manager (FoM).

In the office were two men. One was seated behind a desk and the other was standing next to him; both were pondering over the many papers on the desk.

One of the guys, the seated one, was introduced as the team leader, Mustapha. He was Egyptian, I later learnt. The other guy introduced himself as Papa-Diop; he was Senegalese.

What I had disturbed was a handover of responsibilities. Papa-Diop was to be the new TL for the Diwaniyah field office, and Mustapha was going to replace the TL at the Amarah office, who was leaving.

We spent a few minutes getting acquainted, until I excused myself by asking if it was okay to have a quick walk around the building, meet some of the team and get a feel for the place. It was agreed, as they seemed to have a lot more to get through together. Mustapha instructed Jaffar to show me around (so that was his name!).

Jaffar was the field team's security focal point. He was polite, friendly and very honest in pointing out the gaps in the security management, but as I later found out, he was not very forceful or communicative with his thoughts and ideas, even though he was very well informed and had a very good grasp on the changing situation in and around Diwaniyah.

As the days progressed, I travelled around the project locations to see how the field teams were operating. My very first observation, as I had noticed on the day I arrived, was the signage that each location had in place. In normal circumstances, organisational logos and signs announcing the work that is being done are used to promote the organisation within the communities where they are working; they usually have their donors' logos on them too. With the situation in Iraq becoming increasingly hostile and attacks on Western interests rising in number, it had become a sensible and safe option to take down signage, so as not to draw unwanted attention to those working for organisations from, or funded by, countries that are deemed by many growing terror groups as the enemy.

I had mentioned this to the HoM in Al Kut, but it was seen as alarmist and unnecessary. As I was told, the HoM had a good grasp on the situation and he didn't see any need for change. (Really?)

I spoke with Jaffar about the signs and asked for his opinion. He surprised me by being totally against the signs; further, he told me he had raised the issue only a few days beore and he was roundly dismissed, not only from the Diwaniyah office but from the HQ office at Al Kut. "No surprise there," I thought.

Reigniting my information sources from my last visit to Iraq and tapping into some new ones that I wasn't so sure of just yet, I started to put together a risk map. This would not only show incidents, but would have a narrative explaining adverse changes and highlighting dominant groups that would pose a threat to the organisation and its workers.

A group becoming more influential in Iraq was emerging under the powerful and brutal leadership of Abu Musab al-Zarqawi. Al Qaeda in Iraq (AQI) became an extension of the ideology from the Al Qaeda terror organisation led by Osama bin Laden. Their ideology was absolutely anti-Western, and it was extreme, brutal and growing in influence.

One of the other groups (and there were many based on tribal lines or groups of criminals and bandits that were just out to make money) that were coming into prominence was the Mahdi Army, a Shia group formed and led by the cleric Muqtada Al Sadr. Both groups opposed the 'coalition occupation' as they called it; they opposed Western ideologies and had a special hatred for Americans above all others.[8]

The organisation I worked for was American, and employed alongside the Americans, British, French, Senegalese, Egyptian, Jordanian and Iraqi nationals. Pointing an arrow at where their office was located and where their field locations and projects were operating was, I thought, a very big risk and not thought out in detail, considering the fast-changing context of what was happening across the country.

When speaking directly to me, Jaffar was very clear about the threat as he saw it and how the methods employed by the organisation were, as he put it, "not with the safety of the staff in mind". I asked if he had voiced his opinion to the management here in Diwaniyah or to HQ in Al Kut.

His small frame slouched, and his eye contact with me changed as he looked at the ground. He told me that he had, on several occasions, tried to discuss several issues about safety and security, not just in the field but at the office too, without anyone taking him seriously. At HQ he could not get past the HQ security focal point, who refused to take anything he said seriously.

I told Jaffar that I would be looking and reporting on all the issues I had seen and would support him on the issues he had raised with me during the days we had been observing the operations in the field and at the office, along with the levels of overall security management, which wasn't looking good at all.

---

[8] While it appeared that all things American were a legitimate target, it stretched to being European, African or even Iraqi nationals working for Western agencies and Iraqi organisations that were seen to, or perceived to be, taking money from foreign donors. The brutality inflicted by these groups was shocking and was broadcast across the world's media.

I had started the training, delivering overall awareness training within the context of where we all where and what was happening. We covered the emergency protocols for reaction to incidents, emergency evacuation planning and management and, importantly, we went through reporting and communication.

This first part of the training was very telling. It highlighted a huge disconnect between senior management and field teams. While most knew of the existence of the organisational security plans, it appeared that only one or two had read them and nobody knew how to interpret the instructions into an action plan. There was nothing: no emergency procedures at all written for the Diwaniyah office and field locations. The incident reports from the generic organisational documents were over complicated, when they should have been concise. My six-week plan was looking like it would not be enough, so the two weeks I had been given was woefully inadequate.

I had to focus on what I could deliver that might help these guys if the fan was hit by some smelly stuff, which was highly likely.

I managed to pin down the office management and go through how they would communicate with the field teams if the office was attacked, where they would go, how they would get there and what actions they should take. It seemed like most of the information was being considered for the first time; that was not good. I gave them a framework plan that they (the management) needed to add the details to in order for it to be workable and effective.

I next moved on to all the field staff. We discussed (among many things) their preparedness for when they left the office each morning and went to their respective project locations. I asked about the emergency equipment they carried in their vehicles, spare wheels, water, food and money; all the stuff they might need if they couldn't return to the office.

All the sessions were very focused, but even though we crammed a lot in, it just wasn't anywhere near enough, and I felt my time restriction was seriously impacting on the overall safety of the team; there was so much that needed to be done. The field teams were incredibly hard working and were totally dedicated to the delivery of their programme to give the much-needed help to the communities they worked among. It was management structure and, in my opinion, poor leadership that was letting the organisation down.

The level of communication across all emergency procedures was extremely poor. Depending on who you asked, you consistently got different answers for the same question. This was the key telling point that there had been no consistent training for safety and security and any emergency procedures had been done to a minimum standard.

The original time frame I had put on each of my field visits was now proving to be not only realistic but probably essential. I was now faced with a very short time frame to deliver what I considered to be essential training; even this would not be enough, in my opinion, to be classified as effective.

As I travelled between the different field locations, I got a sense from most of the field workers that they understood already that their safety and security knowledge was not in line with the situations that they were expected to work in every day. While they were individually aware, the collective organisational response was either not present, not known or, more likely, not communicated effectively.

It became apparent that there was a disconnect between senior management, the situation on the ground with the field teams and the fast-changing threat. It was my assessment that the reason I had been brought out was to correct the shortfalls, train all the field teams on emergency procedures and consolidate headquarters' thinking and planning for the dynamic threat that was changing at a very fast pace.

The original time frame I had been given was realistic, with the thorough planning, training and preparation helping the organisation be better prepared and giving greater awareness to the field teams to keep them safe. The amended timeline I was given was woefully inadequate due to the rise in risk around international organisations working in Iraq. Targeting was now a real threat, and trying to cover everything that was required in such a short space of time was, in my opinion a failure of duty of care.

Even today, I still fail to understand. I was employed over a long period of time to deliver the job specification that was given originally. Why it was changed at very short notice is still a mystery, and as it worked out, a grave mistake.

I felt that I had to say something about the situation. Firstly, I spoke to the field manager at Diwaniyah and canvassed his opinion based on the feedback from his team. I had asked him once the training was completed to take collective feedback. In basic terms, to ask if it was too much, too little or just right; what is known as the 'Goldilocks scale' (for obvious reasons). I had expressed to all those who undertook the training that as individuals they could discuss any related issues with me in total confidence, but I guess they felt more comfortable talking to their own manager.

The field manager did indeed express his concerns with the gaps in the training. While I had recalculated the training needs and restructured the programme, I tried to cover as much as I could in as much detail as possible; but even I knew it wasn't enough, considering what was happening in the country.

I was approached by one guy in particular. He was an engineer working on a water-pipeline project, bringing clean water into the town. He was a national member of staff, one I had assessed to be someone others would look to for advice and assistance; he was a foreman type of figure.

Being a local guy, he confided in me that many people not connected to the organisation were asking him questions about his work. Who did he work for? What was he doing? He said some young men had approached him and asked if he was working for the Americans, and they appeared to be quite aggressive with him. This was a concern; it could be the early stages of information gathering. My thoughts were now of the visibility of the programme, signage and advertising, both at the field sites and at the offices too.

I decided that now was the time to speak frankly to the HoM and to hopefully get him to change his tactics around the profile of the programme.

Jaffar burst into my room. He was shaken by something. He was busting a gut to tell me something but he was in too much of a nervous state to tell me calmly.

"Jaffar, sit down. Take a drink of water and a few deep breaths and tell me what is wrong."

"Mr Phil, there has been an incident with our team in Amarah."

I had finished training there just the week before.

"What happened? When was it, and who was involved?" I asked keeping my voice quiet and calm.

It turned out that two of the 4x4 vehicles (with logos) were on their way back from the field sites to the office when a large crowd started throwing rocks at the cars. Windows were smashed, bodywork was damaged but luckily none of the occupants were injured: shaken but no injuries.

I called the field manager at Amarah and asked for more details. I asked him to fill out an incident report form and send it to the HoM, and to copy me and the deputy HoM too.

It was too late to be driving back to Al Kut, so I sat with Jaffar and discussed the incident; how it should be reported and what actions he should take if he was the field manager in Amarah. I talked him through the various options and then we started to piece together an information sheet based on recent incidents, their type and location. We added information from recent conversations. Jaffar chimed in with a few bits of localised information, much the same as the engineer had spoken about, and we started an analysis of what we had.

It was a great process to get Jaffar involved in. He was intelligent, quick to learn and, best of all, he had a very realistic approach to how the situation was developing and the organisation's 'positioning' in the changing context.

One little nugget of information that Jaffar offered up really concerned me and set alarm bells ringing in my head.

Across the street from the office there were some long-abandoned buildings; they looked like office-type buildings. They had been empty for a long time, Jaffar told me, until recently. Jaffar had reports from the office gate guard that over the past week different vehicles had been arriving, and heavily armed men had been seen taking large boxes and crates inside the building.

He said there had been lots of vehicles and lots of men. In his words, "They looked like men from the Mahdi Army." But we had no way of confirming this.

If the buildings were going to be used by some sort of militia, then being just over the road from them was not a good place to be.

I asked Jaffar if there was any way we could confirm who was occupying the building. Was it legitimate? Perhaps a new business? "Unlikely, but it could be a point of enquiry," I thought.

I talked over some scenarios with Jaffar, and it became apparent that some of the boxes, by description, were wooden crates; not dissimilar to weapon crates. Still none of this was confirmed and maybe we were jumping to conclusions, but best to be safe.

I asked Jaffar if he or anyone he knew and trusted locally would be able to find out who the crate-carrying new tenants were. It transpired that a friend of Jaffar used to be the caretaker of the building and was, as far as he knew, a key holder.

Jaffar rang his friend, and a conversation ensued. It appeared to get very heated at times. With Jaffar's face going through a gamut of emotions, it was hard to tell just what was going on.

Eventually the call ended.

"Mr Phil, I think they are very bad men. They are from Fallujah and Baghdad."

I sat quietly, thinking about this information. I then asked some questions about what exactly his friend had said and how he knew where they came from. I asked about weapons; whether he had seen any, how he had managed to see them and what his connection to this group was.

Jaffar, after further clarification and selective questioning, told me that they had arrived at his friend's house and told him to go with them to open the building. They'd paid him some money to take up his role of caretaker. He was to furnish some of the office spaces with chairs and desks, as well as a large conference-type room for meetings.

They'd told him that they would travel back to Fallujah but would send friends from Baghdad in a few days to check he had done what he had been asked.

He told Jaffar that he had seen weapons, but by the descriptions they were AK47s and pistols. Just small arms, only about five weapons in total were seen, but he couldn't confirm what was in the crates.

This was enough. I called a meeting with the office manager at Diwaniyah and got him to bring his field managers in. It took about an hour to conclude the meeting, and I told them to prepare to evacuate the office on short notice, the preparation and identification of key documents to take, what should be destroyed and an action plan for the contents of the safe.

Vehicles and communication equipment were critical, as, too, were the routes that should be taken away from the office. The final location would be determined once safe departure from the office had happened. I told them it could be tonight, tomorrow or next week, but it was likely that it would happen soon, so there would need to be minimum staffing at the office, gate guards had to be briefed to watch all activity without being too obvious and the office manager, with Jaffar, would need to talk with the gate guards every hour to see if there was a build-up of activity that may trigger the pre-emptive evacuation of the office.

The international staff lived in a house two streets behind the office location. It was a quiet residential area, and staff usually walked alone from the accommodation to the office; this was to stop. It was now to be done in twos as a minimum, and if vehicles were available they should be collected each morning and driven home each evening.

I asked Jaffar to get me a driver, as I would be going back to Al Kut immediately before it was too late. I was on the limit now but this was an emergency and I had to get the HoM to initiate a new plan for visibility and programme activity. Should it stop? If so, when and for how long? The coordination across all locations needed to happen and collective emergency plans needed to be actioned.

I had called the HoM and told him of what was happening. I asked if he had the incident report from Amarah; he said no.

After I had finished talking, he told me, amazingly, that Jaffar and his friend might be overreacting and while it was good to be prepared, he wasn't sure it was totally necessary; this was based on what he'd heard from his sources (who I was told were all local government and council people who had a vested interest in keeping the programmes going and would be very frugal with the facts as to what might really be happening). I told him I would brief him and discuss the situation on my return to Al Kut. He agreed but sounded surprised that I was travelling back to talk face to face with him.

The journey back was tense. Every small town or village we passed through had large groups of men out on the streets, many wearing the green headbands and bandanas, and most carrying weapons of one kind or another.

We tried to avoid populated areas but it was difficult, if not impossible. I sat back and low on the rear seat of the car and just hoped that the vehicle didn't attract attention, after all it was a beaten up American Cadillac, not one for converting to a fighting vehicle. Luckily, we avoided any incidents and pulled into the Al Kut office just after dark. I went directly to the office of the HoM and found him at his desk. He was a little miffed that I had disturbed him but he agreed to hear me out.

I spoke in detail about signage, visibility and the safety of field workers with him. I went through the process of information from several sources and my assessment of it. I told him that the office at Diwaniyah was particularly vulnerable due to the observations that had been made over the last few days.

There was a long silence. The HoM was deep in thought.

"Phil," he said in a very quiet and deliberate manner. "While I thank you for your thoughts and consideration, I think you have got this wrong. There was a large explosion at the bottom of this road yesterday and everyone panicked. It turned out to be just a group of guys blowing up the residence of a former Ba'athist; no harm to us, no threat. So I think you and others have just become caught up in some issues that are not really a threat to us at all. But thanks again."

I was furious. I thought, "What kind of person responsible for people working in an increasingly hostile situation just discounts what is happening around him? This can't be for real, surely? At least he could investigate my information and findings for himself?" But no, as far as he was concerned it was nothing to worry about.

"Look," I said in a very distinct and authoritarian manner (as I did, he lifted his head up with a surprised look on his face, almost not expecting to see me still standing there), "if you are telling me that you are going to do absolutely nothing and are not willing to accept what I am telling you, then I am not prepared to put my name to the safety and security of this organisation. I am going away to make a call and to write my letter of resignation. When I return, you have a choice: do nothing, risking your teams, your staff and the programme, taking full responsibility yourself, in which case I leave tomorrow morning, or act, and I will assist you and the teams in any way I can to keep them out of harm's way. The choice is yours."

He immediately countered...

"Phil, there is no need for this. You don't have to resign. Your work here has been great, your training—"

I cut him short. "My training and almost everything I do here is undermined. I get the feeling that I am being used as tick-in-the-box, so you can say you have a safety and security person in place. I can't be effective if you constantly tie my hands and restrict everything I do. I will be back in 10 minutes. You have a decision to make."

I walked out of his office, went to my room and typed my resignation with immediate effect. I already knew, I suppose, that he wasn't going to act; my resignation letter reflected that. I knew at that moment that I would be leaving the next morning.

I made a phone call to Amar at the Baghdad office and caught him just as he was leaving for the night to go home. I asked him to send a driver to collect me at 6am and to book me a flight home. After some explanations and answering Amar's questions, he agreed and then told me that Baghdad was a very dangerous place to be right now. Over the last week, there had been many attacks, more than he had known since the end of the war. This just confirmed my analysis. He said he would get me on a plane to Jordan then onward to London, but it might mean a day's stopover in Baghdad. I agreed. The call was done.

I went back directly to the HoM's office. His deputy was with him, and as I walked in, their conversation stopped.

"Well, what's the verdict?" I asked, already knowing the answer.

"We would both like you to reconsider and stay with us here. If things are as you say, then we will need you here—"

Again, I was abrupt. This just wasn't the time to be blowing smoke up my arse and telling me what a fantastic guy I was. This was about people's lives. "I have made arrangements to leave. I will travel tomorrow morning. You have made my position untenable, and I am not about to take the flack for your bad judgement when things go wrong here, and they will; it may take a few weeks or a month but things in Iraq are turning sour very quickly. The old humanitarian model of being left alone because you are impartial no longer applies."

As I finished speaking, I put my letter of resignation on his table. I told him I had also emailed him a copy and sent one to the organisational HQ and the HR department back in America.

His jaw hit the floor. His reaction told me that he'd thought I was bluffing. He obviously thought I was angling for a better deal on the training or something similar; nothing could have been further from the truth. This was a very dangerous game he was playing, and I wasn't playing at all, not when the potential for harm was extremely high.

I didn't wait for a response; I left the room and went to pack. I called Jaffar at Diwaniyah and gave him advice and information on how to prepare the office and the field teams. I left him with an email containing the emergency plans for evacuation, which the HoM was supposed to have reviewed and signed off (and hadn't), so he could brief the management of his field office and all workers. I told him to pass the information to the other field offices for them to digest. I suggested that time was short and that he had to brief everyone quickly.

I now had an unsettling thought. Was Jaffar's personality strong enough to do what was needed? Did he think he would get into trouble, possibly lose his job, if he did what I'd asked and nothing happened? It was a tough ask from me, and it would be a very tough decision by him. I could do nothing more.

I had a few hours to try to catch some sleep, but I was restless. Different scenarios flashed through my mind. I thought about how stubborn and restrictive the HoM had been right from the outset. His autocratic style had been spoken about by some of the other international staff but none had challenged any of his decisions. Two members of the Baghdad office had, during breaks in training, expressed their concerns about the HoM and his obvious desire to push on regardless of the threats and risks, believing they would never be involved in any targeting or other adverse actions. The red lights were flashing warnings, and I hoped I could provide some calm and clarity, but no; I, like most of the others, became restricted in usefulness, the only difference being that once it became obvious, I challenged it and acted upon the results. I wondered, if enough of those working for the organisation had communicated their issues, could that have forced a change of action? Sadly, I wasn't convinced.

The room was dimly lit and very hot, with no air-conditioning, not even a fan. It was sticky and uncomfortable. I fell into a light and restless sleep, pondering how this would all work out. I woke at regular intervals, roughly snatching about 20 minutes of sleep before waking again.

The night seemed impossibly long. What was only a few hours felt like a lifetime. Time was becoming uncomfortably slow.

I opened my eyes to be met by a shaft of light through the hastily closed curtains from the night before. I glanced at my watch; it was 5.30am. Time to get up, grab a very quick shower and, if lucky, a quick cup of tea. The shower was cold, icy cold, and there was no tea, as the gas canister on the cooker was empty and the main power supply was off (again!); a can of Coke and a couple of biscuits was breakfast. That would do until I got to Baghdad, I suppose.

A car pulled up outside the house, and then there was a soft knock on the door. It was my ride to Baghdad. Again, it was a plain car, some sort of battered American sedan, but it worked and was less obvious than the 4x4 vehicles normally used for the field programmes by INGOs and the UN; they were very high profile.

I sat with the driver for about 15 minutes discussing routes and going through some emergency procedures should we run into trouble. While he smiled and nodded, I got the impression that what I was saying was not fully understood and he would do whatever he thought best in any given scenario, regardless of training or situation. After my bags had been loaded we set off. A bright early morning drive, two or three hours to the Baghdad office. Nothing else to do but try to relax. Yeah, right!

Even sitting in the back of the car, my eyes were out on stalks, observing the road ahead, checking what was left and right of us and constantly evaluating and re-evaluating what to do and where to go if we were attacked from the front or the rear, or from the left or the right. The 'what if' questions were always on my mind, changing plan as we changed environment from built-up areas to open highway to wide, open desert plains to main highways: always thinking, always assessing and always on edge. But it was good to be on edge; it made me more alert and cleared my thinking but was always exhausting, particularly when stopping at your journey's end. One level finishes, another takes its place; buildings, exits, obstacles... it never really stops. It becomes second nature, sometimes even when it's not really needed; old habits die hard (or never quite die at all!).

All along the route there was constant and multiple plumes of black smoke rising on the horizon, far enough away not to be a direct concern but close enough to understand they came from a substantial source. Driving with the windows down allowed the distant, infrequent soundtrack of conflict, with short bursts of distant automatic gunfire and the just-audible sound of explosions which sounded like distant thunder. I wondered if it would carry my way and when, if at all, it would break into a real battle storm.

My driver, a resident of the capital, informed me that there were several checkpoints around the main roads into Baghdad. A few were manned by what appeared to be police, but in the words of my trusty driver, they were bad men; taking money and sometimes cars from people trying to get into the capital. Some people had lost their lives at the checkpoints. Luckily, I would be driven along old routes and tracks to circumnavigate the areas where these bogus checkpoints were often sited.

As we drew closer to the city, the frequency of gunfire had increased but still appeared to be in the distance. There was more activity and the military presence was more noticeable, heavily armed and looking menacing. For all intent and purposes, it looked like the war was still in progress, if not for the groups of civilians trying hard to get on with their normal life, shopping, meeting at cafés and standing chatting, with one eye to the military patrols; it was strange. The atmosphere was hostile and very tense. It was etched on every face, soldiers and civilians alike.

Passing through a marketplace on the side of the main road, we turned off and pulled up at the office. Standing in the doorway was Amar, a big bullish-looking guy with a wide welcoming smile.

He took my bag from the boot of the car and told me to go inside.

Once inside, I sat and looked around to reacquaint myself with the office, its layout, its doorways and its exits. I studied the windows, checking which of them were encased by metal bars and which ones would allow a rapid exit.

Amar greeted me and told me he had put the kettle on. I smiled and noted that he had remembered the importance I had placed on the good old cup of tea, explaining to him on my first visit that a welcome in many places in the UK consisted of the greeting, "Hello, put the kettle on then."

We spent the first half an hour going through the flight bookings, printing tickets and checking passport details. I handed back my organisational identity card and other documents I had been given on my arrival. Amar asked me if I would stay and what it would take to change my mind. I jokingly told him a change of HoM would be a start. We both laughed a rather uneasy laugh.

I was to leave the following day on the Royal Jordanian Airline flight which had recently resumed. The airport inside the infamous 'Green Zone' was constantly attacked by rocket and mortar fire, largely due to the coalition forces that used it as their HQ operating base. Anything coming in or going out was deemed by insurgents to be a legitimate target. That was enough to make you clench your balloon knot tighter than usual.

Once everything was done administratively, I was shown to my temporary room above the office. I got settled, had a shower (warm water at last!), had another cup of tea and sat for a few hours talking with Amar. We talked about his family, his job and his aspirations. We talked about how we would 'fix' Iraq if we had the power and resources; that was interesting. I offered him a piece of advice: I told him that while the country was still in a crazy state of uncertainty and there was an abundance of land that had been abandoned, much in prime locations, it might be worth trying through the local government to either make a claim on some of the land or offer to purchase it, with a crafty eye on peacetime and the eventual rebuilding of the country. Prime land bought now at what could be a bargain price could be worth 10 times its purchase value in the future. He laughed and said on the wages that he got from the organisation, it would take him several lifetimes to save enough to buy land. It was a good idea, but one that Amar knew was out of his reach.

Inevitably, the conversation turned to the situation that had led me to Baghdad and on my way out.

Amar started the conversation quite tentatively, being cautious about what he was saying and always looking around to see if anyone in the office was in earshot and listening in.

As the conversation progressed, he opened up a bit more. He started to tell me of the things he had seen or heard that he disagreed with. He felt that some people in the organisation, international staff, were not sensitive enough to the Iraqi culture. He felt sometimes that although he was the office manager for Baghdad, his opinion or experience and local knowledge was ignored. I sensed it upset him considerably. He valued his job and was proud of being in the position he was in but he thought it could be much better. I kept my council on the reasons that I had resigned, only saying that there had been disagreements about my role. I left him to come to his own conclusions.

Just before Amar left the office for the evening, he went to the market and returned with lamb kebab and a can of fizzy orangeade. "Supper," he told me with a smile. I thanked him and let him out of the building, then I locked up and went to my room.

The night was still hot and sticky. The rotating fan was just pushing the warm air around the room. It was dark; just a small chink of light crept in through the gap where the curtains hung low on the piece of cord that held them up. I could hear sounds of gunfire, some close and some distant; but the fact that the sounds appeared to come from many different directions told me that much was happening across the city. Things were deteriorating, and I had a feeling something major was about to happen: maybe not today, maybe not this week, but I reckoned it would be within a month. I just hoped that those I had trained, and most of all Jaffar, would pick up on the indicators and manage to act before getting caught up in the inevitable chaos that was bound to ensue.

The remainder of my almost-sleepless night was spent thinking about what was happening and what might unfold. I spent some time before slipping into a sticky sleep, thinking about Nasir, Nasiriyah and of Rasha and how her treatment was progressing. I had a pang of guilt for not communicating with Nasir as often as I probably should, but I had a lot on my plate just now, and although Nasir had responded to my last email, telling me how the programme was progressing and what he was doing, keeping me updated on all the work we had started there, he forgot to mention Rasha's progress. I was sure I would hear from him on this soon, but for now, my thoughts as I drifted off were focused on going home.

I woke again and checked my watch; it was 7.30am. I'd had just about an hour and a half's sleep. I felt rough. Everywhere was quiet; no gunfire, no explosions. The silence was broken only by the very infrequent sound of a passing vehicle followed again, almost immediately, by silence.

I got out of bed, washed, got dressed and headed through to the kitchen to put the kettle on and have a cuppa. I brought all of my belongings from my temporary bedroom into the kitchen. As I poured the boiling water onto my teabag, I heard a key being put into the main door lock. I froze for a second before quickly moving to the door in the kitchen which led out to an enclosed courtyard. I quickly but quietly slid the top and bottom bolts open and turned the large key in the mortice lock to open it.

There was a shout from the office space. "Phil, good morning. Is the kettle on?"

It was Amar with a cheerful greeting, and as he came into the kitchen, I saw his smiling face.

This typified my now-instinctive actions: always thinking the worst and looking for escape routes. Luckily, and again from habit, I had taken a peek out of the rear door and into the courtyard the night before.

Feeling that all was well now Amar had arrived, I settled with my cup of tea and a few biscuits. Soon, other members of the office staff started to arrive, and as they did, the noise level grew, with the same chit-chat you would expect to hear in any office anywhere in the UK: greetings, laughter, chairs being moved and computers being switched on.

Suddenly, it went quiet. Just for a moment. Then Amar expressed his annoyance that the mains power had failed again. He left the building via my emergency escape door, and within seconds I heard a small generator starting up, followed a few seconds later by a drop in the generator's noisy tone as the power flooded back into the building.

During that moment of quiet, it amplified the stillness and silence of the day outside. It was still very quiet.

As Amar re-entered the building, I asked him if it was normal for the streets to be so quiet at this time of the morning? It was now 8.15. Amar stood still and tilted his head as though to better hear what was, or rather wasn't, happening outside. Even with the door closed, the muffled clatter of the portable generator was still pervasive.

I followed Amar as he walked through the office space towards the front door. As he opened it, I was just a step or two behind him as he stepped out into the road. One car passed us, then nothing... not a soul, vehicle or anything else.

Amar looked at me and shrugged his shoulders. He said it was strange because the shops and stalls were usually opening and there would be many people, cars and motorbikes on the road.

Was it a day of holiday that we had forgotten about? Had the road been closed further down where we couldn't see? This happened often.

It was eerily quiet, and there were no visible signs as to why.

My thoughts went back, quite a long way, to the riots in Belfast in the very early eighties. "Similar situations," I thought. If there was going to be a car bomb or an ambush set up to attack the police or military patrols, the locals would be warned to stay clear of the area until the attack had happened. This was sometimes followed by what we termed as rent-a-crowd, groups of mainly youths turning up in the immediate aftermath of an attack to stop any rapid follow up and to block off roads, thereby restricting police/ military movement but allowing the perpetrators to escape amid the confusion. "Could this be similar?" I thought.

We went back into the office, had another cup of tea and talked about my flight out. Amar said he would like to come to the Green Zone with me to make sure all went well. I said it wasn't necessary but thanked him all the same.

I had an hour to kill at the office before my driver would take me to the airport in the Green Zone. I spent the time reviewing my emails and checking both my watches (I always kept a spare in my bag). I checked my documents and passport, my three mobile phones, turning the two spare phones off to conserve the batteries. I also set my emergency text message on my phone ready for the journey. This is a pre-arranged message that stays on my screen throughout high-risk journeys. It states who I am, where I am going and the route planned to get me there. If I am stopped with a risk of being abducted, then all I have to do is press 'send' and the message will be sent from my last known position to alert the recipient that something has gone badly wrong and they need to act to start a chain of calls that will hopefully lead to my eventual release; if nothing else, it gives a starting point for a follow-up search and tells the recipients I am in trouble.

In later years, as technology advanced, I would combine an emergency message with GPS latitude and longitude coordinates, sometimes sending several coordinates along the planned route, giving a route that could be plotted on a map. Some satellite phones give this as an option to automatically send location details, which makes it easier to locate people quickly. In the humanitarian world at this time, trackers and GPS systems were not widely known about or used.

I ran through my likely scenarios and what options I would have in each, should I be involved in an incident on the way to the airport.[9] My backpack was correctly packed; I would have to repack it once in the airport, as some of the contents would not be allowed as cabin luggage, but as an emergency grab bag, it would be a lifeline should I need to run.

I spoke with Amar and asked him to brief the driver on what to do if armed aggressors stopped us. Generally, it involves keeping a good distance from the car in front, being aggressive if confronted, usually by 'crashing' out of a line of traffic, keeping revs high, being willing to mount the pavement if needed and in the rare case of an armed aggressor, attempting to shoot through the windscreen, then run him down and keep going at high speed.

I knew, and would put my house on it, that even though the driver was saying he would do what he was asked in these situations, he wouldn't. He would hesitate, and in doing so you lose any advantage of surprise. In all fairness, it is a drill that needs practise and a building of confidence in the vehicle and your own abilities in such environments, neither of which we had the luxury of having. But it was fingers crossed at this level.

---

[9] While the reader may think all these precautions are excessive, they are sometimes critical for the safety of the traveller. While the text messages at the time of sending will not give the final location of the sender, it gives a starting point for searches being conducted and gives an alert that something has gone wrong. It relies on the recipient being pre-briefed and acting quickly to raise the alarm with those authorities that can react.

I now had about 15 minutes before I had to leave the office, so I decided to step outside and take a breath of fresh air and to see if there was any change to the silence.

As I stepped outside, I heard some gunfire in the distance, not a short burst or a series of rapid single shots, but continuous; at a guess, I thought it was medium to heavy machine-gun fire. It was soon joined by other more sporadic gunfire; rifles maybe?

There then followed two very large explosions. I quickly ran into the office as Amar was on his way out. I told him I needed to go now, to get to the Green Zone before the fighting, which sounded to be some distance from the airport, spread and roads were closed. He agreed. The driver was already opening the boot of the car, and I threw in my large bag, keeping my backpack with me.

I sat in the back of the car. The windows had curtains which were tied back, but they obscured a good amount of the window. I thought that if I closed them, it may invite any aggressor to be curious as to why I had done so and want to look.

As we set off, I had my phone in hand, emergency text on the screen and my bag strap looped over my arm, ready for a quick exit if needed.

There were a few more loud explosions. They seemed to be closer now, but it was hard to be exact because the sound was ricocheting off the buildings in the heavily built-up area, and we were moving too.

Traffic was building up, possibly due to people fleeing the fighting. We headed onto a highway and built up speed. There were more plumes of smoke now rising on the visible horizons all around. With my window partially down, I strained to make sense of the noise I could hear. It sounded like a series of battles were taking place. Who was fighting? I didn't know. But linking the large gatherings I had seen the day before made me consider that the Mahdi Army were possibly on the move.

The sound intensified the closer we got to the Green Zone. There was gunfire and explosions, and more and more vehicles were filling the highway.

Suddenly we slowed. We were in some sort of traffic jam; the cause at this point was unknown. I told our driver not to get too close to the vehicle in front. We gained some space and if we took care, we could crash out to the left if we had to. Suddenly, a vehicle appeared behind us and was trying to force us to move over. As I was about to tell the driver to stay where he was, he moved over and allowed the vehicle to overtake. A stream of cars behind him filled the gap and we were stuck on the inside and boxed in.

We slowed and stopped, moved a few meters, then stopped and started again a few times. I was constantly telling the driver to keep the space of half a car length from the one ahead and to try to regain the outside position, but we stayed on the inside.

I was now starting to see many armed men at the roadside. I sat right back and low down. I could see just between the front seats and out of the windscreen. My heart sank.

I could now see the reason for the traffic jam. It was an armed checkpoint; men dressed in black, armed with AK47 assault rifles, were stopping cars and checking the occupants, then allowing them to pass. What were they looking for? Foreigners? I had no idea. What I did know was that if I were to be seen, I would be taken and either shot on the spot or used for the barbaric beheading videos in a bright orange jumpsuit; orange was never my colour. Either way it would not end well. We were still several car lengths away from the checkpoint. With my finger hovering above the 'text send' button, I looked out of the window and ran through my options.

I could get out and run, but run where? With many armed people at the roadside, I would quickly be seen and I can't quite outrun a bullet. I could ask the driver to 'crash out' and make a dash for it by ramming the checkpoint. I doubted he would even try, and with his lack of confidence and experience, plus being scared shitless, it was doomed to fail, particularly as we were still boxed in. I had little choice but to sit well down and hope I wouldn't be spotted and that my driver wouldn't flap.

We were four cars away from the armed guy at the makeshift checkpoint. He was casting a quick look in each vehicle then waving them on. The car three in front of us was searched; the doors were opened, the boot checked and the driver abused by pushing and shoving, with a rifle aimed at him. I feared he would be shot. We waited nervously.

He was eventually forced back into his car and allowed to go. I was now one car away from being discovered.

I spoke quietly to my driver. I told him to stay calm and that whatever he believed in, he should be friendly with the guy with the rifle. I told him to tell the armed guy that he was fleeing the fighting and to be calm...

I was shitting myself. I knew what was coming my way if I was discovered. It wouldn't be nice. I had seen the videos. I was scared, very scared, but calm, still thinking of options, which were getting to the zero end of the scale.

The armed guy seemed to be talking to the driver in front for a long time. My options were reduced to sitting as low as I could and hoping the car wasn't selected for a search or that I wasn't noticed as a result of the stop. He stood back and allowed the car to progress. The car stalled. The armed guy started shouting and pointing his rifle at the driver, telling him to move. We were next.

The car in front fired up and slowly moved away. As he did, there was a very loud explosion about 100 metres to our right, followed by a barrage of gunfire. The checkpoint was abandoned as all the armed insurgents ran towards the explosion and the gunfire. Among the shouting and battle noise, I told the driver in no uncertain terms to "GO, GO, GO!"

As we sped off and the noise of explosions and gunfire intensified, I could see smoke billowing from several areas. The noise of battle was everywhere. We drove on at speed until we reached the drive up to the Green Zone. There were lots of military about, all on edge but obviously they were the perimeter security to the Green Zone.

We were ushered into a waiting queue of cars. The inner security was manned by Iraqi airport security who could have been police, but here and there were American Soldiers overseeing the process almost as though they were in training mode; they just appeared to be observers.

As we drew up to the head of the line, we were stopped. I was told to leave everything in the car and go over to a small building were my documents would be checked. The driver was asked to open the boot. As I got out of the car, I put my backpack on but was stopped and told I couldn't take any bags into the building and that they had to stay in the car until I had been 'processed'.

With a certain amount of hesitation, I agreed, and with my travel documents, I went into the building. My passport was checked, my ticket examined and I was told to go back to the car, collect my luggage and follow the signs into the airport.

As I walked back to the car, I saw the boot still open and the driver sat behind the wheel. I walked to the rear of the car to collect my luggage, only to see the same security guy who'd stopped me, coming back towards me. As he approached, he smiled and said everything was okay and that I could go. I nodded hesitantly, picked up my baggage, said goodbye to my driver, giving him all the Iraqi currency I had, and left.

I walked into the airport to be greeted by the same type of private security that I had seen on my arrival; still appallingly bad at weapon handling and overall appearance, they were scruffy and appeared rather aimless.

I sat down with my bags and observed all that was going on around me, while waiting for the plane to land. I was still running on adrenalin after the very near miss I'd had. I mulled over what might have happened. It brought home to me just how ill-prepared some organisations were and how a simple misplaced belief can get people killed; the 'it won't happen to me' syndrome was out of date and very dangerous to believe in.

I reviewed my actions. Getting out of the car and running; what would that have achieved? In the best case scenario, I would have got away from the immediate area, but in a densely populated area with many armed people on the prowl, I wouldn't have got far and there would have been very little chance of survival had I been caught.

I had thought of just getting the driver to crash through the checkpoint, but I very much doubted his ability to do so, especially after showing that he couldn't take direction during the approach to the traffic jam. He would probably have invited a hail of gunfire into the car.

One thought that had crossed my mind, and it was in total desperation, was to make a grab for the rifle as I got out of the car and try to fight my way out of the predicament, hoping the confusion going on around me would help me get away. But even if that were to be successful, and the chances of that were very, very slim, I would still need to get away, but to where? Additional carjacking at gunpoint? All were thought of in total desperation and dismissed as quickly. I had no chance of being successful with those actions. They were right out of the John Wayne book of bravado and had no realistic chance of success in that scenario.

I thought of the end game if I were caught. How would my wife and family take it? How would they react to seeing me paraded on TV and then executed? How would I react? With brave dignity or as a crying bumbling wreck? I hoped the former, but the latter would also be realistic.

I decided there and then to put the terrible experience out of my mind; to take any lessons and then detach from it. If I didn't, I would suffer from it for a long time. I needed to supress and compartmentalise it; put the memory in a box, fasten it down tight and put it to the very back of my mind. That's what I did. It became a very useful method in dealing with trauma in the future; I just had to learn how to stack the boxes as they mounted up, so they didn't break open at inconvenient times.

The plane was due to land in a few minutes, and all of the departing passengers had been processed and now waited in line to board as soon as it was ready.

I quickly decided to rearrange my backpack and, taking out all the things I no longer needed and the stuff that wouldn't be allowed on the flight.

As I went through the usually familiar contents of my bag, I noticed that my spare watches and mobile phones were missing, as well as a few pens and a flash-drive, which was always left empty and used only to extract information from one computer to another and then wiped, as it only had a small capacity.

The smiling security guard at the Green Zone checkpoint came to mind. He was returning to the car as I came out of the building where I couldn't take my bags. Had he been through my stuff and taken my phone and watches?

"Bastard!" It was the only time my bags were out of my sight and control.

There was nothing I could do about it now. "Live and learn," I thought. "Live and learn."

The plane landed, discharged its passengers and boarded those of us waiting to leave. Within a very short turnaround time, we were boarded and airborne. A steep climb and hard banking to get out of the immediate airspace was the order of the day, done to hopefully avoid any potshots that may have been taken to try to bring the plane down.

After a few minutes, we were clear, levelling off and on our way to Jordan. Iraq phase two was over. I was, at last, on my way home: again.

On arriving in Amman, I had a 24-hour stopover in a very nice hotel. I sat in my room, exhausted. I decided to take a shower, get some food and sleep.

I opened my blurry eyes to the buzz of a text message on my phone. I had slept deeply; it was now 8.30 and the sun was streaming through the open curtains to my room.

I grabbed my phone. It was a message from Jaffar. He told me that during the late evening the office in Diwaniyah had been overrun. The office was ransacked, vehicles with radios were stolen and the gate guard was very badly beaten. The international staff had managed to escape through the rear of the building and were now in their accommodation a few streets away. They were planning what to do next. (A bit late to plan now. I had already briefed the management on rapid evacuation and had told them to get their plans done; apparently all this was deemed to be of low priority for them.) Some days later, I was blind-copied into an email written by Jaffar to the HoM, and the bottom line stated, "We should have listened to Phil Jones but we ignored his advice."

"Little consolation now," I thought.

During the next few days, the organisation extracted all of its international staff and a few select national staff and established a remote operating office in the Kurdish-controlled north of the country. Most of the INGOs in Iraq at that time chose to head north and set up in Erbil or Sulaymaniyah, where it was deemed safer and more secure. Iraq was now well on the road to becoming the most dangerous place on the planet; an unwanted tag that would stick for several years.

The urge to say "I told you so" rang loudly in my head. But for professional reasons, I refrained.

*

Chapter 6.5:

Iraq End Piece Summary: The Final Goodbye

During my second stint in Iraq, I had made contact with Nasir many times. He was never the best at responding but when he did, he conveyed lots of details about how the programme was going, telling me of new interventions and giving me the rundown on the guys at the bakery, the drop-in centres that were now established and the expansion out of Nasiriyah; on and on it went. The only thing missing was news about Rasha. "Maybe," I thought, "he just got lost in the rambling about the programme."

Later, maybe a month or so, I wrote again, asking about his family, the programme and the team, then, as always, asking for a sit-rep on Rasha.

The reply two weeks later was much the same: lots of rambling and an attempt at the odd joke here and there but, again, no mention of Rasha.

Time slipped by fast, and I had other issues to deal with at home, one of which was finding another job. This, and enjoying a good period with my family, kept me occupied.

My emails to Nasir became less and less frequent but I did write, and I always asked for news of Rasha. But then I found myself on my way to Sudan.

Writing to Nasir was not producing the real information I wanted, so I decided to change tactic. I sent an email before I got into my new job and changed my focus. I sent it with a single message, typed in capitals and in bold. It read:

NASIR, PLEASE TELL ME; HOW IS RASHA? IS HER TREATMENT GOING WELL? REPLY, PLEASE.

That was the total content of the message. Nothing else.

Two days later, I was shocked to get a reply from Nasir; I usually waited weeks. His response was as follows:

Dear Philip,

Thank you for your email. I have not wanted to give you news of Rasha, as it made me very sad. I know that you will also be very sad too.

Rasha died a month after you left Nasiriyah. She never went to Baghdad, as our country director who replaced you refused to help and informed me that I could not help, or I would lose my job. I cried many days and nights.

I am sorry. I hope you will forgive me. It was too difficult to give this news to you.

Nasir

I was shocked. I'd had an idea that something was not right, but was hoping either the treatment wasn't working or that her condition was becoming worse. She died within a month of me leaving.

My emotions ran riot; first sadness, deep painful sadness, followed by a sense of hopelessness, then finally turning into absolute rage and hatred. I wanted this guy punished, physically punished. I wanted to inflict damage and pain onto that miserable bastard. I had never experienced so much hate and had never wanted to explode such vicious violence, such as I was imagining, on anyone, but if he was stood in front of me, I would have been unable to contain my anger and rage. It was as if he had deliberately killed my own child.

I still well up with emotion when I mention her name. Writing this book caused me much emotional pain; digging up the details to tell her story, which needed to be told, as it formed a major part of my education in the humanitarian sector and taught me a lot about the person I am.

I will never forget her and have tortured myself over the years about possibly creating a false hope for her; getting everything in place but not following through. Was I wrong? What should I have done?

The thought of her final days causes me more pain than anything else. How did she cope? What was her frame of mind? I don't know; that in itself is hard to acknowledge.

My wife told me that before I met Rasha, her life appeared to be one of sadness. She told me that I gave her hope and that her attitude changed; she was for a time a child again, smiling and laughing. Without my involvement, it would have been unlikely that any of that would have happened and she may have died without any happiness. This was little consolation for what had happened. To this day, over 17 years later, I still feel the same.

My replacement in Nasiriyah was dealt with; fortunately, not by me. Let's just say his employability has become significantly more difficult. I truly hope I never come across him again, for his sake.

I put my return to Iraq down to bad experience at a time when Iraq was under immense pressure and a forced change was happening. The change in attitude towards aid workers and other foreigners made the humanitarian interventions difficult in the extreme. Most INGOs were remotely managing their programmes and some of their national staff had relocated, due to the threat to themselves and their families.

I found myself, in hindsight, looking back, and the situation I was in (which was like hitting a crossroads of what should have been change only to be confronted with an organisational leadership that didn't fully recognise that change for the worse) was already happening. Due to certain senior personalities who had become increasingly autocratic and were convinced that their opinion was the only one that mattered it took a serious incident to convince them otherwise. In my opinion, it was classic head-in-the-sand management, hoping that all would be okay if they ignored it. Well, they did and it wasn't.

I met some absolutely fantastic people in Iraq. The Iraqi people in general are friendly, generous to a fault and have a very strong sense of family values. This was especially surprising considering the hardships they underwent, not only during war but living in constant fear of the Saddam Hussein regime, not knowing who would report you if you spoke badly of the regime; it could be your father, uncle brother or sister who may report you, not only your neighbours or friends or those that may have overheard you in the street, so complete was the fear.

Fear of the consequences of not reporting someone, for example, saying something derogatory, forced many to report members of their own family, close friends and neighbours. To have endured a life like this and still to be resilient enough to welcome strangers is truly remarkable.

*

Chapter 7:

Darfur – My Humanitarian Coming of Age

Being home again and reacquainting myself with my wife and kids was great. Catching up with events at school and listening to how my wife was dealing with work and looking after the kids was amazing. I knew she was adept at coping from the years we'd spent in the military. I was, and have, always been amazed at how she copes with what appears to be consummate ease. I know how difficult it can be dealing with everyday problems and being the only adult in the house. If there were any problems, she never let me know while I was away.

I tried to take over on my return, in a helpful way, but I quickly noted that I was upsetting the routine that she had set up. So, I just conformed as best I could, knowing that at some point in the future I would be off on my travels again.

I had several emails since arriving home, from different organisations asking if I was available for this or that job in this or that country. While it was nice to be in demand, I didn't really fancy any of the offers I was being sent.

It appeared from some of the emails I was getting, that while in Iraq, I had somehow managed to gain a reputation as a security adviser. Some emails came from people I had not met; they had just been put in contact with me on the recommendation of others, some of whom I had met at security meetings in various places during my two trips to Iraq.

There were lots of offers to go back to Iraq from a few INGOs, and I had a very interesting telephone call with a guy from UNSECOORD (later renamed the UNDSS, United Nations Department for Safety and Security), enquiring if I would like to apply for a post with them in Afghanistan. He explained the application process, and after a lengthy conversation and being on the verge of falling asleep while listening, I declined. But that was not the last time I was involved with them.

I was very flattered by the many offers that came in for me from different organisations (some well known, some not so) but nothing really grabbed my attention. That was until a major UK-based organisation advertised for a safety and security manager/adviser in Sudan, with responsibilities in North Darfur. Now this I liked.

I applied and went for an interview in London. It was a relaxed process. They asked about my experience and gave me a few hypothetical scenarios, asking for my reaction and thoughts. Then they told me of a real-time issue they had with landmines, a minor injury that one of their staff had sustained and about the impact this incident had had on the team's confidence and morale.

I thought it through very carefully before giving my answer. I related to my previous life, training I'd undergone and my understanding of mines and mine warfare; I spoke about regaining team confidence by training and understanding the threat and risks; and I capped it off with a sentence or three about leadership, setting the right examples, etc.

They appeared to like everything I had said, telling me that they had others to interview and they would be in touch.

I arrived home that evening and discussed my day with my wife. We talked at length about Darfur, being away again and should I get the job, how long it would be for.

We agreed that the initial period should be no more than three months; we could, if required, decide on a longer commitment if we felt it was workable. We also agreed that if ever I was needed or asked to come home, regardless of the reason, I would do so without question. This was always on the understanding that any request to do so must be deemed to be important. I agreed that if ever asked, I would drop everything and return as soon as possible.

Two days later, I received a telephone call offering me the job if I was still interested. I was, and I accepted.

Four days later, I was in London being briefed on the Sudan/Darfur emergency programme. There was a developmental programme in Khartoum for North Sudan which also acted as the HQ for the emergency programme in Darfur. (There was at that point a conflict with the south of the country, which a few years later, officially became the world's newest country (South Sudan, with Juba being the capital). Right then, though, there was a civil war underway between the north and south of Sudan plus an uprising in the Darfur region who wanted autonomy from Sudan, so there was a complex internal series of wars and rebellions, with the Khartoum government being the major protagonist. Confused? Yep... it gets worse!)

After a detailed briefing and a tour around the extensive office, I was given a voucher for a local hotel where I would spend the night. The following morning, I was to meet with another member of staff who would be travelling with me to Sudan.

After checking in, I went to the hotel bar, ordered some food then retired to my room. I sat for a few hours researching the complex situation in Darfur; I searched the different rebel groups, their leaders, their aims and aspirations and the possibility of opening a line, or lines, of communication to seek some reassurance that the teams could operate with some sense of relative safety. It was a very interesting session of research, which left me wondering who exactly the 'baddies' were in this complex arrangement; it wasn't instantly apparent.

I arrived back at the office at 9am. I signed in at the main desk and waited to be greeted by Simon, the emergencies deputy director, and then taken to the emergency section, were I would be given my travel documents, my new ID card and a final briefing before departure.

I met with Anna, an American lady, who was a nutritionist going to Darfur to join the team delivering a therapeutic nutrition programme for the many thousands of displaced children in the IDP camps and local villages. It formed an addition to the primary healthcare programme that the organisation was delivering.

Anna had worked for this organisation before, as well as a few others. She was an experienced aid worker and was brought in to add her expertise to the growing emergency in Darfur. She had travelled widely and was, by her admission, more comfortable outside of the USA than she was being 'home'. She also had a good sense of humour; that alone meant we would get along just fine.

We flew into Khartoum and were met by a driver with two large brown envelopes, each containing a local map and a welcome note with some simple instructions. We were taken to a house somewhere close to the airport and told to settle in and we would be collected in two hours for our briefing at the Khartoum office.

At the house, and after struggling with the lock to get in, I looked around. The normal routine: entry and exit points, rear of the building for escape, fire extinguishers and fire blankets. I noted that all the windows were secured with fixed metal grills; great to stop people breaking in, but in the event of an emergency, would be a hindrance to get out. In a fire, for instance, the doorway may not be an option to get out, and with the windows barred, you are stuck. "Not the best way to secure a house," I thought.

The kitchen was equipped with the basics: a microwave, a kettle, some tea and coffee, and someone had thoughtfully bought some fresh milk. A cup of tea was the order of the day. Anna frowned and in typical American fashion asked for a strong coffee.

During the trip to Sudan, Anna and I had talked about our jobs, what the expectations were for the Darfur programme and I quizzed her on several humanitarian scenarios, hoping to gain from her experience and maybe get a wider insight to the sector. She had been in several 'unstable and hostile' locations before. She told me about her concerns that if anything would have gone dramatically wrong, she hadn't known of any plans that would have been of help to them, or known quite what to have done other than rely on her own instinct. I was shocked, but it seemed like there was a pattern forming across the sector. Safety and security, while being talked about in the highest regard at a very senior level, was far from effective on the ground. I found this to be true as my second career progressed.

I had also, with my Scouse humour, taken to making fun of Anna and her 'Americanisms', listening to how the Americans had butchered the English language and taken well-established names of items and used them for something else. At breakfast we had toast. Anna took a piece of toast and asked me to pass the 'jelly'… I stared around the table for a moment, then I responded: "Jelly? There is no jelly! Children have jelly at birthday parties. How old are you?" I smiled as I spoke, making it very obvious I was making fun of her.

She pointed to a pot of strawberry jam and repeated her request for me to pass the jelly. I told her it was called jam. She rebuffed that and insisted it was jelly. There was only one definitive argument to throw at this conversation: my trump card. "Tell me," I asked, looking serious but still with a twinkle of mischief, "what is the language called that you speak?" I asked, knowing full well that this question had only one outcome: in my favour, of course.

"Erm…" She stumbled as she realised the point I was about to make. "English?" she said. She was about to follow up with something else when I interrupted deliberately to halt any rebuke she may have.

I dug in. "So," I said with a smile, "It's not the American language. You don't tell people you speak American; you tell them you speak *English*, the language of the English. So the names you incorrectly give to established and well-known items are incorrect: jelly when clearly it's jam, and jello when it's clearly jelly…"

I stopped there because my poker face had given way to a laugh. I continued with just one more jibe, now that I was ahead. "To cap it all, because you Americans can't spell properly, you have altered the spelling of the English language to suit your lazy ways. I mean, spell colour," I said, still trying to supress a giggle.

"C-O-L-O-R," she said as she spelt it out.

"Wrong!" I said laughing. "The correct *English* way is C-O-L-O-U-R," I said, laughing.

Anna responded with a mock-superior look down her nose, and with arms folded, she said, "But we in America are the most powerful nation and we run the world now, so we can spell and talk how we like".

"Touché, my American friend," I conceded, and we both laughed. This became a continuing theme of the time spent in Darfur; humour, as it was that morning at breakfast, was greatly needed in the weeks and months that followed.

At the office, we had to apply for a permit or visa to go to Darfur. It had to be cleared via a government department called the Humanitarian Aid Commission (HAC). This department appeared to be fully integrated into everything connected to anything humanitarian, and in my opinion, too many things not connected!

It took a few days to get the relevant permissions and stamps in our passports. For those few days, we were accommodated in the arrival house and had meetings with all the office-based department heads. I also spent a lot of time with the CD, Katherine, and her deputy, a very nice guy called Mujid.

Katherine talked me through some of the issues that were starting to influence the situation in Darfur. We talked about the different factions: the Justice and Equality Movement (JEM), the Sudan Liberation Army (SLA), which was part of the Sudan Liberation Movement (SLM) who later had a split and became a fragmented 'two group one aim' but achieving that aim under different leaderships and slightly different mandates (if you can call it a mandate; doing things differently because the then leaderships disagreed on a few things, hence the semi-split thing).

Also, coexisting across Darfur was the notorious Janjaweed. As I understood it (and factually and historically I might be wrong, but it is my understanding from the many briefings I received), the Janjaweed were at first a nomadic group (tribe) who roamed the areas of North and South Darfur, West Kordofan and border areas of South Sudan. Their preferred mode of transport was horse or camel, but they had an affinity with 4x4 vehicles which could be transformed into machine-gun platforms (referred to locally as 'technicals'). Often these vehicles were 'acquired' rather than bought; some were, it was suggested, donated by the Sudanese government.

The Janjaweed were (unofficially) courted by the Sudanese government to do the dirty work of what was described as 'ethnic cleansing'. They often attacked the villages and small settlements that the SLA/SLM and JEM emanated from or were supported by. They would kill, rape, loot and pillage, often leaving nothing behind but scorched earth.

There appeared to be a stop-start type of situation going on in Darfur in relation to delivering programmes. The main intervention for this organisation was primary healthcare (PHC), with a nutrition programme delivering therapeutic nutrition as well as feeding and supporting the children who were displaced from their villages; children who, amidst a famine, were in an almost hopeless situation.

My position, as I now discovered, was to take over the safety and security from the logistician, who was 'double hatting' security with logistics. This was a practice that was widespread in the sector; logistic managers were also the safety and security focal point for their organisations. I think the rationale behind it probably emanated from the situation that many of the logisticians were ex-military, and, therefore, were assumed to be knowledgeable about safety and security.

I have two very distinct issues with this situation. The first is that if you are a busy programme (and most are), then your logistics team are always going to be busy. They will constantly be trying to meet the demands of various programme sectors, such as health (trying to source, order and receive medicines and medical equipment for other sectors, such as livelihoods, and food supplements for the nutrition programme). On top of that, you have vehicle and fleet management, keeping all the vehicles serviced and in good order, and the general stocks for the office. The list is endless and with so many people making logistical demands, safety and security becomes (wrongly) a lower priority to dedicate time and energy to.

The second reason is one I have come across many times and have always tried to educate organisations about; it is the misunderstanding about the 'military' assumptions.

Many organisations were making some rather large assumptions about bringing in ex-military to cover the complexities of safety and security, particularly in hostile conflict situations. I met a guy who had been employed by an organisation as a security manager due to his ex-military background. He had been in the army for 12 years and had been to Northern Ireland, Bosnia and Kosovo. While on the face of it, it sounded quite impressive and conjured up visions of great experience, particularly to those who have a limited knowledge of the military, and of a very conflict-wary, experienced soldier, in this case, it was far from the truth. The guy had been an army chef; he was a great cook (apparently) and had a head for food supply, but in the places he mentioned, he wasn't front line. He didn't mix with the local population and he never experienced being under fire directly and having to deal with the immediate actions. Plus, as he was a Lance-Corporal, he was only on the very first rung of the rank structure and had a very limited level of command and leadership responsibilities.

It's just a case of understanding the nature of the role that ex-soldiers have undertaken while serving. This particular guy was, while serving, doing a really important job; an army marches on its stomach and, contrary to popular belief, the food in the military is exceptional in choice and quality. But an experienced soldier with operational front-line experience, he was not. I overheard him in conversation at a security meeting and some of the advice he was giving was, to be honest, dangerous, just because of his lack of operational experience.

Similarly, I have very good friends who have been in the forces for many years and have not left the UK. They have been aircraft technicians and tradesmen of other types who solely operate in UK, and occasionally when they do go overseas or are posted to an operational theatre, they tend to stay far away from the front line, with many staying in hotels in the rear echelons of the logistic supply chain, purely because that is their job. But those trying to indulge themselves in the (false) glamour of working as a safety and security manager or adviser in conflict zones can be dangerous, as the advice, leadership and training that you are expected to deliver is geared to saving people's lives by reducing risk and making all aware of their surroundings while a real threat exists. It gets dangerous if you really don't fully know what you are doing.

Having said that, there are a growing number of correctly experienced ex-military now employed in the sector, and their wide skill base is at last being recognised. It was only a few years ago that the largely stereotyped soldier was, by some, frowned upon. Many saw the harm that some armies had done in the world and painted us all with the same brush.

There are still some ex-military, the disaster junkies, who still give the large majority of the hard-working and professional ex-military a bad name. But by correct selection and with the right background and experience these guys are worth their weight in gold.

While in Khartoum, I was told that a rapid assessment team was being prepared to travel into the far north of Darfur, into a desert region known as Dar Zaghawa (land or place of the Zaghawa). As I recall, it would be one of the first aid agencies to venture that far north. New vehicles had been purchased, all fitted with HF and VHF radios. As the emergency in Darfur escalated, so, too, did the scaling up of the humanitarian response to the crisis; some being quicker than others to take the humanitarian space and to provide the support that the beneficiary groups needed. There was a certain amount of pressure from within organisations, and from donors too, to get the assessment done and to start the process of delivering the multi-sectoral programmes.

Having the knowledge of a trip being undertaken and assessing that it was probably about 300km from the base in El Fashir, I asked several questions about the planning. While the questions were answered in a fashion, there were no details given, leading me to believe that the guys on the ground were doing all the planning and there was not much in the way of communication of details between the field teams and HQ. I got an early impression that the field teams were, within loose boundaries, doing their own thing.

I was reassured that the field manager and his team were very capable and experienced people and would have little problem successfully completing the rapid assessment and opening a new intervention site for those in need in a very remote area. I took this on good faith and face value.

While I was briefed over the following few days, our passports and a copious amount of forms had been submitted to the government department to allow us to travel into Darfur. This, as it emerged, could take a few days or a few weeks, depending who you knew.

Luckily enough, ours (Anna's and mine) came back after only three days. It was a relief to finally get underway, where my work could start properly.

We were booked on an internal flight with Sudan Airways (Sudanair) from Khartoum to the capital, El Fashir (or Al Fashir, depending on who you talk to); 'home' for the next three months. We arrived at the airport, checked in and were quickly on our way to boarding the plane. Our tickets showed seat numbers 13A and 13B but search as we did, there was no row 13. As we quickly found out, we were two of a total passenger list of eight, so we could sit anywhere we liked.

We sat down and strapped in, and soon after, the doors closed and the engines started, or rather they attempted to. Then there was an announcement. We had to get off the plane and wait on the tarmac. We (all eight of us) were herded out to the rear right of the plane and told to wait.

A couple of what I assumed were airport fire crew, turned up with various handheld extinguishers and a larger one on wheels. After some communication with the crew, the engines tried to (I nearly said 'fire-up' and that would have been a bad omen!) start again. They failed. They tried again. There was a bang followed by a puff of black smoke, then the engines burst into life. My next question was would they remain in this state?

The pilot came down the stairs from the plane and inspected the now-running engines. He seemed happy enough, so I approached him as we were ushered back towards the aircraft to board. He was talking to one of the cabin crew when I got close enough to ask what the problem had been and if the aircraft was safe to fly. He smiled and said it was a small problem which had now been fixed and we would be safely underway as soon as everyone had boarded.

I really was on the brink of staying on the ground, but this was the only way, other than a long desert drive which would take days to organise, and I didn't think the organisation would have the manpower or vehicles to undertake the task.

I took encouragement that if the pilot was happy and the cabin crew weren't running away, then it must be deemed to be safe.

Our flight path took us first to Nyala in South Darfur, to take on more passengers and maybe let a few off, then on to El Fashir. I just wanted to get going now.

Soon we were in the air. All appeared to be normal. Anna, who confessed to being a nervous flyer at the best of times, was trying to break the armrest by digging her fingers into it as hard as she could every time there was the slightest bit of turbulence. I smiled and made fun of her to try to take her mind (and mine too) off the flight and the strange events before we were airborne.

After a short time, we descended into Nyala. The sky was heavy with dark rain clouds, and just as we touched down, the rain started, lightly at first but it looked like a full storm was on its way. It didn't take long to board the new passengers and let the three passengers on board disembark. The doors were closed, the engines picked up power and we taxied out onto the deserted runway.

The rain was now coming down heavily. The pilot built up the thrust, released the brakes and we hurtled off down the runway. It seemed as if we were just about to get airborne when I was thrown forward violently in my seat. The brakes were applied and the engines screamed as they went into reverse thrust...

An announcement was made by the pilot, first in Arabic then in English, as we came to a shuddering stop. "Ladies and gentlemen, please do not be alarmed. We aborted take-off, as a herd of goats strayed across the runway. Once they have cleared, we will taxi around and try again. Thank you."

I looked at Anna, who if not for her seatbelt, I am sure would have been clinging to the ceiling. I laughed; it eased the tension a little.

Soon we were back in our position to attempt take-off again. The rain was now really hammering down. With full throttle, brakes off and a bit of wind buffering us, we got airborne, much to the relief of everyone on board.

It was be a relatively short flight to El Fashir, so I just engaged in conversation with Anna, as I could see she was very anxious. I said to her, amidst the bumping and buffeting of turbulence generated by the storm we were flying through, that it would be fine and that we would soon be above the storm and things would be a lot smoother.

Suddenly, there was a very loud bang and a flash of extremely bright light, and it felt like the whole aircraft had been hit by a gigantic baseball bat; the sensation it created was as if the plane had 'leapt' across the sky. My handrest was now getting the same treatment as Anna's had moments before.

I gazed out of the window, half expecting to see the engines on fire or half the wing missing, but nothing; everything looked, from my vantage point over the wings, to be as it should. In the distance, I saw what had probably caused our incident: a large bolt of lightning. I think we had been hit. But there were no alarms, no oxygen masks and no cabin crew running around in panic. We bumped along in the turbulence without any further incident. Not that Anna would notice; for her, every bump was startling and the precursor to a potential crash. It wasn't.

Pretty soon after, we had the announcement that we would be landing shortly and had started our approach.

"Relief," I thought. Wrong!

The rain had stopped, but there was a lot of wind. I felt the pilot battling with it as we got closer to the runway. Suddenly, the plane just dropped (it must have been about 50 feet), regained height then came into land. There were three large bumps, being airborne for a few seconds in between each, then a crunch and a jolt as we made contact with the runway for the final time. As I looked with some relief out of my window, there was a large frame of an aircraft that had crashed at some point and had just been moved to the side of the runway. I remember thinking that could easily have been us!

As we taxied to our disembarkation point, I noticed lots of people, similar to when we took off from Khartoum, waiting for the aircraft to stop; all of them were carrying some form of fire extinguisher. As we disembarked, the fire extinguisher people, the pilot, the co-pilot and all the cabin crew got off the plane and stood around looking at the engine on the right of the aircraft. There were little black puffs of smoke coming out of it; nothing too noticeable and obviously not enough for anyone to tackle with an extinguisher.

While attempting to look calm, I was absolutely glad, happy, chuffed and thankful that I had arrived in one piece. I had three months ahead of me to get ready for my flight out; I just might need that.

We were met at the airport by a driver with a sign showing the organisation's logo, and it had both our names handwritten on it too.

We gathered our belongings and set off to find the vehicle, then we headed off to the office. It was now about 4pm. It was still hot, but a lot cooler than I'd expected. The rainfall had helped.

We arrived at the office. Only a few people were still there. Most of the national staff had gone home and the office was winding down to close for the night.

I was greeted by a friendly Australian guy. He was the logistics manager and safety and security focal point. He greeted us both and told me to take a seat in the logistics office while he took Anna to meet the nutrition team leader.

As he returned, he popped his head around the door and beckoned me to follow him. We went to a shack within the office compound which he called the radio room. Here was the base station for the Codan HF radio set and the Motorola VHF set.

He told me to take a seat and he would get me a drink and quickly talk through some of the pressing issues and the overall situation, telling me between breaths that there were no major issues on the security side to be worried about and much of that he would cover tomorrow.

When we had a cup of tea in our hands, he began his briefing. It was a little scattered in its delivery, jumping from one subject to another then back to the original subject. I stopped him and asked if he had been busy. He paused and confided that it had been non-stop since the rapid assessment had been announced in Dar

Zaghawa: the equipping of the brand-new vehicles, the radio instalments and trying to source things that they needed quickly. He did let it slip that they could and should have waited for at least another week before setting off but deadlines had been given and it was all a rush to get out.

I sensed that this guy was exhausted. That was why I stopped the briefing, as it was not making too much sense. It seemed that his mind was all over the place. I felt sorry for him. This just typified and confirmed my thoughts about 'double hatting' two very demanding roles.

I asked him what time he usually left the office. He replied by telling me that as soon as the radio check with the team on the ground had been completed, he would lock up, brief the night guard and head off to the accommodation.

The radio check was done once a day at 6pm. I was shocked at that; I had expected it to be more frequent. He told me that was what the team leader had set. It was now getting on for 6pm, so he began the radio check.

"Sierra Charlie One, this is Sierra Charlie Base. Radio check. Over."

He paused and waited for a response. Nothing.

He tried again. "Sierra Charlie One, this is Sierra Charlie Base. Radio check, radio check. Over."

Again nothing.

We tried a direct radio phone call to the field manager's radio rather than broadcasting on the open frequency. The radio chirruped, but no answer.

I asked if they had taken satellite phones with them. He said they had but they were only back-up communications as they were very expensive to operate. They would only turn them on if the radios went down.

I looked him in the eye and said, "Like now?"

He picked up his satellite phone, a Thuraya, and switched it on. He dialled in the long number and waited. Nothing. He tried again with a second number. We waited. Nothing.

We were over 300km away from them, meaning that they were 300km away from their nearest help. It was now dark.[10]

We tried and tried on the satellite phone but there was no answer. Suddenly, there was a call on the radio phone. He answered it. It was one of the doctors who was in one of the other vehicles.

I sat listening as the conversation unfolded. They had stopped at a small village for the night and would make camp until first light.

I quickly scribbled a few notes and questions on a piece of paper that was on the desk. I wrote:

How are your food and water supplies? Do you have any medical issues with sickness or heat? What is your progress with the assessments? What is your ETD (estimated time of departure) from your current location tomorrow and your ETA (estimated time of arrival) at your next rest stop? Send coordinates. Are all vehicles in good condition and are you all together for the night?

From the earlier briefing, it appeared that the logistics guy wasn't happy that enough food and water had been taken for the trip so I needed to find out the levels of water and food consumption in

---

[10] In Darfur, being closer to the equator (roughly about 400–500km) night-time and darkness fell quickly; dusk was very short. I likened it to someone flicking a light switch off.

order to estimate how long it would be before they ran out; there were no shops in the desert!

It was always prudent to check on the general health of a travelling team, as what might appear to be a minor health issue could develop into something much more serious; even when travelling with a doctor there is no other support, so early warning and continuous monitoring is vital.

Understanding that the assessment was the main priority not only for the team, but for the organisation and donors as well, it was going to be the one thing that would possibly push the team, if they were falling behind, to make decisions that could be deemed questionable or to take short cuts to ensure the task was complete.

When under pressure, this is always a consideration, and such a situation needs strong leadership and discipline. Keeping informed of progress is a critical management tool for situations like this; it meant that the senior management teams back in El Fashir or Khartoum could override any decisions that were made for the wrong reasons or that might border on reckless or dangerous.[11]

Having a grasp on how long they were likely to be in one place gives an indication of how much rest they as a team are getting and also, for that time, you know or have a good idea that they are in one place, so coordinates can be mapped, giving a good start for location-finding if anything were to go wrong ; you would also

---

[11] I had come across several 'leaders and managers' in this sector who refused to accept the dangers while pursuing the aims of their programme, thinking they could not let down the beneficiary groups who they were hoping to support with the aid they were bringing. My argument was always in favour of the teams; if they got sick, had accidents, became incapacitated, or at worse were kidnapped or killed due to not taking the relevant advice or making bad decisions, the programme would fail anyway and would have more and wider-reaching consequences.

know from their ETA at the next stop, where they should be and when.

As the vehicles were brand new, it was always wise to see how they are performing: fuel levels, oil, engines running okay and coping with the sand and the heat, etc. Again, there are no garages out in the desert. While the drivers had some knowledge, a major mechanical failure could be a disaster.

Knowing that all the vehicles and all the team are together, as they should be each night, is also an indicator that things are going well; no one has been left behind, so all is good.

But as the answers came back, all seemed positive until the very last response.

They were not all together. One vehicle hadn't joined them at their village camp. It appeared that the plan was to hop from remote village to village or settlement; the teams would conduct the multi-sectoral assessments then move off and set up a camp for the evening. The locations were pre-planned but as many of the groups to be assessed were nomadic the locations were flexible within a few mile radius. Once found, the coordinates, via satellite phone, would be recorded.

It appeared that the individual assessments were taking more time than they had originally thought, and as darkness was about to fall, they still had one village to assess before setting up camp for the night. The team leader made the decision to send the remainder of the convoy to the pre-arranged campsite while he, with his driver and a water engineer (who by chance was very familiar with the Dar Zaghawa region, as he had grown up there) would go to the last settlement and conduct the assessment before joining them at the pre-arranged campsite. The single vehicle left the convoy and set off to find the last settlement of the day.

I now put my pen and paper away and gestured that I wanted to speak directly to the doctor. I took a second or two to decide on what information I now needed.

"Can you confirm you have one vehicle missing? Over."

"That's correct but we are expecting it to rejoin us within the hour. Over," was the reply.

I needed some details now. "Can you confirm what time the vehicle left the convoy? Over."

After a moment of hesitation, as I guessed he was confirming with others, his response came back. "At about 3pm, but not sure of the exact time. Over."

I quickly responded. "Was an ETA back to your campsite given? If so, when are you expecting the vehicle to return? Over."

"Yes, an ETA was given and it expires in 30 minutes. Over," was the response.

I instructed the doctor and the remaining members of the team to stay in place and get some sleep but to ensure that the radio was manned throughout the night and that they should try to call the team leader on the radio and satellite phone every five minutes until we next communicated. I told him to report back the moment the missing vehicle joined them or they established communications. I finished by telling him that I would call him in 30 minutes, the ETA expiry time.

The radio call was finished for the moment. I asked the logistics manager for an emergency contact sheet, a list of in-country numbers of those who may be in a position to help or should be informed in the case of an emergency. I was handed a sheet of A4 paper with what appeared to be every phone number of every organisation in Darfur, and lots of Khartoum numbers too.

I thought again, "This isn't good enough." There should be a list of critical numbers, no more than six or seven, of who to call in case of emergencies. I spent the next 15 minutes going through each number, crossing off the contacts which were of no use, and came up with a list of, hopefully, some numbers of people or organisations who could help.

From the sifted numbers, two possibly had assets that could help: the UN and a number for the African Union Military headquarters[12] here in El Fashir. I had noticed on arrival that there were a number of white UN helicopters at the airport, so there were air assets to be utilised, I hoped.

We waited, with another cup of tea, for the time to slip by, half expecting to hear from the team that the vehicle had rejoined them before we had to call.

No call came. The ETA arrived, and I called the team. They answered immediately, and I asked for a sit-rep.

The vehicle had not arrived back. It was now very dark. Time was ticking on. I had a decision to make. I told the doctor to stay at their campsite until he received further instruction from me. I told him again to maintain a radio watch but to try to contact the missing vehicle every 15 minutes until midnight and then every 30 minutes until I communicated with him again. I stressed the point that they were not to move until they received instruction from

---

[12] The African Union Military sourced from the militaries of African countries. At this time they were Nigerian forces, who had a joint commander/adviser who was a senior french officer with an American officer as his deputy as part of the AU command structure that had been sent to Darfur to act as peacekeepers. The then Sudanese government refused to have Western UN military forces; indeed they expelled a senior officer from the British Army due to some spurious reason linked to past colonial bias and the unconfirmed rumour of spying (although I never saw any reports). It was a growing rumour and had been exaggerated over a period of time.

myself or from the programme management in Khartoum. I finished by wishing him a safe night.

I then started to make phone calls. The first was to the UN. There was a number listed for the UNOCHA party leader. I called it. It rang about four times before it was answered.

I established who it was I was talking to and explained who I was and who I was working for. I got to the point straight away, informing them that we had a vehicle unaccounted for in the Dar Zaghawa region that was not responding to radio or satellite telephone and was now past its ETA at the main convoy.

The last confirmed sighting was at 3pm or there-about, when the vehicle left the convoy en-route to a nomadic settlement to the west of the team's eventual camp location.

There was a silence, as though this was the last thing this guy expected to hear, so I continued with some suggestions-cum-demands.

"I would like an immediate heli-borne search of the area, if not by the UN then can a formal UN request be put to the AU for help from their air assets?"

He began to speak, and what he said wasn't good news.

"Unfortunately neither the UN nor the AU helicopters have night-flying capacity. They can't fly at night."

"Shit!" I thought.

The UN heli-fleet that I had seen consisted of a few Russian Mi-8 helicopters: a workhorse helicopter, mass produced, used globally, unsophisticated and pretty industrial, but if maintained well was reliable, in daylight. There was also a huge Mi-26 helicopter, the largest helicopter in the world (at that time), but again, it was stripped of any sophisticated night-flying technology, so again was useless.

I pressed the guy for options.

Unfortunately, he replied by telling me clearly that there was nothing that could be done until first light. He told me to be ready to receive a call from him very early in the morning and to be ready to travel to the helipad at El Fashir Airport. At least he was thinking the same way I was and was gearing up to make things happen. I thanked him and awaited his call.

I then immediately called Khartoum. I spoke to the country director and told her of the situation and of the plan in place for the morning. She was very obviously shaken, but she told me to keep in touch as things developed.

I also called the organisational HQ in London. I had the personal number of the director of emergencies. His phone rang and was immediately answered. I went through the entire scenario and plan with him. He had nothing to add other than the fact that he and his deputy would fly into Khartoum on the first available flight. We swapped information and details about what I knew so far, and he wished me good luck for the morning, whatever it had in store. I thanked him and hung up.

I had been in El Fashir for less than 24 hours and was already in the driving seat of a potentially major incident. Part of me was still thinking or hoping that this was just a very bad case of procedural ignorance, failing to abide by procedure, and everything would be okay come daylight.

I split the night on radio watch with the logistics manager. I took the first five hours and woke him at 2am. I told him that I would need the duty driver to take me to the airport at 5am and he would need to set up a roster for the radio throughout the day while I was away, ensuring it was always manned. He agreed, but from the look on his face, I thought it may cause an issue in doing so; but he had to make it happen until we got some type of result from this growing crisis.

I didn't really sleep, as I was in someone's office on the floor. I was awake before the driver arrived, and the logistics manager made me a nice cup of tea. There had been no news. I took the radio and spoke to the team, taking their precise coordinates. I briefed them on the plan to get a heli-search, telling them that I hoped to be with them at some point during the day.

Throughout the north of Darfur, the Janjaweed, the JEM and the SLA/SLM patrolled. The Janjaweed were looting and killing and the SLA/SLM were fighting them and attacking the Sudanese army who had remote outposts in the area. It was a very unstable and hostile place to be, especially in a vehicle on your own.

I arrived at the helipad at about 5.15am. I was soon met by a tall guy who introduced himself as the head of party for the El Fashir office of UNOCHA. He told me that he had been contacted by the commanding officer of the Sudanese military base in El Fashir, telling him that a man had staggered into one of their remote outpost garrisons in Um Baru. He was badly injured, mainly burns, and had collapsed. The soldiers there were giving him immediate first aid.

We stood on the helipad while the pilots ran their checks. We had three helicopters: one was manned by a South African medical team (their helicopter was almost a mobile hospital), one was just a transport helicopter, which I would travel in, and the third was on standby should it be needed.

I spent some time with all the pilots. I gave them the coordinates I had, the last known position before the team split and the coordinates of the guys still at their overnight camp location. I suggested that both helicopters fly and land at the Um Baru military outpost to see who it was that had wandered in. Was it just a local who may have escaped a Janjaweed attack or something similar, or, worst case scenario, was it one of the team? We had to land and find out.

After the pre-flight checks and the quick map check, we all agreed the plan and loaded up. Very soon we were in the air.

After a short while, we were circling above the military outpost in Um Baru. The pilot selected a landing site, and we set down. As we landed and were getting out of the helicopter, a Sudanese army officer came over and in very good English explained that the man, who was now being wheeled out of a tent on what can only be described as a wooden cart (the type with two large wooden wheels that a horse might pull, but in place of a horse were four soldiers) had wondered into the camp saying that he had been in an explosion with others who were dead. He had walked most of the night until he reached the military outpost, then collapsed as the soldiers challenged him.

His body was covered with rags, which had been improvised makeshift bandages doused in water and applied to the burns which covered the majority of his body. As the cart got close, the medical team took control; they loaded him onto their helicopter and quickly set about trying to stabilise his obvious injuries. A saline drip was put in and his ragged bandages were removed. He was examined, then new, clean, sterile dressings were applied. He was lucky to be alive.

After a few minutes of talking to the Sudanese officer, who could give no other useful information, I boarded the medical helicopter. I spoke to the medics who told me that over 80 per cent of the casualty's body was burnt (but luckily it wasn't too bad in terms of the depth of the burns), his fluid levels were down and he needed emergency hydration, which the drip was applying. He was sitting up now, taking very small sips of water.

It was made clear that he was the driver of the missing vehicle. He managed to tell us that the vehicle blew up. The other two had died in the large explosion and fire. He pointed roughly in the direction from where he had walked, telling us the approximate location he had walked from. Looking at his condition, I guessed that the site of the incident was only a short distance away; he couldn't have walked very far in his injured state.

I asked one of the medics if the casualty was fit enough to sit in the crew seat between the pilot and co-pilot and try to direct us to the incident site. My concern was that if there was a remote chance that either of the other two were still alive, we would need to get to them ASAP. The medic nodded his reluctant agreement. He hung a drip against the bulkhead of the helicopter, and once we moved the casualty into position and propped him up comfortably, we set off.

The details were still vague. I still had no idea what had happened to cause the explosion. Was it a critical fault on the new vehicles? Was it an attack by some group or other? Could it have been an air attack by the Sudanese government, mistaking the lone vehicle for a rebel vehicle? I just had no answers... yet.

As soon as we were airborne, the driver started to point in a general direction. He was having trouble speaking due to the burns he'd suffered in his mouth and throat but he made himself understood with simple gestures. We were now, according to his gesticulations, in the rough area. Looking out of the window, I shouted to the pilot to circle the area in a rough three-mile radius. He gave thumbs-up, and I strained my eyes looking for anything that may give away the vehicle's location or anything that looked out of place or unusual.

We were now flying over a wadi bed (a dried-out riverbed) which had trees growing along each bank, giving an obstructed view, as the branches and the little foliage obscured the sandy riverbed and some of the bank from clear view. As we started to circle away, something caught my eye. There was a colour change in the trees on the bank, and the ground that was visible was also in contrast to the sand-coloured surroundings.

I shouted to the pilot as I pointed out of the open helicopter door.

"Look low. Nine o'clock. Dark patch in the riverbed."

We were just starting our circling bank over to the right, when the pilot heard my shout and corrected to bank left. Looking down, I could now see from a slightly different angle that the ground, the trees and some foliage was charred: burnt from what must have been a substantial fire.

The pilot got as close as he dared at a hover. I sensed he was about to land but I shouted for him to stay off the ground. I was now thinking mines.

The carcass of the vehicle was totally destroyed. It was on its roof, although the roof had little structure to it, as the intensity of the fire had melted much of the structure. Here and there were pools of what looked like liquid mercury but was in fact solidified pools of molten aluminium from parts of the vehicle and its engine.

I asked the pilot to set down next to a small settlement, where people and animals were moving about; at least we had a good feeling that it was safe there and nothing was going to go bang.

As we landed, roughly about 400 metres from the blast site, some of the villagers came over to the helicopter. Two of the guys from UNOCHA were Sudanese and held a conversation with the locals. As it transpired, both the Sudanese army and the SLA had visited their location at different times on patrols. They also said that there was a rumour that bombs had been planted in the ground (mines) but they didn't, or wouldn't, say who had planted them. They stayed away from that area.

It was ascertained that the blast had happened roughly between 4 and 5pm. The locals thought an animal may have set off a mine, so apart from staying well away, they did nothing.

It was obvious that no one else had survived. But now I had a new problem. If mines had been laid in this region (which was against the signed treaty that all sides had agreed to), did I want the remainder of the convoy to drive back across wide expanses of desert that may have had mines placed at obvious choke points?

My other problem would be the recovery of the bodies.

I called HQ in Khartoum on the satellite phone. I spoke with the country director and relayed the bad news. Two dead: one being the team leader and the other being the water engineer. The driver who survived was badly burnt and would need much in the way of hospital treatment.

We discussed the problem of the remaining team and their convoy. Over the following 20 minutes, we communicated with Khartoum and the team on the ground, told them of the situation and the findings and asked if the vehicles could be secured anywhere very local while the team was heli-lifted back to El Fashir. We would do a vehicle recovery later. It was agreed and a safe location was found. The vehicles were locked up and the third reserve helicopter flew out to pick up the remaining team members.

Now, how to recover the bodies?

The medics took the badly burnt driver onto their helicopter, made him as comfortable as they could and returned to El Fashir. I, together with my new friend from UNOCHA and his two colleagues, stayed with the final helicopter to brainstorm the recovery of the team leader and the water engineer.

After some deliberation, I suggested we return to the Um Baru outpost and see if the army had a de-mining team. It was a long shot but it was the only option available at the time.

On landing, we were taken to meet with the outpost commander. He described himself as a brigadier. In reality, he had a comparable command of a British major: a company commander possibly.

He said he had a de-mining team and dispatched a soldier to go and get them ready. I knew the Sudanese army was not as highly trained as the British army but detecting mines is detecting mines; get it wrong and you go home in a bucket, well the bits they find do!

Four what looked like hastily dressed soldiers appeared, all carrying long, thin metal rods, about a metre in length. These, I assumed, were their prodders. Apart from their rifles, they had nothing else.

I decided, with the help of the English-speaking captain we'd met earlier and one of the UN guys, to conduct a quick bit of individual mine-detecting training before we boarded the helicopter; the last thing I needed was more casualties, least of all to become one myself.

I went through the motions of the slow and careful methods of locating or 'prodding' for mines, the marking of cleared space and how to mark identified mines; identify, mark, prod around it and move on, then repeat until you have a completely cleared path.

There was lots of nodding and smiling, as well as, I noticed, a bit of piss-taking at the white man on the floor: me.

I asked if everyone understood. They nodded, and I told them we would land a safe distance from the blast, then they would clear a path up to the incident site and clear around the carcass of the vehicle so the casualties could be recovered. I wanted that final bit done with as much dignity and respect as was possible. All agreed. I loaded everyone onto the helicopter. They would be first off to start the slow clearance, then we would follow.

We took off and were quickly over the blast site. We set down, and after the rotors stopped turning, I gave the thumbs-up to the leader of the de-mining team.

To my shock, horror and total amazement all four soldiers leapt out of the helicopter and ran at a sprint to the blast site. I carefully stepped out of the helicopter and watched them 'de-mine' the area around the upturned and burnt-out Land Rover Defender. With their metre-long prods, they stabbed, beat and whipped the ground around them; no careful prodding and no thought of the fact that if they hit a mine they would kill themselves and a few others. It was mayhem, catastrophic mayhem.

I had watched for about 10 minutes when the leader eventually waved for me and the others to come down. I had to think carefully about this.

I looked down at the multiple footprints left in the sand by the sprinting de-mining team and thought the safest way was to stick to stepping in the footprints of those who'd gone before. I gave the same advice to my UN friend who had agreed to help me recover the casualties and place them carefully into body bags. This was not going to be easy or particularly nice.

We managed to get to the vehicle without being blown up, so that was good. I now had my first close-up look at the incident site; I could still see the tyre tracks in the sand leading to the point of the explosion. I took some photographs of the scene. I also took a couple of photographs of the remains inside the upturned vehicle. This would help identify who was who by where they were sitting.

It looked like they were searching for a crossing point to get across the wadi. The banks were fairly steep on either side except for a slight depression which I guessed the animals had been using, along with the villagers who probably herded animals to drink and cross from one side to the other. It was the only point a vehicle could have crossed. The blast was in the centre of the dried-out riverbed. The explosion had lifted their vehicle up and thrown it about 15 feet, flipping it on its roof next to a tree. The vehicle had also been carrying reserves of fuel for their prolonged trip, and that had ignited as well. How the driver escaped is a miracle. It would be some time before we got his full account of what had happened.

The team leader would have been sitting in the front passenger seat. The remains in the rear seat could only be that of the water engineer. The remains were charred beyond physical recognition. Some parts had been dismembered in the initial blast. It was horrendous picking out charred skin and bone which had once been a fully functioning, caring, responsible human being; both were sons to fathers and mothers and had families, brothers and sisters. I tried hard to supress these thoughts, as we had to get as much of what was identifiable into the body bags, while remaining as respectful and meticulous as possible, before we ran out of time and out of light.

The soldiers were getting a bit twitchy too. They said that the rebels would be in the hills and mountains watching and planning to attack them once it got dark. They were now making me nervous, not because of the rebel issue but because of their insistence on not standing still and constantly changing positions; a foot in the wrong place could still be fatal.

Soon we were done. I marked the coordinates on my satellite phone and between the soldiers, the UN guys and myself we carried the remains back to the helicopter.

The rear dome-shaped cargo doors on the helicopter had been opened. We carefully placed the remains inside, secured them and closed the doors.

I made a call to Khartoum and told them our passengers had been collected. It had been arranged that we would drop off the soldiers at their outpost, go to El Fashir, drop off the UN guys then I, along with the two 'passengers', would fly on to Khartoum where the bodies would be received by the organisation, which would be waiting with the appropriate authorities to deal with the ongoing formalities that would be required. We would land in Khartoum, hopefully just before nightfall.

We finally landed in Khartoum, and on the landing pad stood the country director and the emergencies director and deputy who had only moments before our arrival landed direct from London.

I disembarked, still focused on the task at hand, and went around to the cargo doors which were now being opened.

As the officials with the ambulance arrived, I had to show them the temporary labels I had tied onto the black body bags stating who was who.

I helped with the transfer from the aircraft to the ambulance and then watched them leave. I really hadn't registered the other guys who had stood back until the ambulance left. I remember watching it drive away and thinking, "How do I get back from here? Too late for the helicopter to fly, and I ain't walking." The Scouse humour kicked in like a safety measure.

Only then did I turn around and almost bump into the country director, who on taking the cigarette out of her mouth gave me a massive hug and thanked me, saying she hadn't known what to do and wouldn't have coped if I hadn't been there.

She had the unenvious task of informing the next of kin and with the help of the London office would be the one to talk with the family of the international staff member. I guessed there would still be a decision to be made about who would be best placed to break the sad news to the national member of staff's family; someone who knew him best, I hoped.

After prising myself from the embrace, I fully recognised both the director and deputy director of the London HQ-based emergencies section. Both of these guys were seasoned humanitarian workers who had many years' experience under their belts. The deputy director came over, slapped me on the back and just said, "Well done." I appreciated that.

The director of emergencies was a little more emotional in his appreciation, asking not only if I was okay, but if I needed to see 'anyone', as it must have been awful for me. By 'anyone', I am sure he meant some sort of counselling. I smiled at him and said, "Thanks but no." I was fine.

I still had to ask the question: "How do I get back to El Fashir now?"

I was told that after a good meal, a few beers and a night's sleep, a UN flight would take me.

"Thank fuck for the UN," I said. "No more Sudan Airways flights."

The next morning, after possibly the worst cup of tea in history, I was driven off to the airport, loaded onto a small aircraft and with a bunch of other UN and aid workers set off for El Fashir via Nyala.

The flight this time was without incident, and on arrival I was met by the logistics manager and his driver. It was a very short drive back to the office, whereupon I collected my luggage from where it had been left two days before and was taken to my new 'home' for the next three months. My 'home' was a compound in a residential area close to the edge of El Fashir. The compound had a high wall surrounding two main buildings and a small outbuilding housing a toilet and small shower. The open space between the two facing buildings was large enough to take two vehicles. A set of large creaky metal gates covered the only entry point into the compound.

I was eventually shown to my sparsely equipped room in the house. I put my bags down on the tired linoleum floor and sat on the thin sponge mattress on the metal-framed bed which was covered by a white sheet and a thin blanket.

It was hot. I felt drained just thinking about everything that had happened in the two days since I had arrived. It was a severe introduction to the hardship, risk and violence that existed, never too far from the surface of what looked like normality. I wondered if I would be dealing with any more similar incidents during my stay. As the adrenalin subsided, the emotion and horror of what I had witnessed hit me.

After sorting myself out, I decided clear my mind and acquaint myself with my new surroundings, so I went to explore my new compound.

Stepping out into the open courtyard, I noticed that close to the front gate was a generator, used when the mains electricity went down: which was often. The generator was older than God, or even his dad. It was cast iron and heavier than Everest. It was started up by hand cranking a large flywheel, and took several attempts to get it started before it noisily cranked into life.

It was the night guard's responsibility to start the generator. One of the night guards was an elderly man, tall and very thin with no teeth but always a smile on his face. He looked very frail. I feared that when cranking the generator, he would forget to let go of the cranking handle[13] and would get spun around with the flywheel like a cartoon character. Several times, I told him that I would start it up, but he insisted it was his job. He was more robust than he first appeared

My normal day-to-day routine consisted of meetings within the organisation in North Darfur, getting to know the programme and the people making it all work. Assessing the threat and risks was a constant, and identifying the organisation's vulnerability to it was the underlying theme to all training I had to give.

Travelling to the programme sites was my favourite activity. There, I got to meet with the field teams, observe their work and see first-hand the problems and difficulties they faced, but even more importantly, I met with the village leaders, those who had influence in their communities. I also made friends with the local ancillary workers: the guards, the cooks, the cleaners and the drivers. These are the people who know what is really going on in their communities. Would they confide in me? Only time would tell, but I hoped so.

In every field location I visited, I always took a small football. Football, even in the remotest of places, is played; some kids in very remote outreach locations would often appear out their homes, mud huts or tented shelters of nomad or IDP camps, wearing a football shirts, largely from the Premier League. They may have been old and ragged, but they were always worn with pride.

I used to gather the kids to have a 'kick-around'. I would try hard to impress them with my 'keepie-uppies' but would often fail, much

---

[13] The cranking handle of generator could easily break your wrist if you failed to let go in time as the generator started up. Failed cranks had a habit of spinning in the opposite direction giving a whiplash effect to your wrist and arm. It was all about timing and became a bit of a spectator sport at times.

to the amusement of the kids. It was a great way to gain acceptance; trust would come later.

While with the field teams, I explored emergency escape routes, looking at where to go should the village be attacked while we were delivering the much-needed aid, thinking about how to gather all the field team together to get in the vehicles and flee and predicting from which direction the threat was likely to come from while planning a compass-wide plan if an attack came from any direction.

One of my earliest identified training objectives would be how to safely negotiate road checkpoints in convoy, by day and by night. This could be a fraught experience, with those manning the checkpoints varying from the Sudanese military on the entry and exit routs to El Fashir and at the airport approach roads, to those set up by the rebel groups, ensuring that no uninvited guests get access to their villages, at least without warning.

All checkpoints, regardless of who manned them, were subject to attack. This was a frequent activity, and ranged from long-distance sniping to drive-by shooting and grenade attacks to a more substantial full-on attack.

I remember leading a convoy from El Fashir to a village a few miles away called Tawilah. Tawilah is a strategically placed village on the main route to Chad. The road, which then consisted of a sandy track, gave way in places to a rocky and uneven surface which shook you to the bone for a few miles. The route was one of the only roads for the Sudanese military to supply their troops in the outposts and the military border posts. Tawilah also had a police station which on occasion housed small military patrols, again inviting trouble. The road was often the location, along its length, for ambush attacks.

At the final road checkpoint on the El Fashir town limit, every vehicle had to stop and present documents and ID. The vehicles were then checked (for INGO vehicles, it was usually just an external, visual check) then vehicle by vehicle you were allowed to continue. As these checkpoints were regularly attacked, the soldiers were often nervous. The Sudanese military in El Fashir were also largely ill-disciplined and were prone to getting drunk or high, or sometimes both, while manning the checkpoints, to kill the boredom in-between activity or attacks.

I was once confronted, while waiting for the road barrier to be lifted, by two very drunk or very high soldiers. One carried an RPG rocket launcher and stood immediately in front of the vehicle at a distance of about five metres. He aimed the RPG right at me. If he'd fired, it would have come straight through the windscreen and right through my head, exploding inside the vehicle, killing me and the three passengers I'd had. The second soldier, who struggled to walk in a straight line, came over to my door, instructed me to wind down the window and then put the business end of his AK47 in my face. He was spoke in a drunken calmness, his eyes were bloodshot and the stench of alcohol was almost overpowering. He asked who I was and where I was from. He asked if I could give him money or a computer or my watch. With each sentence, he used his rifle to prod me as he spoke, as if for added emphasis; as if he needed it!

I tried to remain calm and looked him in the eyes and smiled. I told him I had no money, explaining that we were not allowed to carry money while we were working. I told him that the laptop computer, which he had seen on one of my passengers' laps, who was foolishly and against my advice using it at the checkpoint, was the only one we had and it was used to ensure we could help all the people we were giving aid and support to. My watch, I told him, was a present from my father; he had given it to me on his deathbed, telling me never to be late, as being on time was a sign of a good man. All of the above were, of course, totally fabricated lies, but my calm, slow and deliberately monotonal speech was designed to bore the living crap out of him without being aggressive or inviting any confrontation.

With the RPG pointing at me, a rifle to my head and both soldiers totally intoxicated, it would take only a minor spark, a sudden movement or the perception of aggression, for one of these two guys to get twitchy and pull the trigger. Luckily we were allowed to progress, with both soldiers laughing loudly as we departed.

It became a bit of a lottery at the military checkpoints as to what frame of mind the troops were in. It appeared to me that there was a rotation of troops, with some being more disciplined than others. Some commanders were more professional than others. Once or twice, I had a decent chat with the soldiers and the situation was very friendly. As I said, it can be a bit of a lottery.

During my early days, I was very active in the joint meetings held by UNOCHA and UNDSS. These meetings were for all INGOs to attend and gave a situation report on the whole of North Darfur. They gave the UN-agreed no-go areas, due to reports of possible or actual attacks. The UN would sometimes put whole areas or roads out of bounds, not always giving an explanation as to why.

As time went by, I found that the UN information got less and less informative and also became even more UN-centric. I decided on several occasions, as I had done in Iraq, to challenge the information and to ask for more detail. When it was denied, I threw the argument that we were all in this together... weren't we? This was usually followed by a statement explaining that it was information they had, but had not yet confirmed, and once it was confirmed, they would brief the details; they never did.

Following the model of the INGO security forum I had established in Iraq, I decided to do the same here. Many INGOs with people who had been in El Fashir much longer than I, all had, from what I gathered, good information sources. I put it to the group. It was agreed. Immediately following the weekly UN briefing, we would hold an INGO security meeting to swap notes and get a much better understanding of the situation on the ground.

The INGO security forum proved to be an important and effective tool for all INGOs in El Fashir, so much so that some of the UN staff asked if they could attend. One UN group confided that our information was of more benefit to them, as there was more detail and it gave a region-wide picture, not just were the UN worked. Every INGO representative had an equal platform and we challenged each other's information and cross referenced it to try to ensure that we had the best possible picture of events and that any patterns of activity became clear.

The UNDSS guy who was in charge of the UN safety and security briefings didn't agree that we, the INGOs, used what he deemed as his conference room for our meetings and set about kicking us out. I tried to reason with him, and my friend from UNOCHA chipped in on our behalf too, but to no avail. I think there was a bit of jealousy, as his audience was dwindling and ours was growing. We even invited him to attend but he said there would be no benefit for him. So the INGO forum just moved to a different INGO office each week. We still invited any UN staff who wanted to attend. Considering we should all be helping each other, I thought there would be no room for individual empire building, that would be detrimental to us all, but obviously some just didn't want to play.

I had been introduced, via a colleague who worked with our logistics manager, to a very influential member of the SLA/SLM (who later moved over to JEM): Suleiman Jamous.

Suleiman Jamous was, by his own creation, the humanitarian coordinator, liaison or spokesperson for the SLA/SLM. (Later, when the SLA/SLM divided and there were in effect two SLA factions under different leaderships, he changed his allegiance to JEM.) To me this was a very new ideology; never before had I come across a rebel group with its own appointed humanitarian representative. Strange... but true!

This strange appointment indicated to me that the group(s) he represented had a responsibility to the people they were fighting for, which was a tad more complex than I'd first thought. The people of Darfur were being brutally oppressed by the Sudanese government and were, according to reports, being, or attempted at being, wiped out. In effect, it was being reported on the world stage as genocide of the non-Arab black Africans of Darfur, as opposed to the Arab-African Sudanese which formed the basis of the government.

The fighting and the rebel uprising was not, as many thought, based on religious grounds. Muslims counted for over 95 per cent of the Sudanese population. In Darfur, Islam is followed as the majority but so, too, are the traditional religious beliefs, in contrast to South Sudan which is predominately Christian. A conservative approximation for the south is Christianity (60.5 per cent), traditional African religion (32.9 per cent), Islam (6.2 per cent) and others (0.4 per cent). In my opinion, and from conversations I'd had in Darfur, the issues were based more along the ethic and tribal lines of non-Arab black Africans versus the Arab militias and the black Arab Africans in power in Khartoum; I think?

The Darfur situation was complex; with the rebel groups, the factions formed from or by different leaders and those who were (unofficially) government sponsored, supplied and directed. Not forgetting the North/South Sudan war which was largely religiously divided but also driven by the oil wealth that emanated across a disputed border.

Yep! If you were not careful you could easily become confused as to who was who, and who was fighting for what. I tend to simplify it as those who want to do me and my teams harm and those who don't. You can keep your politics and religious beliefs.

I had a hard time convincing the logistics manager to agree to my meeting with his colleague to give me the contact details for Suleiman. It all appeared a bit 'cloak and dagger'. I did eventually get a satellite phone number but was told that it was for emergencies only.

I fully understood that Suleiman and those close to him had to be very security conscious. Being connected to any of the rebel groups was seen as a huge crime, and someone of Suleiman's importance, if captured[14], would be a major propaganda coup.

Now in possession of the contact details, I wasn't any better off, as I had been warned not to use them other than in an emergency. According to my reasoning, if it was an emergency, then in some cases, it would already be too late. This defeated the reasoning of wanting to have a contact in the first place.

I spent the next 24 hours mulling this over. Then I made a key decision. Would it be the right one? Who knew? Only time would tell.

I found a quiet location where I wouldn't be overheard and punched the number into my satellite phone. It rang. Knowing

---

[14] Suleiman Jamous had been held captive several times by the Sudanese government. In 2005/6, he became critically ill and was taken by the UN to a hospital in East Darfur. He was 'held' in his hospital room and not allowed to leave; if he did, he would have been instantly arrested by the Sudanese government. Many stated that the UN were complicit in his detention and should have flown him to Nairobi for more in-depth treatment. The UN were seen as being supportive of the government, or at least not opposing it, and raised little in the way of petition for his release. Due to much international pressure, he was eventually released for treatment in Nairobi, Kenya, after over 11 months of being detained in a small hospital room. Mr Jamous was famously labelled as the 'Nelson Mandela of Darfur'.

there is a delay on these phones, I waited. Nothing. I hung up, waited 10 minutes and tried again. Nothing.

This continued for about an hour or more until eventually…

"Hello, who is this?"

The voice, amidst some background noise from what sounded like moving vehicles, came out of my phone.

"My name is Philip. I am the safety and security adviser for a large humanitarian organisation in El Fashir." I waited for a response. It didn't come so I cut to the chase. "I would like to meet with you to discuss our programmes of delivering aid and possibly the incident in Dar Zaghawa."

He answered in exceptional English, and was very calm in his reply.

"I am travelling now. I am meeting with UNOCHA tomorrow morning. Please be on their flight and we can meet then." With that the phone went dead. He'd hung up.

I thought, "Wow, that was easy enough."

I now had to call my new friend at UNOCHA to see if I could hitch a lift with them. The relationship I had established with the head of department at UNOCHA in El Fashir was good. He was a tall fair-haired guy in his late fifties, I estimated. My first impression of him was that he was a retired school headmaster, probably of a prestigious school somewhere in an affluent part of the UK. He was a well-spoken, quite serious character, slow on the humorous uptake but a very likeable, straight-talking guy, and I guessed he was a man of principal and integrity. The reality, I found out much later, was that in his 'past life' he had been an antiques dealer, semi-retired.

I decided to speak to him face to face, so I drove the short distance to the UN offices in El Fashir, not that far from our accommodation and offices.

I was greeted with a handshake and a smile, at least I thought it looked like a smile. Maybe his teeth were hurting? I told him of my contact with Suleiman and, as I put it, his insistence that I attend the meeting tomorrow, meaning I needed my backside on a seat on the UN helicopter.

After a bit of convincing, he agreed. He also mentioned that the UN were to conduct an investigation into the mine incident and I would be invited to be part of the investigation process. This was one of the main reasons for the UNOCHA/Suleiman Jamous meeting.

We were to meet again on the helipad at 7.30 in the morning.

With the news of the UN investigation being planned, I called London to speak with the emergency directors about my part in it. I also thought that we, as an organisation, should conduct our own internal investigation, prompting, from our perspective, a look at our procedures and hopefully leading to lessons learnt.

I had already taken copious notes, not quite in report format, on my involvement and findings. This was without any of the preparation and briefings that had happened prior to my arrival, but I'd already made a start.

The emergencies directors agreed with the internal investigation, and they promised to make the international staff who had left the programme, such as the logistics manager who was already in the throes of his handover, available for questioning when required.

I then called the country director in Khartoum and explained the situation to her. She welcomed the investigation by the UN and our internal one but I sensed some nervousness, as she seemed a bit unsure. I didn't pursue the reasons why, but I guessed she thought she may not come out of this too well.

I now looked forward to the meeting with Mr Jamous.

I spent the next few hours in a double session of meetings. The first was the UNDSS security meeting followed by the INGO security forum. During the UN meeting we were shown a large map of North Darfur and on it were several red lines indicating routes and areas that were out of bounds (OOB). There was also a time limit of three days that these routes were not to be travelled. I asked why.

Why were the marked routes out of bounds? What was the reason for the three-day timeline? And were they aware of the impact of delivery, or rather suspension of the delivery, of aid in those areas and what it would actually mean?

The answer was very evasive. The UNDSS guy had no explanation as to why they were out of bounds, he had just received information from his HQ that this was the case.

"And the timeline?" I enquired.

Again, no explanation. This was frustrating, and other members of the INGOs chipped in with their annoyance, largely at being told that they couldn't travel.

I wasn't sure that the UN could actually stop the INGOs from travelling. While there was a bit of to-ing and fro-ing, I gathered my thoughts to challenge the UN's governance over the INGO community.

"Excuse me, guys," I said loudly over the growing conversations that were all heading to a dead end.

My next comments were directed exclusively to the head of UNDSS.

"Please do correct me if I am wrong, but as I understand it, we as INGOs are totally independent organisations and are associated with the UN out of a shared understanding that we coordinate our interventions and other issues, so as not to duplicate effort and to share common safety information for everyone's good."

I paused for effect, as I now had everyone's attention, then I continued. "You are telling everyone in this room, UN and INGO alike, that you are placing the marked routes as out of bounds, yet you can't tell us why and you can't define whether it is a safety or security issue or just that the route is impassable due to the heavy rain we've had."

There was now lots of nodding and little whispers of agreement across the room.

I continued. "Unless you can clarify the reasons with your HQ, then we as INGOs have every right to assess the risk for ourselves and decide our best plan of action. Those of you here who are UN staff, unfortunately have no choice but to abide by the UNDSS instructions, but in all fairness, we do."

I added a warning. "I must be clear to everyone here, UN and INGO, that by taking the risk to travel these routes, it is the decision of your organisation alone, based on whatever information you can gather. For the UN: if you have information that the routes are out of bounds for reasons that may impact our safety and you fail to make that clear when questioned, as you have done here, then that is a huge failure of duty of care and you will be accountable for it. If there is a valid reason, we need to know because there are, across the area you say is out of bounds, possibly thousands of men, women and children who need our support on a daily basis."

The room was silent. I now finished with a request. "Can you please make contact with whoever gave you the original information and ask for clarity based on the reasons I have given? It would be appreciated by us all. Thank you."

By the look on the face of the UNDSS guy, I assumed he had never been challenged like this before. I understood he was an ex-lieutenant colonel from Jamaica, which explained his over-authoritarian approach to his briefings; he still thought he was talking to soldiers and his word would not be challenged.

He concluded his briefing and left the room, saying he would send an email to us all, answering all our questions, by that night. It didn't materialise.

We decided, due to the nature of the first meeting, to stay and occupy the conference room for our next meeting. As I was chairing it, I asked if everyone could take a break for 15 minutes and try, if they could, to scrape up any information on the out of bounds areas from their staff and those national guys who lived across the areas that were out of bounds.

Everyone left the room, lighting cigarettes and drinking from bottles of water as they went.

Mobile phones, satellite phones and Motorola VHF radio handsets were all used to get some information.

About 20 minutes later, we reconvened. We discussed the OOB issue and shared some interesting information. It appeared that two UN vehicles had been stopped by several unknown militia soldiers who wanted to know who they were and where they were going. They asked for money and their telephones. The UN staff then did everything that was requested of them and they were allowed to go on their way.

This, with some minor differences, was the information provided by three independent INGOs. While being stopped by armed people and having them make demands or pilfer items from you can be a frightening thing to experience (note that this was the nature of the location and the conflict) this happened to INGOs almost every day. It was something you learned to navigate, reading and assessing the situation quickly and deciding whether it was serious and aggressive or just bored rebel soldiers chancing their arm to blag some stuff while on a random road checkpoint.

There was no other information that could be accessed that gave any other reason why this road should be OOB.

After a short but productive INGO forum meeting, I went to the office of my best friend in the UN: the UNOCHA boss. I just popped in (again) unannounced to discuss the OOB areas and the conversations we'd had about travel. I told him about our information. He smiled (again, I think it was a smile. It always seemed like his face didn't know what his mouth was doing. It was the most awkward smile I had ever seen) and told me in confidence that two vehicles had been stopped by armed men, or as it had been reported to him, armed gangs, and several items had been taken. He concluded that this was the most likely reason, as he had not heard of anything to do with fighting or any attacks in the areas shown on the map.

He also told me that the UNDSS guy had been in his office asking questions about me. I laughed when he told me that he'd said I was a retired colonel (meaning that I outranked him) with the British intelligence. I laughed loudly. British intelligence? Me? I laughed again. Now that was a complete contradiction.

I asked him to put him right and tell him that I had a military background but was not a colonel or officer at all. "I worked for a living," I joked[15] (but part of me meant it).

As my friend was the humanitarian coordinator for the UN, I gave him the same scenario about INGOs not being bound by the UN. He agreed but stated that it would be unwise to distance too far from the UN, as they had more assets than the INGOs and it would be a long walk to meet with Suleiman without UN support. Wise words from a wise man. I thanked him and said I would see him in the morning at the helipad.

As I left, he said quietly, "Don't worry about UNDSS. They can be a bit over zealous at times and full of their own importance. There is good and bad in all of us and in all departments; it's just learning how to play them, my friend."

I smiled, nodded and left. I thought to myself, "My smile is way better than his."

I spent the remainder of the day talking to the various team leaders and getting a better understanding of their particular interventions; getting to know the problems they had, their perception of the risk and threats that existed and what they had done thus far to ensure their safety when in the field.

---

[15] It is well known that in the British army, the new officers, fresh out of training and given immediate command of 30 soldiers, are guided by their platoon sergeants who may have anywhere from 6 to 12 years of experience. This is repeated up the chain of command. Behind every major, commanding a company of roughly a hundred men, there is a company sergeant major making sure things happen. A lieutenant-colonel who would be a battalion commander, would have a regimental sergeant major as his guide and disciplinarian, again ensuring that commands are followed and giving words of wisdom when needed. Some refer to this structure as the common, hard-working man keeping those who are of well-educated and privileged backgrounds on the straight and narrow.

It was amazing and varied work that the teams were doing; from health to education to child protection to livelihoods to shelter to food and nutrition, all were working flat out. When not in the field, they were planning and preparing for their next trip out. Their approach to the threat and risk varied from one team to the next. All relied on their team leaders, who were of different backgrounds and had different levels of experience. Most were reactionary, waiting for things to happen and only then trying to fathom out their plan of action.

Everyone had their own ideas: some were okay but some were, well, pretty poor and unworkable. This was typical in a sense, as everyone's focus was on the work they had to provide to the many displaced people who needed their support and, of course, the pressure to deliver was at the forefront of their minds, giving their own safety and security a lower priority; in some cases, a much lower priority.

I kept reminding them that if anything happened to the team, there would *be* no delivery. I encouraged them to keep this in mind. Their dedication to their work was fantastic, although at times it could be somewhat disjointed and viewed with tunnel vision.

My task was to get everyone on the same page and to put together a safety and security plan that was simple, flexible and easy to understand. I had seen the organisational planning consisting of huge documents of confusing instructions, many trying to cover every eventuality (which is impracticable), giving page after page of generic instructions. These documents were often full of dust and kept on a high shelf were no one could see them, let alone read them. Most knew of their existence but few had read them and fewer still understood them. I had not met one person who had applied them; not in practice, nor in a real-time incident.

The key to any safety and security instruction or guideline is ensuring that everyone knows the basic aim of the plan; knowing what is available to you, such as communication equipment, first aid or trauma kits, and understanding the threat you are facing.

I have seen many very well-equipped medical trauma kits with lots of all-singing-all-dancing-equipment in them. Teams were very proud to show off how well-prepared they were but no one was trained in how to use them. Nobody had thought to train every person who might use them in their correct application. It was the same with the vehicle radio sets. It was usually the team leaders who knew how to correctly operate them; no thought had been given to the locally employed drivers who might be the only uninjured person in a position to use it, but couldn't because he had never been shown how.

I remember running a short exercise scenario in DR Congo. I was a rear-seat passenger in a vehicle. The team leader was sitting in the front passenger seat and the driver was a national member of staff, employed solely as a driver. The driver kept his vehicle clean and well serviced. He knew the roads and was, without doubt, a good driver.

Our little trip, by my design, took us out into the jungle. It was a remote route. At roughly halfway, I asked the driver to pull over and stop the vehicle. Looking quite puzzled, as too did the team leader, he pulled over and stopped.

Both the driver and the team leader shuffled in their seats to look at me.

What I said next took them both by surprise. "Okay guys, we have just come through a rebel ambush. We were shot at many times. The driver pushed the vehicle hard to get us out of the killing area as quickly as he could. We are now about two kilometres away from the ambush location and it appears that some of the shots fired at the vehicle have hit the engine and the vehicle is now immobile; plus, we have two flat tyres."

Immediately, the driver looked at the team leader, who was about to speak when I interrupted him.

"Sorry, I forgot to mention that the team leader was killed and I am critically injured. What are you going to do?"

The look of shock and horror on the driver's face told me all I needed to know, so I led with a few suggestive questions. "Would you radio for help? And do you know where exactly you are?" I followed on with: "Can you apply emergency first aid to my wounds to stop me from bleeding out?"

The answer, much to the embarrassment of the listening team leader, was a resounding no to all questions. He had not been trained on the radio, nor had he been given any basic first aid training. A management or an organisational failure? Either way it had to be addressed.

This type of scenario role play is vital in driving home a message, or messages, highlighting how under-prepared some people or organisations are. Many locations where humanitarian aid workers intervene are rife with difficulty, danger and, in most places, conflict. Everyone has to be considered for training, everyone should be given basic and life-saving first aid skills, and everyone should be taught how to use the equipment they are expected to carry, radios for one.

This knowledge is often 'assumed' by some organisations, so training is not asked for or given. My job was to ensure that all staff had the same basic understanding and skills and to ensure that their emergency procedures were understood and practised, not just taught then forgotten.

My conversations with the staff, team leaders and senior management were always productive, often showing the gaps that needed to be filled by the training of new skills or by reiterating the threat and risks that many people at all levels can, if they have been in a conflict location for long enough, become complacent to, which leads to bad or sloppy decision making, which can cost lives.

Anyway, the next morning, I was up early. My day sack was packed for the day's adventure, my cup of tea had been drunk then I left to meet with the helicopter and the UNOCHA team at El Fashir Airport.

I was the first to arrive, followed a few minutes later by the UNOCHA team. We stood and chatted while we waited for the pilot and co-pilot to complete their checks and get the 'chopper' ready to take off.

It was a bright morning. The heat of the day was already starting to build up. As the blades of the main rotors began turning faster and faster, it washed the engine exhaust fumes across the helipad. The smell of aviation fuel filled the air as we were given the thumbs-up from the co-pilot to board.

Walking briskly to the steps to get on the 'chopper', you automatically stoop down, thinking the rotor blades may decapitate you. On this type of helicopter, the rotors are high and even if the tallest of people stood bolt upright they wouldn't touch them.

I have heard grizzly stories of freak accidents where the tips of the rotors have been blasted by freak gusts of wind and have dipped dramatically, taking off the heads of those boarding.

I have been a frequent passenger in helicopters of all sizes over the years and have never witnessed an accident caused by hitting the rotor blades. That's not to say it doesn't happen (maybe on the smaller helicopters whose blades rotate closer to the ground) but I have never witnessed it, nor do I know of anyone who has. The bowing down and hunching of the shoulders is just, I think, a reflex action; a good habit to have, I suppose.

Soon we were airborne, flying over some mountains then over the brown, featureless desert. Every now and then there would be a splash of colour; the green of a few trees, as sparse as they were, next to the empty wadi beds and a few dwellings and the thatched mud huts looking black in contrast to the pale sand on which they stood.

We had flown for about 15 minutes when a small village came into view. We circled, looking for a good place to set down, and as we did, lots of children ran towards the aircraft. Their clothing and the clothes of the women who had now all come out of their dwellings to look at the helicopter, were a splash of vivid colour (bright reds and greens), and took me by surprise.

A few armed men were now 'herding' the children back and away from the aircraft. As we stepped down, we were pointed in the direction of a large lone tree on a dry riverbed, on the very edge of the village. We walked over, through the very soft sand, to where a few men sat under the shade of the tree. One man, dressed in white, traditional robes (this was called a jellabiya, a long loose robe which was usually white and consisted of an immah (a white scarf), a sarwal, (loose pants) and a large turban with a hanging piece of fabric that could quickly be pulled across the face to protect from sandstorms or the heat of the sun), stood up and looked directly at us as we approached.

As we reached the shade of the tree, we were invited to sit down on the soft sand. The man in white was, of course, Suleiman Jamous. His grey beard was a sharp contrast to his dark skin and his face was etched with lines and furrows. It was a face that without speaking could tell a thousand stories.

After a few opening pleasantries and introductions, the real conversation began. Soon we were discussing the incident of the landmine explosion. Suleiman was very quick to establish that it could not have been the SLA/SLM rebels who had planted the mine, as they had stuck to the agreement that no landmines would be used by either side. He stated that all landmines that the rebel factions once had were either destroyed or long surrendered and taken by the Sudanese military. He expressed his deepest sympathy for the families of those whose lives had been taken and wished the lone survivor a quick recovery.

It was made clear by the UN that they were looking for evidence of those who would have a reason to lay mines. They wanted to establish who would have access to them and what purpose it would achieve, knowing that whoever did lay the mine was in contradiction of the mine and arms embargo,[16] and they would, without doubt, be condemned by the UN and the international community. It was here that the waters got well and truly muddied.

After listening intently to the UN dictating the talks, I decided I needed to add my voice to the mix. I had questions, some based on the tactical use of mines, then a question of intent.

"Suleiman," I began, trying to pick my words very carefully, "if I was a military man, let's assume a Sudanese military man, I would want to place mines, if I had them, along my outer perimeter and at bottleneck and choke points, such as the wadi crossing point where my colleagues met their untimely deaths."

---

[16] In July 2004 Security Council Resolution 1556, not unanimously adopted, imposed an open-ended arms embargo on all non-governmental entities and individuals, including the Janjaweed, operating in the states of North Darfur, South Darfur and West Darfur. This was in response to the ongoing human rights abuses and deteriorating humanitarian situation in the region.

Security Council Resolution 1591, not unanimously adopted, expanded the arms embargo to include all parties to the N'djamena Ceasefire Agreement (including Sudanese government forces active in the region, the SLA/SLM and the JEM) and any other belligerents in North Darfur, South Darfur and West Darfur, Sudan. The resolution established the Security Council Sanctions Committee to monitor the enforcement of the embargo and to consider requests from the Sudanese government for the movement of military assets into the Darfur region.

I paused while I tried to read his face. It showed no emotion; he was just staring at me, eyes locked on mine, waiting to hear my conclusion. I continued. "This would not only inflict casualties upon my enemy but it would also give me, at my outpost, and any of my patrols an early warning of a potential attack. Would you agree?"

Before I continued, Suleiman responded. "What you say is true, and if you follow your line of thought, the same could be said of the rebel groups or, in fact, the Janjaweed. We would all have the same or similar gains. I think that is where your question is heading."

He'd taken the words right out of my mouth. A very clever man.

"But," I added, "who has the least to gain from such an action?"

My direct question took him and the UN guys by surprise. No one offered an answer, and that in itself was telling.

These were my thoughts: the Sudanese government were really on a hiding-to-nothing from the international community over the fighting in Darfur. Yes, they wanted propaganda headlines that they were doing everything possible to create peace, but on the ground that was not really a true picture. They could absorb a few bad headlines.

The SLA/SLM and JEM relied on the support of the international community to put pressure on the Sudanese government to stop the killing in Darfur and to assist the many displaced people with vital and lifesaving humanitarian aid and assistance. So who had most to lose?

Now to really stir the muddy waters. The Janjaweed, who were a tool often used by the government to do its dirty work, could have planted the mine with a view to discrediting the SLA/SLM and JEM, sparking a backlash that the rebel groups were at fault. The fact that humanitarian aid workers had been the victims would only amplify any growing concerns about the rebel movements' causes and objectives and may lose them critical support within the international community.

At this point, there was no conclusive evidence one way or the other. Would the following investigation uncover any conclusive evidence? I wasn't sure it would.

My friend from UNOCHA made a request for the SLA/SLM and JEM to make their regional commanders available to the joint investigation for questioning. He asserted that a similar request would be made to the Sudanese military commanders in El Fashir.

Suleiman pondered the request and gave a very non-committal answer, stating that he would make a request but could not guarantee the cooperation of the regional commanders.

It was agreed that a timeline of one week would be given to get an answer and to arrange meetings with those who agreed. The meeting was winding up, and we got back on our feet. My legs had gone dead sitting on the ground for over an hour. I deliberately hung back as the UN guys said their goodbyes and thanked Suleiman for his time and cooperation.

As they started to walk away towards the helicopter and Suleiman was about to leave the shaded canopy of what he called his office, I quietly called out and walked over to him.

He stopped, turned and with a gesture of his eyebrows as if to say "there's more?", I walked over and got close to him. I smiled and spoke in a very low voice. "Suleiman, I hope you don't mind a bit of straight talking away from the ears of the UN. I believe in straight talking, and I appreciate your position and what you are trying to do for the advancement of aid delivery but…" As his dark brown African eyes stared into my blue English eyes with an emotionless expression, I continued. "...I know that you already have information about what happened. I would take a good guess that if you don't already have the answers to who placed that mine, I guess you will soon. I understand the consequences at stake but I ask you to trust me. I will put my trust in you, as I believe you to be a good man who wants the best for the suffering people of Darfur, as we do. I will no doubt speak to you again but please, and in total confidence, communicate with me. Thank you."

I knew the minute I approached Suleiman that whatever I said had to be impactful. I had to give a message of understanding, while at the same time make it known that I knew he would be inside the information loop and would without doubt want to know the whos, hows and whys of this terrible incident.

When I had finished speaking, he responded, almost in a whisper, "God willing, *Insh' Allah*, Philip. Not all is clear and not all can be clear."

With that parting comment, he turned and walked off in the direction of the village.

I walked back through the soft sand, which was now hot under my feet, to the helicopter and was given a glance and a knowing nod by my UN friend. It was as if he was saying, "What have you said and why did you say it without me?" The flight back was full of ifs, buts, whys and wherefores, but the content of my brief conversation with Mr Jamous was not mentioned.

On landing in El Fashir, we disembarked and stood for a minute on the helipad discussing the next moves. It was there that I was told that the UN would coordinate the meetings with the Sudanese military and that they would be conducted at the military base in El Fashir.

I asked, then quietly demanded, that we also went back to the Um Baru outpost to interview the commanding officer there. To the UN, this didn't appear to be a popular request, but after some debate, it was agreed. Agreed, at least to try to get it organised.

I also suggested that we visit the village close to the blast site; just to ascertain if there had been any unusual activity that might help with the investigation. This, again, was met with hesitancy, but eventually, it was also agreed.

On the way back to the office, I was thinking about the events of the day; I thought about and chewed over the conversations that had taken place, the attitudes, the body languages and the suggested sequence of events of how the investigation should be constructed.

As I reflected, I thought that the UN appeared to be a little disinterested. I hoped I was wrong, but the lack of thought regarding who to interview and the slight reluctance to revisit the location of the village and the military outpost suggested otherwise. I really hoped I was wrong. The thing needling me were the constant reminders I'd had from various places and people of how political the UN could be, as much as they argued otherwise.

One of the benefits of meeting Suleiman Jamous was the tapping of information when the situation became a bit more tense because of the attacks. Other INGOs had got into the habit of asking permission from Suleiman to travel a particular route or to deliver aid to a particular village. This I thought was wrong; wrong in the sense that as a humanitarian organisation, we should not be asking permission from rebel groups to deliver our aid. Doing so could easily lead down a road of manipulation, giving rebel groups the final say on who we could deliver aid to and when.

My stance was that of course we had to communicate, but the importance was the terminology and trying to maintain some control. For example, my organisation was about to deliver some healthcare to a large community in a fairly remote area. Knowing that the location was a border region of disputed ground, the rebels sometimes had control and the Sudanese military, likewise, would assert control. There were no fixed straight lines where one side held the northern side and the other the southern side. It was scattered pockets of disputed territory and mixed areas, making it very hard to identify who was controlling what.

I called Suleiman and 'told' him that we would be sending a mobile clinic to a village, asking if he knew how safe it was to operate there. Sometimes he would answer immediately; other times he would ask me to call him again in 20 minutes to an hour or so.

If there was something planned, he would tell me that it would be unsafe or unwise to travel to a particular location on that day; advice such as this was usually followed by an attack of some type in the same general area. The control issue for us was not asking if we *could* go but stating that we *would* be going, putting the onus on him to advise otherwise. It just made our independence a little more authentic, which was important.

I managed to strike up a reasonable relationship with Suleiman over our satellite phone calls. They were short and to the point, but I always managed to get some general chit-chat in as well. It helped that I had called Suleiman to tell him the location of our mobile health clinic to see if he would offer any advice. He asked what time we would be arriving and leaving. I told him we would arrive at 10am, or close to it, and would leave at about 3 or 4pm.

"Philip, be sure that you and your team leave the village by 3pm, and no later."

I asked why, and he responded, "No later than 3pm. After that, your safety cannot be guaranteed."

I took that as being a pretty clear message that 'something' was about to happen in that area, so I told him we would do so. I then thanked him, asked about his health and wished him a safe day.

We arrived at the village just before 10am. Our group consisted of three Land Rovers, two doctors, Anna the nutritionist and three Sudanese nurses. I was in the lead vehicle; just me and my driver.

We arrived and set up a rudimentary shelter as a waiting area. It was a white, lightweight, portable gazebo type of thing. It was set up with a few foldaway tables and chairs. A small building next to it was given over as a doctor's room, allowing some level of privacy for examinations, etc. This hut was divided by, what could be best described as, a couple of bedsheets on a string, giving three separate flimsy rooms. It worked and it was accepted, so the team cracked on, checking babies, pregnant women, the old, the sick and anyone else who needed any level of treatment.

I, however, didn't have the luxury of staying in the shade of the shelter. I went out with my driver, who would act as an interpreter if needed, to observe life. My main aim was to keep an eye open for any change in the situation. Danger could swoop down at almost any moment under the threat of rebel groups, the Janjaweed and the Sudanese military; the worst case scenario being that they all turn up at the same time! Now that would be bad.

I engaged a group of kids who, out of curiosity, had gathered to see what was going on. The kids, like kids the world over, were laughing and being inquisitive. Their personalities were always emphasised at times like this; kids who were generally bold became bolder and those who were generally shy kept quiet and just observed without any involvement.

I walked over to my vehicle and retrieved my trusty football. I walked over to the group of kids and kicked the ball skyward as hard as I could. Screams of delight and laughter filled the air as the kids, boys and girls alike, from the ages of about six or seven to maybe about eleven or twelve years, all ran off chasing the ball.

The kids were dressed in what could only be described as loose rags of sand-dirtied and stained robes. There was the odd splash of faded colour from a ripped and faded shirt or t-shirt, which was probably older than the child wearing it, but regardless of the obvious poverty and total lack of any material wealth, they were happy at that moment; running, kicking the ball and chasing after it. It was so uplifting to see in such a barren and desolate desert location of abject poverty and hunger.

I joined in the game and showed my football skills by doing some 'keepie-uppies', finishing with a high kick and a 'back-heeler', powering the ball back into the waiting throng of wide-eyed kids. I don't think I could have replicated that skilled sequence if my life depended on it; it looked very skilful but was, in all honesty, a fluke.

I left the kids to play with the ball while I, together with my driver, went on a little walk about. We hadn't gone very far when a man and woman emerged from one of the mud-hut type dwellings and beckoned us over.

As we walked over, I noticed that they had set a blanket on the ground and there was a large metal flat dish at its centre. On the edge and spread around the dish were pieces of local flatbread cut into small squares. In the centre was a local food called Asseeda (Sudanese porridge). It was almost grey in colour and had the consistency of a lumpy blancmange. It sat in a liquid-soup type of fluid which was also greyish in colour.

I felt both shocked and immensely privileged to be invited to eat with this family; they had nothing, but were willing to share what they had with me, a total stranger. I felt overcome with emotion. I knew only too well that this food could be their only sustenance for a few days. I was so overwhelmed by their generosity.

I sat and waited for a simple prayer to be said, then I was invited, as the guest, to be the first to eat. I cautiously took a piece of bread and a swipe of the porridge, scooping a small amount and placing it quickly into my mouth before I dropped any of it. My hosts smiled as I indicated for them to eat.

This was my very first introduction to communal eating; seated on the floor, using only your fingers and little bits of bread to scoop up the porridge and the soup it sat in.

I was very mindful not to eat too much; just enough to show my appreciation and give thanks but not so much that I dwindled their weekly food supply.

Even though I was being encouraged to eat more, I used the tactic of talking more than I was eating, allowing the family, whose four kids had now joined us, to eat more than me.

I was told later that it would have been viewed as a great privilege for them to have a guest, and a white guest at that (giving the perception that I was important in some way), to join them at their meal.

I nibbled on the same piece of bread until the family had almost polished off the meal.

To refuse their hospitality could have been seen as rude, bad mannered and a direct snub to the head of the family. To eat until full would also have been seen as rude and insensitive. Finding the right balance became an art form.

The sentiment and hospitality were very genuine. It always left me emotional, and I reflected on how out of touch, as caring people, we had become in our wealthy, industrialised, food-abundant little worlds. These guys are among the poorest in the world in every sense except human kindness; if that became a bankable asset, they would easily be the richest people on the planet.

We sat for a while and listened to the head of the family telling tales of the hardship and violence inflicted on them from all sides, of the dwellings that had been burnt out and of the days spent hiding in the mountains after fleeing attacks on their village, trying to keep their children fed and walking many, many miles to new locations with only the few possessions they could carry. This family, and many like them, had every right to be bitter towards their fellow man. They had such a poor impoverished life, living on the very edge of life and death. The parents, with their yellowish, bloodshot dark brown eyes, had all the years of hardship etched in their faces, but there they were showing nothing but a sincere kindness to my driver and me. Astonishing.

I finally stood to give thanks, preparing to head back and see how the team was getting on, when my satellite phone rang. Making my apologies and asking the driver to thank the family for their kindness, I stepped outside to get a stronger signal and answered the call.

"Philip, you must leave now. Gather your team and leave. You have little time. Go! Go now!"

The tone in Suleiman's voice was one of urgency. Something was happening, or was about to happen, and we had to get out.

I shouted for my driver to get to the shelter pack it into our vehicle. I ran quickly into the makeshift doctor's surgery and shouted for the team to pack up and get in their vehicles.

One of the doctors started to protest. I cut him short and told him I would explain later, and that we had to go, and go quickly. The urgency in my voice told everyone this was a real emergency. There was a flurry of activity, vehicles were rapidly packed and the whole team scrambled to climb into a vehicle; any vehicle at that point.

I physically grabbed one of our Sudanese nurses and told her to explain that it was possible that some kind of attack was likely to happen, instructing her to tell the young man standing in total bewilderment to go and warn the people in the village. She did, and the young guy sprinted off to warn the people.

I quickly conducted a headcount, making sure we had all of our team, and rapidly asked if everyone had their laptops and phones; the answer was yes, and everyone was accounted for. I went to the driver of each vehicle and told them to keep up with me, maintaining a distance of about 50 feet or less between our vehicles until we were well clear. After ensuring that the instruction had been understood by all, I ran to my vehicle and told the driver to 'floor it'. He looked at me with a puzzled expression and I told him to go, and to go fast. The wheels spun on the soft sand and we lurched forward as the vehicle built up speed. As we did so, I tried to spot the other following vehicles in my wing mirror. Between the gusts of soft sand being churned, up I eventually accounted for all the vehicles.

I had been hesitant to use the VHF radios to communicate between the vehicles; if there was an attack about to happen, it could draw unwanted attention from anyone listening in. I waited until there was about a two-mile distance between us and the village, then I called all the vehicles and told them to slow down to a regular speed, as we had been pushing the limits and bouncing around on the soft sand and often-rocky tracks. After two miles, I stopped the convoy and ran to each vehicle to brief them quickly on why we'd had to make such a rapid withdrawal. I instructed each team member to lower their windows, remove any headphones, keep the music in the cars off and to listen and observe as we made our way back to El Fashir.

I told the commander of each vehicle to radio me if they had any problems. They were to call and use (say) the number 'one' if they heard any shooting or saw any groups that could be a threat, the number 'two' if their vehicle was having difficulty and had or was about to break down and the number 'three' if they had to stop for any other reason. I gave clear instructions about distancing and checked (again) that the vehicle logos and the logo flag were clearly visible so it could be established without error that we were a humanitarian convoy, not a rebel or military group. Within minutes, we were moving again. Hopefully, without stopping, we would get back to El Fashir without further incident.

After about five minutes, I heard the sound of an aircraft engine. I looked up and saw an Antonov AN-24. This was a Russian-made twin-turboprop cargo plane that the Sudanese air force had used to deliver barrel bombs.[17] I then heard the unmistakable 'rotor slap' of a pair of Mi-24 attack helicopters as they over flew our convoy, heading in the direction we had just come from. Fifteen minutes later, we were confronted by a convoy of Sudanese military vehicles carrying soldiers; they were heading straight towards us. We moved over, off the rocky road, to allow them to pass us. I assumed that they were heading in the same direction as the plane and two helicopters. Five large trucks with about 20 (at a guess) soldiers in each, bounced and rattled past us, leaving our convoy in a cloud of sand and dust as they went.

---

[17] These are typically made from a large barrel-shaped metal container that has been filled with high explosives and nuts and bolts, as well as other small metal objects that contribute to the shrapnel effect, then dropped from a helicopter or aeroplane. Due to the large amount of explosives (up to 1,000 kilograms (2,200 lb)), their poor accuracy and indiscriminate use in populated civilian areas (including refugee camps) has resulted in devastating detonations. Critics have characterised them as weapons of terror, and they are illegal under international conventions.

This was what Suleiman had warned me about. He'd known that something was going to happen and that we were in harm's way, so he gave us just enough warning to get out.

I thought of the kids I had been playing football with and of the family and their four children who had shown me immense kindness and told stories of hardship and survival. I hoped they would survive whatever it was, if it was in their village.

As the military convoy disappeared and the sand clouds dispersed, I stepped out of my vehicle, holding the HF radio handset in my hand. I studied the horizon behind me, looking for evidence of an active attack, smoke or the audible sound of a battle. I couldn't make out any but I knew something bad was happening.

I radioed the UN radio room and reported what I had seen. I gave directions and timings. I described the aircraft I had identified and the troops I had seen. Once done, I checked (yet again) that everyone was okay, and we set off back to El Fashir, a place where the airport would have, some minutes before, seen the Antonov aircraft and the two attack helicopters take off to destinations unknown; unknown for now, but their direction was clear.

It is hard to keep a tight rein on your feelings when operating in a conflict zone. Knowing that people, such as we had found in that small village, were possibly being hammered by an army of well-equipped, well-fed and heavily armed troops.

The usual tactic was for the fixed-wing aircraft to fly in and drop the barrel bombs, causing devastation and panic, and the two attack helicopters to support, like a hunter looking for ground targets to attack, giving close ground support to the troops who arrived to clear up (by that I mean kill) any survivors and, as had been reported in several different attacks of this nature, commit terrible acts of brutality, including rape, execution and other such atrocities, such as torture.

Some attacks on villages were justified as being retribution upon those who'd helped the various rebel groups, offering them food and shelter. While this did happen, it was the innocents who paid the highest cost; the rebels often faded into the background, living to fight another day.

It had been known for the Sudanese military to fully close off villages and refuse humanitarian aid to get through, knowing that the result could be starvation or death from illnesses that could be prevented by simple mobile medical clinics, such as the one we had brought to the village before Suleiman had made that all important call.

War; conflict, battles for freedom from oppression, the putting down of rebel insurgencies by governments, the guerrilla warfare[18] waged by the oppressed for whatever the reason. There are always opposing sides, and within the mix, there are always the innocents, who just want to live a peaceful life and bring up their families in a safe and secure environment, with enough food to fill their bellies and a secure place to call home.

Whatever the reason, the justification or the intent, the human cost is always too much. Displaced people walk for days to get away from attacks on their homes and villages; mothers with children feel a sense of total desperation; fathers feel defeated and humiliated; young women, some still in their teens, give birth in a transient state between what they were forced to leave behind and the unknown ahead of them. I once witnessed a mother holding a newborn, having given birth under the stars in a location completely alien to her, being surrounded by people who

---

[18] Guerrilla warfare is a form of irregular warfare in which small groups of combatants, such as paramilitary personnel, armed civilians or irregulars, use military tactics, including ambushes, sabotage, raids, petty warfare, hit-and-run tactics and mobility to fight a larger and less-mobile traditional military. Guerrilla groups are a type of violent non-state actor.

were starving and massively dehydrated, struggling to keep up with the straggling crowd, not understanding why her new baby was so quiet and 'slept' for so much of the time. Due to her shocked state from the initial horror of what she had witnessed during the attack on her village and the trauma of giving birth without any medical help or assistance (just a few other women who had tried to ease the pain with nothing more than words) at sixteen years of age, she hadn't realised that her new baby had died three days previously.

The process of realisation for this young and very vulnerable girl was probably the saddest situation I have ever witnessed. On arrival at the IDP camp, she was met, as they all were, by medical teams who are ready to assess the new arrivals and to provide a shelter as their temporary home.

Listening to and observing the conversation, with doctors trying to find the right words that a young, frightened and traumatised girl would understand, was heartbreaking, especially the moment she finally realised that the child had died. The sudden loud, almost primal, screaming and wailing that came from her frail body was shattering. She was alone; she had no husband, and now the only blood relative and memory of her husband was gone too.

A nurse eventually took the small bundle from the girl and said she would care for the baby and call for her when it was time to bury her.

The crying continued for a long time. Other women in the camp came to offer comfort, but she was totally distressed. One of the doctors eventually gave her a sedative to calm her and help her sleep. Nearly three hours passed since her realisation of her baby's death, before she finally, out of exhaustion, fell into a deep sleep.

Stories like this were sadly common. In Darfur, survival was an everyday battle and the enemies were numerous: government attacks, rebel attacks, hunger, thirst, sickness and drought. It was a very hard existence, which was made all the harder by the raging conflict.

The humanitarian workers, all volunteers who worked tirelessly helping people who often found themselves in dire situations, frequently end up exhausted, working well over their contracted hours; 16-hour days are common, 18 hours are for many a baseline and for some, finding a few hours of sleep a day is sometimes the best they can hope for.

There are no canteens or cafes to quickly nip off to for a coffee and a rest and no hotels to grab a drink from before slipping into the crisp white sheets of a self-contained room. No; life here is hard on the humanitarians, who are drawn from all over the world. They give up all the luxuries of home to help people who don't have the means to help themselves. They forgo a shower or bath for days, sometimes weeks. Their 'homes' are often not air-conditioned, so they struggle with the oppressive heat, not sleeping and constantly feeling exhausted. They have very meagre meals, often losing a lot of weight and ending much lighter than when they first stepped off the plane.

Why do they do it? Why do they endure the hardship? The answer is simple. It's not the money, as no one ever got rich working in the humanitarian sector and it's not the glamour, as often no one can see what they do (they are the often unreported, unrecognised and silent workers amidst almost every war, post-war and natural disaster in the world). They do it because they care, because they want to help and for them, it's the right thing to do.

As an ex-soldier with a full 22-year career behind me, having served in conflict and war zones, I have to acknowledge the world of the humanitarian sector, in the locations I have been privileged to work, as providing the most difficult, dangerous and challenging situations I have ever experienced.

As the days flashed by, the investigation with the UN got underway. Meetings were arranged, then cancelled, then arranged again. Some were informative and productive whereas others were set out to create confusion and to throw doubt into the mix. Nothing, it appeared, was as clear as we had hoped.

Two meetings, for me, highlighted the issues we were dealing with in a more succinct manner and gave a level of clarity among a confusing sandstorm of information and misinformation.

The first meeting I had insisted upon, was to meet with the commander of the Um Baru outpost. This meeting had been previously cancelled several times, due to insecurity in the area, the danger involved in travelling there and the availability of the commander, who seemed to vanish at times.

When we finally arrived, we discussed the sequence of events. The UN led the questioning, focusing, as it appeared to me, on what we already knew. I was getting bored and restless with this line of, what I called, politically correct questions. It appeared that the UN were deliberately avoiding any direct questions about who might be at fault or who may have placed the landmine and why?

During a pause in the conversation, I took my chance. "Can I ask?" I announced, noticing all heads had now turned to face me. "As a military force, you may feel vulnerable and want to secure your borders with what is perceived (or not) as rebel territory, knowing that they could attack at any time; it would be in your interest to deploy mines along routes you think attackers may use to gain access to your base."

The commander looked at me and smiled. He responded, "Yes, that would be a tactic that would favour us here and give an early warning, but we don't have any mines. It is against the arms embargo agreement, and to have mines would mean we would be in violation of that agreement."

I jotted down his response. I noticed that the UN guys were whispering between themselves and I was getting a few sideways glances. I had upset their politically correct and ineffective questioning technique. I didn't care. I wasn't bound by the UN rules, so like it or not, I was going to persist with my more direct questioning.

While this was going on, the commander, without prompting or questioning, made a second statement connected to my first question. "Some weeks ago, one of my patrols stopped a rebel vehicle and after a short firefight[19], we killed the two occupants and took their pick-up, which had 21 mines loaded on the back."

My eyes were now as wide as saucers. I asked, "And where are these mines? Can we see them?"

The commander answered with a smile and told us that he had sent them all back to HQ in El Fashir.

I casually acknowledged his response and stretched my legs, asking if we could take a quick break to take some water and, for those who partake, a smoke too. It was agreed.

Upon leaving the tent, I grabbed the UN guys and told them to call their office in El Fashir and get someone to the military camp to verify this 21-mine story.

I thought the commander had been a bit naive by offering this information. Was he trying to discredit the rebels by pointing out he had captured mines from them? As far as I was concerned, he had now clearly stated that he had been in possession of mines. Had he kept some for himself and sent the rest back to El Fashir? Was the story just a rouse to put the blame on the rebels? Either

---

[19] Firefight is military terminology for a small 'gunfight' between two opposing sides.

way, he had clearly stated that he had been in possession of mines, were previously he'd denied it.

After our water and smoke break we got back to the final session at Um Baru. The conversation returned to the UN's political correctness and there was nothing more of any significance to come out of the meeting.

We stood, shook hands, gave our thanks and said goodbye. We left the tent and walked through the soft sand back to our transport.

As we walked to the chopper, my UN friend's satellite phone rang. It was the call I was waiting for. The UN representative in El Fashir had met with the garrison commander there, who denied that any mines had been delivered to his camp. He stated he had no knowledge of any contact with rebels who were carrying mines nor of a firefight on the day in question.

This meant one of two things: either there were no mines and the outpost commander was just trying to mislead us into thinking that the rebels did indeed have mines, or he had taken the mines and kept them for his own protection. Either way, it appeared strange that he would, without any prompting, make the statement that he had.

Our next meeting, a few days later, was arranged by Suleiman Jamous. We would fly by helicopter to a pre-arranged location and hopefully would be met by local commanders of the SLA/SLM.

As we circled above the meeting place, it was immediately noticeable that this place was in stark contrast to the location where we'd last met. It was open desert. No dwellings, children or women; just a few vehicles and groups of heavily armed men sitting around chatting while they watched the chopper land.

As the rotor blades stopped turning and the mini sandstorm it created subsided, we stepped down from the aircraft and were directed to a lone tree about 200 metres away.

"Aha!" I thought. "Suleiman's office."

As we got closer to the tree and its large canopy, I could see it was set on a bank of another dry wadi. In the dip of what would be the riverbed, sat a circle of men dressed in robes which were draped in bandoliers of what looked like 7.62mm bullets. Each had a side arm, a pistol and a rifle of different sorts. These were the local SLA/SLM leaders, all seasoned fighters, and they looked every inch the part.

Sitting at the base of the tree was Suleiman. He was talking to the group of leaders in a very serious manner. The group looked serious and angry; then suddenly all eyes were on us.

All conversation stopped. We were greeted and quickly told to be seated. This was going to be yet another torturous session for my knees.

Suleiman addressed the gathering first in Arabic then in English. He told his fighters why we had come and that we would be asking questions which he hoped they would answer.

As in the last meeting at Um Baru, the UN led the questioning, this time proceeding slowly and carefully, allowing Suleiman time to translate. The pattern of questions followed the same path as they had last time. I found myself getting very frustrated as the questions and the responses seemingly led nowhere. I was just about to interrupt when the noise of a vehicle broke the silence of the pause I was about to jump into. The one point of interest, we were told, was that there was no evidence or acceptance that the military had taken the mines from any of the SLA/SLM rebels, let alone any confirmation of a firefight and loss of rebel soldiers.

Suleiman told us all to wait as the overall SLA/SLM commander of North Darfur had just arrived.

Suddenly, a figure in black robes emerged from over the bank of the wadi and quickly descended into the dip before walking directly into the centre of the gathered circle.

He was only about five-foot-five or six. On his face, he had a few scars; whether they were tribal markings or scars from battle, I couldn't make out. One thing was instantly apparent, though; he was really pissed off. He was an angry man. To make matters worse, he was holding his pistol in his hand and while furiously talking and shouting at the assembled group, he was using it to point at various people. I thought someone was going to get shot, I just hoped it wasn't me.

As the commander ranted at the group, I could see people averting their eyes so as not to make direct eye contact with this really pissed-off guy.

He had his back to me, shouting and pointing his pistol at two or three of his commanders, then he spun around pointed his pistol directly at me and continued shouting.

The pointing of the pistol was exactly that; he was using it to point in a jabbing motion as opposed to aiming with a mind to shoot, so I remained calm(ish). Unlike his commanders, I didn't avert my gaze. I looked directly at him, not because I was brave or trying to show him I wasn't afraid, but if he changed his mind and stopped pointing the gun, deciding to shoot instead, I wanted as much visual warning as I could get. An old instinct, I guess. There probably nothing I could do to stop him, but that was my reasoning. Self-preservation, I suppose.

When the rant ended, he called to Suleiman to walk with him. They left the group and walked away from Suleiman's office and out of earshot.

I could see the commander still ranting and using the pistol to point at the chest of Suleiman and then back at the group still nervously twitching under the tree. Then it went very still. Both men stood face to face. The commander placed his hand on his heart and lowered his head. Suleiman reciprocated. That, I thought, was a true sign of mutual appreciation and respect.

The commander, almost in a speed march, hurried back to the waiting group and shouted something as a command. The other subordinate commanders stood, picked up their weapons and departed towards their vehicles. I could hear the engines firing up, and within seconds the noise faded as they drove away. "Meeting over," I thought.

Suleiman stood alone for a few moments, then slowly returned to greet us again.

I asked if he could tell me what had happened and what had been said. What I learnt next really shocked and surprised me.

Suleiman began, "As you arrived, I was speaking to the commanders and reminding them of the incident and why you were coming to speak with them. Some did not like or trust you. They thought you would betray them to the government and the military. They thought you were spies." He paused, smiled and then continued. "I had to explain the humanitarian nature of your work and why you were in Dar Zaghawa, which is the homeland to many of the commanders. This, Philip, stopped them from wanting to shoot you," he said with a very enigmatic smile.

"Thank you," I replied with a similar smile and a sarcastic tone.

He continued. "He was very angry and has promised to kill any of his commanders who might have been involved with the landmine. He told them that if he has information against them, he would not only kill the commander, but also his family. He told the gathering that you are here to help their families and all the people of Dar Zaghawa and that using landmines would damage their cause in the eyes of the watching international community. But he will take revenge if you are guilty; his uncle died in that vehicle."

I now understood his anger and his passion and knew full well that he would carry out his threat. The driver, a Sudanese national, had survived; the team leader, a Brit/Scot, had died; and the water engineer, a Sudanese national who had said he knew the area, had also died. This was his uncle.

Although I got the drift of the message had been given, I think Suleiman had added some points of his own in order to make the interpretation a bit less frightening and more palatable for the UN and myself.

The investigating team from the UN and I convened a final time to assess our findings and to hopefully agree on a conclusion to the final report, which would be a UN report. I would get a copy and so would my HQ office in London.

As it turned out, there was a difference of opinion. While not all events and conversations are included here (that could be a book in itself!), the UN concluded that it was probably the rebels who had placed the mines. The rebel group could not be identified, as there was no direct evidence to say exactly who it was. When visiting the nearby village, the villagers there confirmed that both military patrols and rebel groups regularly passed through their village, so nothing concrete came from them.

Similarly, I could not be precise in my conclusion, but from my observations, I concluded it was the military that had placed the mine.

The mine explosive experts had told me that it was a double-strike anti-tank mine, meaning it was two mines placed one on top of the other. One anti-tank mine is lethal enough, but two?

My conclusions were based on the statement of the commander at Um Baru (who was the only person on either side to state that he had been in possession of mines) which later could not be confirmed even by his own HQ and senior commander. So where were the mines?

The actions of the mine-clearing team from Um Baru, particularly as I had revised the mine-clearing process with them, were really strange. A de-mining team, such as they claimed to be, would never run into a suspected minefield and stamp and whip the ground in such a manic way... unless they knew there were no other mines. Did they place it? Acting in the manner in which they did in what could have been an active minefield would have meant certain death. De-miners know this. They understand the effects of mines. So this behaviour, in my opinion, could only have been demonstrated if they knew that there were no more mines to endanger their lives; possibly because they had planted the mine themselves.

I think, finally and again inconclusively, that the rant at gunpoint of the rebel commander and his obvious anger at realising his uncle had been killed in the mine strike told me that it was something he would not condone. His expression that the international community was something the rebel groups needed positively on-side was an indicator of his prioritised thinking.

We agreed to disagree, but I requested that my thoughts and findings be included in their report for consideration, as both of our lines of thinking were inconclusive. It was agreed, and the final report alluded to my findings but didn't really include any details.

I wrote my independent report, stating all the observed points and the inconclusive thinking and findings of the UN. I added the details I had mentioned and finished with a militaristic viewpoint that the location of the Sudanese outpost was very vulnerable, being surrounded on all sides by what was perceived to be rebel-held land, and the troops there would have possibly been outnumbered in any attack, so by defining boundaries and setting up defences, it would give the outpost early warning and possibly reduce the numbers that would prosecute any attack against them.

Keeping an open mind, the rebels (whichever group it may have been) could have set this up as an ambush for the military. An attack on them without committing manpower? Maybe.

The organisation took some time in assessing its next steps. The senior management team back in London, in conjunction with the programme director and her senior management team (including me) spent a long while deliberating over the findings of the joint investigation and the two reports. It was suggested that maybe the organisation itself had been targeted; maybe to make an international statement by one group or another in order to taint the response and support of the international community. A black propaganda plot maybe?

It was also discussed whether, if the incident was indeed targeted, the organisation should pull out of Darfur altogether. There wasn't any evidence or even rumour that this was the case, so it was discounted, and at this point in time it was agreed that the programme would continue to deliver the much-needed aid to the many identified and growing groups of beneficiaries that were filling up the IDP camps,[20] as well as those in remote locations, such as villages, who were under the constant threat of attack.

---

[20] Due to the large numbers of displaced populations across Darfur, many IDP camps had opened up. The largest was the Abu Shouk camp, seven miles north-east of El Fashir, is one of the biggest camps of internally displaced persons (IDPs) in North Darfur. It contains 30 blocks and more than 80,000 people from nearly all ethnic groups in Darfur, but mostly from the Fur, Tunjur, Berti, Zaghawa, Gimer, Fellata and Hawara.

Unfortunately, two months later in South Darfur, two staff members, clearly identifiable as humanitarian workers, were taken from their vehicle and shot dead as they made their way back to Nyala from the clinic they were supporting in South Darfur.

I was at El Fashir Airport when I received the news. I immediately ran to my vehicle to retrieve my satellite phone and punched in Suleiman Jamous's number. It rang and was immediately answered.

"Suleiman, this is Phil. I have just had news that two of our staff in South Darfur have been shot and killed just outside Nyala. It is being reported that they were shot by the SLA/SLM. Can you confirm this, and can you tell me why this has happened?"

I waited for a response.

"Philip, I, too, have just had news but I have no information. I will call you when I do."

I never heard from him again.

The line of acceptance of the safety of staff had now been crossed. Even though Nyala was in South Darfur under the South Darfur programme, I was invited to investigate this incident too.

As it transpired, the vehicles the aid workers had been travelling in were clearly marked as humanitarian aid workers, with the logo clearly printed on both sides of the vehicle. The two that were shot were wearing organisational t-shirts with large organisational logos on them. There was no mistaking who they were. The story evolved that a couple of SLA/SLM rebels were drunk and decided to take action against the vehicles and their occupants. Several staff managed to flee as the first shots were fired. One, as he fled, was shot in the hand.

It was at this point that the organisation, who had suffered the death of four staff members (killed in the line of their humanitarian duty), had to make a very serious and extremely difficult decision. Could they realistically stay in Darfur? If there was to be another incident and staff were killed, could it be justified? At what stage would they say "enough is enough"? After the death of five or six? That was the dilemma faced by the organisation.

As it unfolded, the decision to pull out of Darfur was made. The organisation had been operating in Sudan for over 20 years and had been delivering humanitarian aid in Darfur since the crisis began.

Luckily, in a sense, the programme activity, all of its assets and the funding to sustain what had already started, was given over to other aid agencies to continue the great work that the organisation had begun.

It was a very sad time; losing four valued members of staff in two separate incidents in two separate locations, yet all from the same organisation.

Other incidents in Darfur were numerous. In a small town called Tawilha, there were several INGOs with staff operating on a daily basis. Some national staff often spent days in the field clinic and were visited almost every day by the mobile teams who would bring supplies, doctors and other things to continue the support to the population there. People from other villages would walk several miles into Tawilha to access the medical facilities there.

At the far-eastern end of the village, there was a police station. This housed a para-military police force and often a patrol of Sudanese military. The whole village was in the shadow of a small mountain range which was believed to be the hidden base of a large rebel group.

After various tensions in the village following a previous attack by government forces, the rebels, one random morning, decided to attack the village, making the police station its main target.

They swooped down from their mountain bases and attacked the police station. It was a chaotic attack and many innocent villagers had to flee in fear of their lives.

As soon as the news hit El Fashir, the Sudanese air force took off in their helicopters and Antonov aircraft.

We had teams in the village, as did several other INGOs, and there was also a team from the UN.

I managed to persuade the African Union (AU) commander (who was actually a French lieutenant colonel supported by an American major) to get airborne to bring the teams out.

At first the lieutenant colonel was reluctant to help but his American counterpart managed to persuade him to get three helicopters and fly to Tawilah.

I used a satellite phone to talk to our guys on the ground, who had been relaying information to us since the attack had started. Most INGO staff took shelter either in the clinic or in the school building not far from the western edge of the village.

I told my guy on the ground that he had to get all the INGO staff to the large piece of flat ground about 200 metres outside the western edge of the village and split them into three equal groups ready to be evacuated by helicopter. They should lay low in the dip in the ground until the helicopters came into view. I told him he would have to keep very tight control of all the people and ensure they didn't rush to the aircraft as they attempted to land.

I went back to the American major and told him of the plan. I gave him the coordinates that I had previously recorded and confirmed with my guy on the ground from his Thuraya satellite phone, which has a GPS function.

As the lieutenant colonel came out of the building on the edge of the helipad, he turned to me and said, "You cannot come on this mission. You are a civilian and, therefore, not authorised. You stay here. It is too dangerous."

The American major who was standing at his side just caught the last bit of the conversation but then heard me say, "I am coming. It is largely my people out there. I can identify them. Can you? Will you know who is boarding the aircraft? Would you have a fucking clue who is a rebel, a civilian or an aid worker? The answer is clearly no. Plus, I have socks that have had more military operational experience than you. So, are we going to waste time arguing while good people are potentially in the process of being killed?"

The lieutenant colonel looked embarrassed and the American major was trying hard to supress his smile that almost led to a laugh. So I said I would be on the lead chopper out and the last chopper back. Then off I went and boarded.

We were quickly in the air. The lieutenant colonel was frantically talking to a military liaison on the ground at El Fashir, telling them that three AU helicopters were in the air and that the Sudanese aircraft were not to engage them, commanding them to cease all air activity over Tawilah.

I was still in contact my guy on the ground, telling him to look and listen and let me know when he could see our helicopters. It only took minutes for us to arrive.

Looking out of the doorway as we circled the proposed landing site, I saw plumes of smoke rising at the far end of the village. Some dwellings were burning, but just where I expected the police station to be, there was a large plume of billowing black smoke and a continuing exchange of gunfire.

As we prepared to land, I told my guy to have the first of the three groups ready to board the helicopter that I disembarked. I told him I would wave them forward but the other two groups had to stay still.

As we landed, I was out the door as soon as we touched the ground. I spotted my guy and waved him and the others to come to me. As he approached, leading the first group, I pulled him to one side while the others frantically climbed aboard.

"Are all the others in the same place as you were?" I shouted to him over the noise of the engines.

"Yes," he replied, pointing to where he had just emerged from.

I pointed at him to get on the chopper. The lieutenant colonel and the American major had now joined me on the ground.

As the last person climbed aboard, I gave a thumbs-up to the pilot who then took off and left to return to El Fashir. I then whistled loudly for the next group. While the lieutenant colonel and the American major ran towards the next chopper, I ran to the next group of people who were just emerging from the dip in the ground. In a nice neat row, still lying on the ground behind them, was the final group.

I told them to stay there and keep low and I would be back for them. I then led the second group to the second chopper. They were loaded by the two waiting military men who, when everyone was on the helicopter, gave the thumbs-up to the second pilot who in turn took off and headed back to El Fashir.

I then ran back towards the final group and collected them and led them to the last chopper. Once loaded, we all found a seat and took off. As we climbed into the sky, I could still hear some gunfire. We took a wide turning circle to face back towards El Fashir but as we did, I could see in the distance some bodies lying motionless on the floor. There was a trail of destruction leading up to the police station, where it looked like more bodies were strewn around the building. Some of the mud hut dwellings close to the police station were burning, sending plumes of smoke straight up into the air. There didn't appear to be any movement on the ground. I thought that the attackers were either inside the police station, ransacking the place, or had already left to return to their mountain hideouts.

Touching down at El Fashir airport, we were met by representatives from several of the INGO groups whose staff had just been extracted from Tawilah. They included the UN, Oxfam and my own organisation; all in all, about 35 humanitarian workers had been brought to safety.

A small group of Sudanese aid workers, upon hearing the initial attack starting, decided to flee on foot. They took off in several directions but somehow all managed to meet up and walk back to El Fashir, taking time to stop and rest. They were very cautious and took a rather long route, taking care to stay away from any traffic or local villages. It was another 24 hours before we had accounted for everyone.

It was reported by eyewitnesses that 14 police/soldiers were killed in the attack. I returned to the village two days later to see the aftermath for myself and to talk with the villagers in an attempt to risk assess the likelihood of humanitarian work continuing.

Close to the school building was a crater in the ground. According to eyewitness statements, it was caused by a barrel bomb that had been dropped by an Antonov. Our education team had been in the school and had moved to the helicopter landing zone minutes before the bomb had landed and exploded. A lucky escape for sure.

On reflection, incidents such as this highlight the need for coordinated training on how to act in an emergency, understanding the assets available and how to access them, and who the decision makers are that can, for example, get helicopters in the air. Having emergency contact numbers is critical so that contact and planning can start without delay.

On my first visit to Tawilah, I identified potential helipads in four different locations based on the compass points. Using the village centre as the middle point, I allocated one site to the north, one to the south, one to the west and one to the east. So, if an attack came from, or was active in, the north of the village, then the safest evacuation point would be the one located in the south (the furthest point from the fighting). The nominated sites could also be used as a reference point if they were impractical to actually use; for example, telling your team to move 300 metres east of one of the known helipads would give a good indication of where they should go. Everyone had to know where the sites were and be familiar with the actions necessary if requested in an emergency to go there.

Fortunately, I had the chance to conduct some training with our field teams, so the basics were already understood; that explained the discipline they showed at the helipad as the choppers landed. The urge for all to just run towards the chopper would have been compelling, but with my guy on the ground being calm and capable, he was able to put the plan into action and direct as needed on the ground. The American major later commented on how disciplined the evacuation was. He was surprised at how organised it had been. Full credit to the teams on the ground for sticking to the plan and not panicking. Training works!

My time in El Fashir was busy; busy with incidents such as this.

When people talk about being an aid worker, thoughts of doctors attending sick children and hungry populations getting food aid come to mind. Often, the white vehicles with the blue UN signage can be seen hurriedly rushing to a location you never get to see. It all appears to be risk and danger free, after all they are the good guys helping those in need.

What is often missing in people's minds is the hardship and the dangers, for those who regularly volunteer to help those in need in hostile locations are themselves in harm's way. They have to know what the risks are and understand their contingency plans so they can react quickly when things go wrong. They have to be calm in a crisis and decisive when needed. I have seen some very courageous people, some of whom you would least expect, taking control of emergency situations and organising their teams in order to keep them safe. I have seen the opposite as well, though; those who when not under pressure are self-assured, good at their jobs and are effective managers but when a life-threatening situation occurs, they freeze or become very indecisive. With most people, you can never tell how they might react until something actually goes wrong; then it just might be too late.

Having good training, being aware of the situation you are working in and anticipating what is likely to go wrong is always a good place to start when imparting understanding and confidence.

Good trainers are those who have had direct experience and can relate to the fear and confusion that can often arise. They can advise on what to expect in terms of being scared and how to control the inevitable panic that may surface.

INGOs working in very difficult locations deal with dangerous and risky interventions regularly. They volunteer to help because it's needed. They are good people with a selfless outlook. Part of my role was to embrace that quality and to train the INGOs in the knowledge and know-how of how to stay safe and what to expect when things go wrong. Having a basic plan that is familiar to all gives a basis upon which additional and immediate decisions can be made by those operating in the field, to enhance the team's safety.

Plans are the foundation; good people making effective and rational decisions during moments of crisis is what saves lives and makes the plans succeed. Have a plan 'A' but be sure to have plans 'B' and 'C' just in case plan 'A' fails.

A famous military quote I learnt many years ago was a quote used by the German commander, Rommell, but pinched from the military teachings of Helmuth von Moltke the Younger who was born in Biendorf, Germany. He was a German soldier who served as the chief of the German General Staff from 1906 to 1914 and attended the War Academy between 1875 and 1878, joining the General Staff in 1880. The quote was: "No plan survives contact with the enemy."

Basically, this means that all plans are great up to and including the point when someone does something you hadn't anticipated. That's why a plan 'B' and a plan 'C' are always good to have in reserve. It is also important to train or explain to people that regardless of basic plans, you will always need to think on your feet and remain flexible in order to make a plan work in whatever form it eventually ends up.

Darfur was a tough teacher. I learnt hard lessons. I finally understood my expanding role and the responsibilities I was entrusted with.

I took all of my work as being deeply personal. I found I had built upon the skills I had learnt in Iraq and in my 22-year military career.

The military gave me discipline. It gave me the ability to assess situations quickly and to act in an effective and decisive manner. It taught me the value of good training, and I gained much from the operational tours and from warfare.

What lacked was the personal or interpersonal understanding. The military, for good reason, is a very rank-structured and almost dictatorial environment. You have those of higher rank who tell those of lower rank what to do and in many cases how to do it. In several instances, I found that rank does not always assume knowledge. I have experienced some very poor commanders who because of their rank assumed they knew better.

I witnessed some who, with rank, abused their position; they became very autocratic and bordered on being bullies, just because they held a higher rank. Some were often in very important positions and actively discouraged opinions or ideas that were opposed (or better than) their own.

Maybe that is a generalisation within my experience, but it does exist. The British Special Forces have a different approach; they believe in the individual and what they bring. They believe in challenging plans and orders to ensure they reach the best possible and most thought-through solution to any problem, but they also manage to marry that ethos with decisiveness when needed.

Horses for courses, I suppose, but I do believe in the individual and in the knowledge that being senior doesn't necessarily mean you have all the answers or that you are always right.

In the humanitarian world, I found that the actions I would be marked down on in the military (for instance, by challenging some decisions) became a strong point for me. I found the INGO world to be totally open to this particular way of working. This ideology instilled a deep respect and a better understanding of what needed to be done and how best to do it.

Don't get me wrong, there are a few 'dinosaurs' in the humanitarian world who are autocratic, who can't see the wood for the trees and who like the sound of their own voices above all else; but they are few and far between. In my experience in the military, during my service, there were a lot of 'dinosaurs' about. Some may have been good soldiers in disciplinary terms but were totally unrelatable as people.

My grounding in the military from the age of 17 and a half, gave me a great education in values. It taught me respect and it gave me the general tools to lead a decent life. The courses I attended gave me the skills to be an instructor, understanding the methods of learning and how to get the best out of individuals, as we all have different methods of attaining and retaining information and skills. It taught me methods of rapid assessment, how to make decisions quickly and of course good leadership traits that many never put into practice.

All of the above gave me a fantastic basis for later life. But the best and most critical lessons I learnt were not from the military, but from the humanitarian sector.

I have what has been described as a rebellious streak, a personality that doesn't always accept the immediate picture and a very enquiring and questioning mind that was always frowned upon in the military. I had it at school, where conforming was not my best attribute. The military was the same; the higher I climbed in rank, the more pronounced it became.

I appeared to have finally found my niche. I was accepted for who I was and for the experience I could offer.

Following Darfur, I took the job of global safety and security adviser for a very large international humanitarian organisation. I was part of the emergencies team but was also responsible for the upkeep and management of safety and security for over 60 global programmes in as many countries.

It was while attending a meeting I had been invited to attend, that the penny finally dropped as to my actual self-worth.

Let me make it clear. I had no real education to speak of. University was totally out of my academic reach. I went to a comprehensive school and hated every minute of it. I joined the army as a last resort to keep me out of trouble. I was (and still am to a large extent) a nobody.

Sitting in the organisational HQ offices in London, researching a country I had prioritised for a visit, I was called by the emergencies director and told I needed to be available for a senior team meeting in 15 minutes. I shrugged my shoulders, said okay and asked who else would be in attendance.

I was told that many country directors had flown in for a series of training sessions over a span of a week. They would be attending, along with all the top-level management from the UK, including the CEO and board members.

This would be my very first formal meeting with all the bigwigs from the UK, and some from the US too.

I must admit, I had always felt slightly inferior to such people. They were all university educated, with master's degrees falling out of their ears, and when they spoke, they used really big words; some I knew, some I didn't.

The meeting was called, and I was told that I would be an observer. I simply had to listen to what was discussed, listen to how issues were debated and see who was pulling the strings. Good advice, I thought, would hopefully give me some experience to fall back on once I had my feet firmly under the table.

As the meeting wore on, I found myself doodling in my notepad instead of taking notes.

The conversation then turned to the planning of various intervention programmes and some potentially new interventions. This was interesting.

Several people very excitedly read through some of the baseline plans they had put together.

I returned to note taking.

There was an excitement around the room as they discussed the implementation of the programmes and what would be needed in terms of resources and funding. This went on for over an hour. While deeply intrigued, I was puzzled too. Something very important was missing, or was being grossly overlooked, but no one even got close to addressing it. I was in a bind. Should I speak up and say my bit or should I wait until it was all over and approach the emergencies director with my issue?

Just as that thought went through in my mind, I heard the emergencies director mention my name. "Phil, do you have anything to add to the planning? Phil is our first full-time, dedicated global safety and security adviser. Would you like to add to the meeting?"

At first, I thought this was a question that I was supposed to decline from answering. After all, I was just supposed to be observing. But I took the question and responded. "Ladies and gents, I have listened with great interest to the plans that have been put forward today, and I hope they come to fruition as you are envisaging."

The room of nearly 40 people was focused on me and what I had to say. I continued. "In all of the planning I have heard regarding the different sectoral needs and requirements and the aims and outcomes that will surely be produced and gratefully received by all the targeted beneficiary groups, there is, in my opinion, one very important area that has not been included in either the budgetary requirement or the investment of your teams."

I had to make this good, as I had everyone's attention.

"Two out of three of your proposals are for interventions in areas of conflict, yet not once have I heard of any planning for the safety of the field teams or the threat and risks they are taking to deliver the programmes you have outlined. Your financial planning leaves no room for safety and security management, and no one has mentioned the need for a security manager within the staffing framework."

I looked across the crowded room and not one person met my gaze, except the director of emergencies. I noticed that many of the gathered intelligentsia were fervently writing, making notes and muttering to each other. I continued. "As planners and employers, we all have a duty of care to give our field teams the best possible support we can offer. We need to include HEAT[21] packages to prepare them for the environment they will be working in. We need a safety and security manager as an independent role, not as a second hat for a logistics or administrative role. We need the right equipment, such as first aid trauma kits, with staff training so that all staff members know how to use them. We need radios too, plus the training to go with them. Ask yourself these simple questions: can you afford to deploy without this training and associated equipment? Will you wait until there is a fatality before acting? Prevention, in every case, is better than cure. If there are any questions, I will be happy to take them over the next few days, as I am sure there needs to be some more collective discussion on this subject. I am happy to advise if needed. Thank you."

I looked at the emergencies director, who was beaming from ear to ear. I now realised why he had invited me to the meeting.

As soon as the meeting concluded, I was almost swamped with people asking for advice, information about HEAT providers and if

---

[21] HEAT: Hostile Environment Awareness Training.

I could conduct some pre-training and first aid training. My little addition to the meeting had, in my opinion, been a success. No longer was the focus solely on delivery of programme; it now went hand in hand with the safety of the teams delivering it.

Although this, for some, was a light-bulb moment, I was made aware that some didn't see it that way. Some still thought that it was over-indulgent to have a dedicated security manager for a country programme. This became all the more evident as I moved from INGO to INGO.

Darfur taught me so much. At times it exposed my shortfalls, but at the same time it taught me many lessons that I quickly learnt from. Being in head office was also a pretty steep learning experience. I gained a deeper understanding of the internal politics; I learnt that whatever you did and whatever decisions were made there will always be some form of opposition; not the type you could talk to and reach efficient compromises with, but the type who whispered behind your back and took pleasure in discrediting you when the opportunity arose. As in any large organisation or business, petty jealousies existed. In this case, it was largely by those who were desk bound and hardly ever by those who had worked in the field. Such is life.

Working in HQ had its benefits: the travel opportunities were many and the work itself was interesting. But the biggest downfall and my greatest dislike was the internal office politics. The sniping from the developmental programme desks about the emergencies section was a 'tortoise-and-hare' scenario, with the emergencies team being the hare (but not quite so side-tracked, and largely faster at responding and more decisive) and the developmental programmes which, while very important and much needed, were perceived to be very slow and ponderous with much in the way of resistance to change, being the tortoise.

On several occasions, I was tasked with forming part of a programme audit team. I travelled to whichever country programme was being audited and assessed their safety and security protocols for effectiveness and organisational compliance.

It was amazing to find that almost every programme, sometimes projects within the same programme, had a different methodology on how to react to a given emergency. Some even had completely different ideas on what the threat they faced actually was!

Compliance and general understanding of the safety and security plan wasn't fully understood by the country programme staff. This was due partly to having no dedicated management for it and lacking any training based on their individual country and the threats it presented. Almost everything was a generic, non-specific approach; both vague and ineffective.

I had already started to modify the organisational directives to make them less voluminous. The generic organisational document had been co-written by several people, and various consultants had added to it, so it was far from a cohesive read. Instead, it was convoluted, contradictory in places and was just not read and understood by those who needed it most.

According to the generic, country programmes were supposed to write their own location-specific safety and security guidelines. Some did and some just didn't bother. Excuses ranged from a lack time or not really needing anything more than the generic, as all staff were experienced, to one shocking admission by the senior manager of a very busy programme based in a hostile location who said, "If things go wrong, I will tell everyone what to do. I don't need directives for that."

He found himself lost for words when I put it to him that he could be out of the country or perhaps even kidnapped or killed; then he wouldn't be in a position to give verbal direction to his staff.

It was going to be a long road to getting everyone on the same songsheet. I covered the immediate gaps by writing some simplified template documents that allowed the programmes to insert their own location-specific information yet gave a clear direction on how to deal with various situations. With specific scenarios in one country programme, I made document templates for the following:

- How to approach a road checkpoint by day and by night
- Actions to be taken on hearing gunfire or explosions
- How to communicate an incident report
- Safe travel-planning requirements
- Actions to be taken and preparation for hibernation after a no-movement order
- Emergency evacuation planning:

  o as a lone INGO
  o in partnership with other INGOs
  o as part of a UN-directed evacuation
  o under military control

There were other document templates that related to location-specific threats. The checkpoint issue could, particularly at night, be a lethal situation if you judged it incorrectly. Revving your engine too aggressively might be enough to spook those manning the checkpoint into opening fire, as they would likely perceive your action as threatening (they may well have been attacked more than once while at their check point). Approaching too fast could create the same perception.

Identifying the intent is always critical. Is the checkpoint a formal one, manned by a legitimate police or military forces? What are their general intentions and attitudes to foreigners? Or is it a random checkpoint, set up to hijack vehicles, steal valuable items or kidnap?

Merely approaching a simple checkpoint can, in hostile locations, become a real danger if you are misunderstood. Knowing at what speed to approach, which lights to have on and what your demeanour should be are all critical to the safety of the travelling team.

I learnt, to my detriment, just how unforgiving approaching a checkpoint at night can be.

During my time in Darfur, it was generally accepted that each organisation would host a function (more like a get together); an informal relaxing way to swap stories of the week and catch up with people who you may not have spoken to for a while. It also served, more importantly, as a tension reliever. The situation in Darfur was at times very intense, and the need to relax (with the absence of a pub, club or bar) in an alcohol-free society was paramount.

I announced at one of the security meetings that I, with my organisation, would host the coming week's party. My proviso was that men were to dress as women and women as men. I said that written invitations would be sent (no invitation, no admittance), knowing full well that there would be an invitation for every organisation rather for individuals; just so we didn't miss anyone out by mistake.

I took the time late one night to design the invitations and print them off ready to hand out at the next security meeting.

I went to our international female staff to borrow a long skirt, a blouse, a bra and a headscarf. I was offered shoes, but decided my boots were good enough.

I tried on my outfit in what I thought was the privacy of my accommodation compound, only crossing the open courtyard to go the loo. As I did, I heard shrieks of laughter from the two Sudanese cleaners and the cook. Embarrassed? You bet I was.

The ladies had me parading up and down the courtyard with oranges in my borrowed bra and my headscarf and skirt blowing in the breeze. They thought it was hilarious.

At the security meeting in El Fashir, I handed out the invites to a very grateful crowd and gave one to my UN friend. I sensed a bit of unease as he took it from me.

After the meeting, I was invited to join my UN friend in his office. On entering, I was asked to close the door. It was a bit like being summoned to the headmaster's office.

I asked if there was a problem and he said "No, but..." He then asked if I thought it was culturally correct for men to dress as women in an Islamic-Muslim country. I laughed, then asked him if being a Muslim meant you had no sense of humour. I went on to explain how our cleaners and cook had reacted. He looked somewhat embarrassed, so I told him he was invited, of course, but the dressing up wasn't compulsory. So whether he did or didn't, he and his team were still very welcome. With that said, I left.

The night of the get-together came, and I welcomed everyone at the door to our compound and showed them to the drinks and food. We had some very low music playing, and the atmosphere was very relaxed.

People arrived by vehicle, parked outside and walked in. As the UN vehicles arrived, I stood by the entrance to greet them. My UN friend led his contingent of UN staff to the slightly open door and politely knocked. I opened the door and stood there in my best skirt, with an immaculate headscarf on my head and the best pair of oranges in El Fashir trying to burst out of a 'fit-where-it-touches' blouse. I greeted my guest with an immaculately well-practised line. In my deepest (and badly attempted) cockney wide-boy accent, I said, "Welcome, matey. By night you can call me Wendy. Come in an' enjoy the party."

His face was a picture. He was shocked. He said nothing, turned around, got back into his vehicle and drove away. His team stayed and had a great night. Almost everyone turned up dressed as per the invitation. A six-foot-plus muscular, bald-headed guy turned up in a dress borrowed from the only female in his organisation, who was just about five feet tall; what would have been a full-length dress on her was nothing short of a mini-skirt on him.

One of our team, the vehicle manager, turned up at the door with two very large watermelons, one under each arm. I invited him in and thanked him for bringing such a wonderful and refreshing gift. He laughed and asked where the orange juice container was. I pointed to the five-gallon, blue, plastic, chilled container on the table. He smiled at me and told me to follow him.

We had two orange juice containers on the table and some cans of cola and lemonade, as we were alcohol free in Sudan. He placed both watermelons down on the table and removed the lid from one of the containers. He then carefully, with the aid of the tip if a butter knife, removed a cut-out square of watermelon, which had been acting as a plug. He then tipped the contents of the inside of the watermelon into the orange juice. I remember thinking that the watermelons back home didn't have as much juice as these did. Each of the melons had their contents emptied into the orange juice until the container was full to the brim.

It was home-distilled alcohol, smuggled across the town from his home, with the knowledge that if he was stopped and the alcohol discovered, it would be prison, not a party, for him.

With this new source of refreshment, I made a subtle announcement, telling the gathering that they could leave their vehicles at our compound for the night and I would drive everyone home.

There was a curfew of 9pm in El Fashir. No vehicle movement unless you had a special permit, and that, we most certainly didn't have. So at 8.15pm, I started to ferry everyone home. The town was only small, so each journey with a full Land Rover only took a few minutes. My last drop-off was a team whose accommodation was on the opposite side of town, past the airport which had two checkpoint barriers, one at either end of the airport road.

I passed through without incident to drop everyone off. One young lady, a bit the worse for having too much melon juice, took longer than usual to thank me for the night's entertainment and thought I looked 'fetching' in my skirt and blouse (quite what I was fetching was beyond me), but after helping her out of the vehicle and setting off back, I knew time was getting tight.

It was dark. I approached the airport road, hoping the barrier would still be open. It wasn't. As I approached, I switched from headlights to sidelights, turned on my interior light to show I was alone and was not a threat and took my foot off the accelerator, quietly slowing to a halt at the barrier.

A Sudanese soldier came to my window. He asked for ID which I gave to him. He looked at it, looked at me and then looked at my ID again. "Get out of the vehicle!" he demanded. I did, but left the engine running. He called over the rest of his section who all formed a circle around me. It was hot. I was sweating and thinking about what the punishment would be for breaking curfew, even for the few minutes that I was late.

We stood in silence for a few seconds; one rifle was pointed at me and the others were just casually held. The soldier who'd ordered me out of the vehicle said something I didn't understand to his comrades and they all fell about laughing, pointing at me and having hysterics. It was then that I realised I was still dressed in a skirt, blouse and head scarf. One of my oranges had gone south. I must have looked a real sight.

I was allowed to proceed, but on reaching the barrier at the other end of the airport road, I went through the same process again.

The first group had obviously radioed ahead to the second checkpoint, telling them to stop and check out the crazy British man dressed as a woman.

Luckily, the humour of the situation diverted from the fact that I was out after curfew. "Worth a laugh," I thought. "I bet I would have done the same if I was manning a checkpoint and came across a bad drag queen."

It pays to know your vehicle checkpoint drills though!

Nights like this were much needed and most welcome. They were a stress reliever and gave a weekly opportunity for an informal chat, almost a medicinal counselling session. We were able to discuss how the incidents of the week had affected us as individuals and we could speak to others, who were not from the same organisation, producing refreshing and open conversations without getting tied up with organisational politics. Some good friendships were formed. Trying to keep these functions upbeat was sometimes hard, but generally we all managed to achieve it; for our own sanity, I suppose.

*

Chapter 8:

The End Game – The Road to Ebola and Beyond

Working as an employee to some of the world's largest humanitarian charities can be extremely rewarding. At times it can be dangerous, and for many reasons it can be frustrating too.

As an employee, you are tied to organisational politics. If you speak out of line, there is a consequence. You are, in effect, like any other employee in any other walk of life: conscious about your job safety and tending to be careful or mindful, sometimes unrealistically so, when you speak out.

There are many different policies, including the whistle-blower policy which is designed, in theory, to protect those who wish to speak out against bad practice or any other issues that need addressing but can be too sensitive to report openly. There have been cases of whistle-blowing that have not served their purpose at all, with the whistle-blower often being ridiculed or alienated by those who are involved.

As a consultant, it is far easier to operate totally openly and to highlight issues that some employees know about and disagree with but won't report, even if this may lead to severe consequences.

When, as a consultant, I am hired by any organisation, I am very clear and I push the organisation hard to define my parameters.

I also include, as an offer, to help and assist the management teams on the ground if I see gaps in knowledge or know-how and I agree to work hand in hand with individuals for the betterment of team and programme safety.

As an example, one organisation working on a programme in Syria but based in Turkey, had contracted me to complete a very defined piece of work. A few days into my contract, their safety and security manager resigned. He claimed that the organisation didn't listen to his advice and they often ignored protocols.

I was asked at very short notice if I would step in and fill the post until they got a replacement. I agreed. I immersed myself in the details of the interventions and took time to talk with all staff about what they do, how they do it and it could be done better. This for me was standard process, as it helps to understand what is happening and why, while flagging up areas for concern, which can then be addressed.

After talking to the field teams across education, livelihoods, health and child protection, I very quickly understood the reason that the last guy had resigned.

It was claimed that he was very abrupt. Many of the teams said that they had never been asked about what they do and how they do it from a safety and security aspect, so they had developed their own sectoral procedures that were inconsistent and lacked any support outside of their immediate field-team structure. So health had a different emergency procedure than livelihoods, and child protection and the other sectors were different again.

The generic organisational directives and protocols were not understood; several admitted that they had no idea they actually existed.

The plan of action was to bring everyone together to train then mentor them, in order to ensure that there was a workable plan with clear aims and a level of flexibility, allowing critical and timely decisions to be made by those on the ground in any emergency case.

All of the above was documented; a report on my findings, and of course the solutions, were clearly stated. This was all be very factual with no hidden agenda. I was not concerned about my position because I was a consultant: self-employed and hired to do a well-defined job. I offered additional help if it was accepted, then I reported my findings, warts and all.

In my early days, I found that there was a strong inertia to change. Some organisations were slow, sometimes dangerously slow, to react and adapt. Some were better than others while some were just poor.

I was very fortunate to have gained work often because of my reputation or through recommendation, generally by word of mouth, by organisations I had worked for. (Often, in multi-organisational meetings, I agreed to assist some organisations who had no safety and security management of their own but obviously needed help. This was not charged).

The sphere of INGO interventions is a close one. It is very often that the same organisations deploy to the same emergency locations, often with a sprinkling of the people you met at the last disaster. Friendships are quickly forged, but with such a huge turnover of people, can be just as quickly forgotten.

Having good relationships across the different organisations is critical, and those on the ground, at the sharp end so to speak, value the inter-organisational partnerships and information sharing much more than the senior leaderships at the country or organisational HQ level. As mentioned earlier in this book, rivalry in the sector can be fierce and there have been times that information sharing between organisations was not as popular (with some) as it should or could have been. Towards the end of my time in this sector, I noticed an improvement, but generally it was quite slow to change.

The move from one disaster to another can be swift and unexpected. Enter stage left: the Asian tsunami.

My time in Sudan and Darfur was cut short, as I was redirected from my R&R[22] which had been negotiated prior to my contract to be over the holiday period.

It was Christmas 2004. I was still full from my Christmas dinner and relaxing with a beer in hand, thinking about the contrast between Darfur, which I had left just a few days before, and the situation at home in the UK.

I felt pangs of guilt. I had a house, a family, safety and security and more than enough food to eat. Coming home from some locations where hardship was the everyday way of life, where people were constantly on the edge of starvation, living in extremely basic dwellings with maybe just one or two items of clothing, was hard for me to reconcile. I had often heard the clichés from seasoned humanitarian workers who were dismayed by the sight of children screaming and crying in supermarkets because they wanted sweets or toys, and throwing tantrums if they didn't get them. I think of the privileged lives my own kids have: their own bedrooms and all the comforts and gadgets that kids in the UK have. They've had a good education in a well-equipped school. (Regardless of how much the teachers and headmasters bleat on about not

---

[22] Rest and recuperation. This is a set period of time allocated within your contract as time off. It is pro-rata, so the longer the length of your contract, the more R&R days you accumulated. Some organisations allow you to travel back to your home country, while others insist that it be taken in a named safe country or part of a country, where you are away from work. R&R is critical, as those who take it work extremely long hours and often in very stressful environments. It doesn't stop burn-out but does help towards easing the stress.

having enough facilities. They want to go and teach in some of the locations I have been to. That would be a real reality check.) They were fortunate.

At times, I wanted to scream and shout at what I saw as over-indulgent, when people elsewhere were starving and dying because of the lack of basic healthcare and the scarcity of food.

It would have been wrong to rant for those reasons. I gave my kids the life and material things they have. The screaming kids in Tesco are the product of their parents; they know no different.

I do, however, educate my kids on the world around them, and through comparison they clearly see how privileged they are and how under-privileged some people in far-flung (or not so far-flung) places can be. I can't blame regular working people and their kids in the UK for the hardships in other countries but it is something that's always on my mind. It's a dreadful comparison, but one I struggle to shake off.

At around 1am GMT (8am local time) on the 26 December 2004, a huge megathrust earthquake struck just off the coast of Sumatra, Indonesia. The earthquake produced a massive tsunami which killed over 2,500 people across 13 countries. An estimated five million people lost their homes and livelihoods. The worst place hit was Banda Aceh on the northern tip of Sumatra.

I woke up on boxing day to the horrific news. I rang the director of emergencies of the organisation I was working for.

"Hi, Phil. Glad you called. I was just about to call you. Pack your bags. You are not going back to Darfur; we are sending you out to Indonesia. I will talk to you at the airport, but briefly, you will fly to Jakarta, then take an internal flight into Aceh. It may be a UN flight, but we are still trying to book our emergency teams on now, so be ready to go on a phone call. Oh, and by the way, Merry Christmas."

A day later, I was in the air and on my way.

It took almost another 18 hours of traveling to get to Banda Aceh, and as we flew in, the scenes of devastation were instantly apparent from the air.

During the days immediately following the disaster, bodies were still being recovered from the rubble and from the debris-laden storm drains all around Banda Aceh.

Large fishing boats were found in the middle of residential streets. Against one bridge over an inland tributary, about ten or more boats of all descriptions had been crushed, stacked and broken on top of each other. It was obvious that there were still bodies either inside some of the boats or trapped under them, as the smell of death, a smell that is unmistakable, lingered in the humid air of what was becoming yet another hot day.

One of the reasons I had been sent to Aceh was to manage the safety and security of all the new emergency teams that the organisation had sent into the disaster area. Aceh had been a region in conflict with a group whose name translated means 'Free Ache Movement' but are known by the acronym GAM (Gerakan Aceh Merdeka).

Since 1975/6, this group had been fighting for the independence of Aceh from Indonesia. Banda Aceh, being the regional capital, had much historic conflict and was seen as being different to the rest of Indonesia, a conservative community. It was the only region in Indonesia to be practising Sharia law as its main judiciary law.

The rapid onset of this disaster in Aceh was for me a time for new thinking and a much-needed rapid change of approach. There had been an organisational developmental programme running there for many years. It was routine and was classed by some as a sleepy backwater in a prime Indian Ocean setting with some conflict in areas, but it never really hampered the programme activity too much or in prolonged stages.

The tsunami changed all of that in a blink of an eye.

GAM rebels, who sometimes hid away in the dense tree-covered mountains, usually relied on sympathetic villagers to provide food and sometimes shelter, but such was the impact of the disaster that the food, for a short time, became limited. Whole fish beds along the coast had been uprooted and destroyed. Fishing boats, too, had been badly damaged or completely destroyed. Swaths of land where crops grew had been polluted by sea water, with the yields totally destroyed as the salt in the water rendered the soil infertile.

This, in the short term, brought GAM down into more villages, making them more mobile, and so more easily tracked by the government forces. The TNI-AD (Indonesian army) was a well-equipped and much-feared force. They were aggressive and lethal. Due to previous agreements and ceasefires, there was, prior to the tsunami, a cap on how many Indonesian forces would be in Aceh at any one time.

The Indonesian government, during the disaster and under a homeland military aid to the civil community-type response, poured more troops into Aceh to help its citizens to cope and to help with the clean-up operation that was badly needed. This was true and those tasks were undertaken, but other things were happening too.

I began logging the locations of large military groups on a map. I debriefed the teams each night and asked if they had come across any military formations that were not in the disaster zones.

Once plotted on a map, it appeared to me, with my military, strategic mind, that there was a lot of pre-positioning, particularly around the mountain regions where it was known that GAM rebels frequented. Was this the real reason for such a massive influx of troops?

The Indonesian government, via its police force in Aceh, kept a keen eye on any foreign organisations. Aceh was not a place that many tourists visited, largely due to the ongoing conflict, but the government wanted to keep Aceh under control.

During the response to the tsunami, communications equipment was strictly controlled. No HF radios and no satellite phones were allowed. All information and communication was tightly controlled; that was until the Tsunami hit.

Suddenly, with the international response, the UN arrived with all its HF radios, and various organisations under the UN umbrella did exactly the same.

It was critically important that INGOs could communicate with one another and that teams could be tracked when venturing out to more remote areas.

I had made an urgent request to HQ in London to procure radios and to get them out to us ASAP. Someone in the organisation's partner HQ in the US countered the request, stating it was unlawful to have radios in Aceh. This person had been the head of mission to Aceh some years before and, in my opinion, was way out of touch. Many organisations had brought in and were using their radio kits, applying retrospectively for permission from the government. I didn't, at the time, know of anyone who had been refused, but this very senior person was insisting that we shouldn't be bringing in, let alone using, HF radios, as we would be seen in a bad light by the government.

What he'd failed (and glaringly so) to understand was that all the previous rules had changed, almost overnight, with the organisation struggling to cope with timely information and the teams on the ground struggling with a very poor and weak mobile phone network which was far from having region-wide coverage. That is a prime example of failing to understand rapid change and adapting to it.

Within all the death and destruction in Aceh, I witnessed a very touching moment. The organisation I was working for had set up a family repatriation programme. Many families had become separated during the initial moments of the disaster. Many believed that all family members, aside for themselves, had been killed.

Through a series of verification stages, the hope was to find close family members, or even extended family members, and connect them again.

I had just returned from a day in the field when I noticed a lot of activity around the grassy area in front of the office. I noticed a little girl holding the hand of one of our national child protection team members. (Through the repatriation programme, some children who were found frightened and alone were cared for by various groups and organisations in the hope that some relatives would be found.) They walked into the building, followed by several other team members. A few moments later, I saw another member of our child protection team with what I assumed to be another member of our national staff who I had not yet met enter the garden at the office. The pair stopped and chatted casually in front of a large window.

Moments later, the little girl, still holding the hand of our team member, emerged from the building. She got very excited and was pulling to get away from her chaperone. She girl shouted, *"Ayah"* (daddy or father), as she broke away and ran crying towards the man chatting in the front garden of the office.

The man looked up and ran to the child; it was his daughter. Both had believed the other had died as the wave violently swept through their house. They met and hugged, the father swinging his daughter around and kissing her head. Both cried uncontrollably.

Everyone watched what was the first successful organisational repatriation, clapping and cheering at the newly reacquainted pair. It was an amazing sight. Both had thought they had lost everyone and had believed each other to be dead. The relief and joy must have been overwhelming. I had a lump in my throat. I must have got something in my eye too, as they watered a little; I think it was dust?

The issue with radios in Aceh was never resolved during my time there. Many other organisations did fit radios and were granted licences, with some licenced under the UN, but the organisation I worked for had no long-distance communication other than mobile (cell) phones; all because one very senior director refused to budge on a decision based on historic facts.

I stayed on in Indonesia for a while, rewriting emergency protocols and creating travel-tracking plans. These included the introduction of disciplined booking in and out of field teams, which would give us the best possible understanding of where our field teams were located and provide an expected time of return to the office. We had limited call-in facilities, but I produced a mobile phone 'dead spot' map based around our fieldworking locations and the routes normally travelled, getting teams to report when entering a 'dead spot' and calling again when the exited it. Not perfect but it worked.

There was a similar issue many years later in Myanmar or Burma. I was employed to assist with the safety aspect of working in a cyclone disaster. Cyclone Nargis brought a tougher type of government control, and communication equipment was controlled to a massive degree. At one stage we had to hire regular office phones (the old numbered type with a dial) and take them with us on our travels, hoping to find a plug-in point in one of our field offices. The phone was the commodity, not the use of the landline it connected to. The phones were extraordinarily expensive too.

As most of the disaster was centred around the more remote Irrawaddy delta region, which is based around water inlets, much of the travel was by boat. So apart from trying to waterproof a 1970s-type office phone, I also had to teach watermanship to the new emergency teams who were arriving every day.

It was also a huge job to train many national staff, who were all born and bred in the big city of Yangon (Rangoon) and couldn't swim, how to stay calm and have confidence in their life jackets if they fell into the water. The aims were achieved, as we didn't lose anyone to drowning during the response.

It still amazes me now that the behind-the-scenes issues of preparedness and training are seldom known by the general public. All that's advertised in the media are the programme delivery images, the starving children eating nutritious, specially prepared foods or the doctors and nurses attending to the sick and dying, which is an ongoing traumatic situation in itself. The risk of being in harm's way in many locations and being subjected to the high chance of kidnap and torture (being killed in horrific ways, such as beheading, being dowsed in petrol and set on fire or being shot or blown up) are not portrayed. These risks are, in many countries, realistic ones that humanitarian workers face when applying their skills to help people. Those who volunteer to help people they have never met understand the risks, but they still go. It is this that should be recognised alongside the good that the programme delivery achieves.

But, alas, many humanitarian workers are very modest. They don't seek the limelight; they don't shout about their achievements. To most of them, it is simply a job. I know from my own experience that it is much more than that, and the demands are at times equal to, sometimes even exceeding, those of the military, police, ambulance service, hospital workers and fire fighters here in the UK. But do they get recognition for it? Mostly not. Should they? You bet they should.

On my travels, I have come across several contrasting attitudes and perceptions of the environments in which humanitarians work; I have seen the blasé, the over-confident, the ignorant and those who openly dismiss the threats and risks. Complacency is a big issue, and trying to re-set people's thinking once they become desensitised to the threat and risk is very hard work.

When working in Nigeria, I ran a safety and security awareness course and a field first-aid course. This was given to a UK-based organisation who were educators. They were teachers of varying experience, very well educated and intelligent (or so I thought), who would be running educational programmes in the northern part of the country where religious conflicts had been evident for a long time.[23]

On the course, we had both national and international staff, which was a good mix because listening to the local staff speak about their experiences gave a genuine ground-level feel. The international staff, mostly from the UK, were, I found, quite set in their ways. Two of the UK teachers were in the same hotel that I was booked into, and on the first evening I sat with them in the bar.

---

[23] Violence in northern Nigeria has flared up periodically over the last 30 years, mainly in the form of urban riots. It has pitted Muslims against Christians and has seen confrontations between different Islamic sects. Although there have been some successes in conflict management in the last decade, the 2009 and 2010 troubles in Bauchi, Borno and Yobe states, involving the radical Boko Haram sect, show that violence may still flare up at any moment.

One lady in particular, a very senior member of their organisation (let's call her Sarah) was quite formidable. She was very self-assured and offered a confident and apparently knowledgeable response to every topic we discussed.

She later expressed an opinion that shocked me, not only the content of her statement but the confidence and belief in what she had said.

"Phil, this is the second training of this type I have attended here and I hope you are going to be more realistic than the last instructor we had."

I assured her that all my instruction and advice was based on first-hand experience, real time, and all my information about the situation was verifiable, so no problem there... I thought.

"You do understand," she continued, "that all this talk about Boko-Haram[24] is nonsense. They don't exist, so are not a threat. They are a figment of the media's imagination."

I was shocked. How could she think like this? Where was her evidence and reasoning? This set the climate for the training, which didn't go as well as I had hoped.

---

[24] Boko Haram, also known as the Islamic State in West Africa or Islamic State's West Africa Province (abbreviated as ISWA or ISWAP), is a jihadist militant organisation based in north-eastern Nigeria, but also active in Chad, Niger and northern Cameroon. The organisation was founded by Mohammed Yusuf in 2002. On the night of 14–15 April 2014, 276 mostly Christian female students were kidnapped from the secondary school in the town of Chibok in Borno State, Nigeria. Responsibility for the kidnappings was claimed by Boko Haram, an Islamist extremist terrorist organisation based in north-eastern Nigeria. Over the months that followed, 57 of the schoolgirls were rescued by the Nigerian army. Some have made appearances at international human rights conferences, where they have described their capture. Boko Haram militants have killed five hostages, including four aid workers who were abducted in north-eastern Nigeria.

Another typical comment was made during the training that also shocked me a little, but showed clearly just how complacent and desensitised people can become if they are subjected to a situation for long enough.

During one session, I asked the national staff what the situation was like in their home towns. One lady raised her hand to answer. She said, "In my town everything is calm. It is very peaceful. We have no worries. Sometimes, a bomb will go off and there is gunfire, but it never lasts long. It's okay."

"Woah!" I said. "Can I just recap what you just said? In the same sentence you said that everything is calm and peaceful, then you follow up with, 'Sometimes a bomb will go off and there is some gunfire '"

I looked at her, waiting for her to realise what she had just said.

She spoke again. "Only sometimes. Not every day. Maybe only once a week or every two weeks."

She seemed to be justifying her statement.

This situation was typical of many people. They become almost comfortable with violent situations. Because they happen regularly around them for a very long period of time, they become desensitised. This is a very important situation to understand.

We generally take information about any particular area from the locals who live there. If they are desensitised, as this lady clearly was, then the information given about the safety aspects of a town or village will not be accurate or reliable, as it is based on a level of understanding of what is normal or safe.

I found that, in that particular scenario and for that organisation, it was very difficult to get the aims of the training across. Sarah was manipulating the sessions. She was subtly intimidating the students and trying hard to talk down or even dismiss the genuine risks that existed in northern Nigeria at the time. She was almost trying to nullify our information in order to give confidence, a false and dangerous confidence, to her colleagues so that they wouldn't either resign or refuse to teach in the locations we were focusing on. Her denial, if not so serious, was almost laughable. She, in my opinion and from my observations, was a complete control freak and micromanager; if the information didn't come from her then it couldn't be correct or true.

I reported this attitude back to the consultancy company I was working through. I stated clearly that we (a team of two safety and security consultants) were having problems getting our message across, and we were unrealistically challenged at almost every session on issues that were absolute fact. Such was this lady's opposition to anything that posed a threat, that after one particular session, I left the building to make several telephone calls and send some emails to re-verify my information, which was correct. She caused so much uncertainty and confusion that it degraded the training significantly.

I have seen the good and the bad in terms of charitable organisations who offer help to communities in need in underdeveloped countries. One in particular that I was employed to run as a start-up not-for-profit organisation, was based upon educational support and was being developed by a very wealthy businessman. I was introduced to him in the UK, as he was looking for 'someone' with INGO experience to set up and run an organisation under his direction 'somewhere in Africa'.

I agreed to meet with this guy and listen to his ideas. His original idea was good; he wanted to partner international private schools with schools in remote locations in Africa. This would benefit from the support that a partnership or 'twinning' brought.

After attending an education conference in Ghana together, we decided that the far north of Ghana would be a good starting point. We would look at some schools in the remoter areas and select a few to partner with the more affluent schools in the UK and across Europe.

After visiting several schools, we decided to take on eight schools that were, what I considered, urgently in need of support.

I was assured that money would not be a problem when providing equipment and giving basic infrastructure support to make the 'twinning' process more attractive and viable for the schools who would hopefully support them as the project advanced.

The idea of not needing to drum up donors to fund the programme and to have a one-man direct line of management (largely I was in total control and just had to report to one person) sounded idyllic, so I accepted the job.

My aim was to establish an internet link from the remote schools in Bolgatanga[25] in the upper east region of Ghana. For each school, I had to purchase a portable generator, a BGAN satellite modem, computers, printers and a TV. The aim was to connect one teacher to another and the students in Bolga to students from their chosen twinned schools in Europe or the UK.

Eventually, the twinned school in Belgium, for instance, would conduct yearly fundraising events to buy educational materials or to help build additional classrooms for their twin in Bolga, making strides towards becoming a sustainable partnership outside of the organisation we had set up. The timeline between Ghana and

---

[25] Bolgatanga, colloquially known as Bolga, is a town and the capital of the Bolgatanga Municipal District and Upper East Region of Ghana, adjacent to the border with Burkina Faso.

Europe and the UK was at worst only ever one hour different, so a school day in Ghana was a school day in their partner school.

The benefits that would be received by the schools in Ghana were endless. Many of their teachers had very little or no training, so via skype, teacher-training sessions could be conducted. Also, children could swap their cultural differences with each other and learn about the wider world, see things they may never otherwise get to see.

Another aim was to eventually organise school visits. I had already engaged in renting suitable accommodation in Bolgatanga to house up to 20 students and teachers.

We purchased new sports equipment and sent books, pens and pencils and some school furniture, all to get set up.

I later found out that our wealthy businessman had only started this venture to better the projects his father had already set up and was running in Kenya. He wanted to outdo him; it was an expensive competition.

I found that over the months that followed he became disinterested in the programme and it was increasingly difficult to gain the funds from him that he had originally promised. I decided to try to find alternative sources of income to help sustain the schools project should he decide to completely pull the plug.

I engaged a local INGO who specialised in agriculture, subsistence farming[26] and how to expand crop yields in harsh climates.

---

[26] Subsistence farming is when a farmer grows and raises the right amount and a wide enough variety of food to feed themselves and their families. It's not about having any extra goods to sell. It's more of a survival or self-sufficiency technique; and a way to considerably lower one's expenses.

I spent over a week with this organisation, discussing how we could intervene in schools with agricultural programmes.

My idea was simple: one day a week, initially, would be given over to agricultural teaching. This would involve the preparation of a strip of land on or very close to the school's property, which, by the creation of composting heaps made by the children under the guidance of a member of the agriculture INGO, would produce fertile ground to grow basic staple crops.

The initial crops would go directly to the school to give the children something to eat during their school day. As the plots and yields expanded, there would hopefully be surplus to sell at the local market to bring a small income into the school for new seeds and then, hopefully, to pay for some school equipment.

The idea was simple and cost effective to set up. The purchase of basic tools for each school and some start-up seed packs was agreed for the first year, as was the finance to provide payment to the INGO for hiring one staff member per school for one day a week to assist with the agricultural teaching and training.

I had just set up all of the above when the wealthy businessman finally pulled the plug. He stated that some of his other businesses were in financial trouble and he could no longer afford to run his new charity.

While his other businesses were indeed in some trouble, it was obvious to me that the novelty of competing with his father had finally worn off, as it became clear that he had won the competition, whatever it was.

I had secured funding for the first year, but after that it was up to the international schools and The Agricultural INGO to find a pathway for themselves based on the foundations we had left behind.

The disinterest left a really bad taste in my mouth. Such a fantastic and promising project was abandoned due to a lack of interest. The single source of funding was a mistake from the outset. If it dried up at short notice, as it did, the programme would stutter to a halt. Another harsh lesson learnt.

I was privileged, or unlucky, depending on your viewpoint or political standing, to have been involved in some significant history-making situations during my time working in this sector.

I was in Libya during the fall of President Muammar Muhammad Abu Minyar al-Gaddafi, commonly known as Colonel Gaddafi, who was killed in October 2011.

I was contracted to supply the emergency security plans for a de-mining group based in Benghazi. They had de-mining programmes across the entire northern coastline of the country, from Benghazi in the east through to Tripoli and Zintan in the west. I was called in after they had an armed raid on their offices and were for a short time held at gunpoint. This was one of the first indicators that change for the worse was on its way. Sirt, the town where Gaddafi was finally captured and killed, was also a location identified for a de-mining programme.

It didn't take very long, once Gaddafi had fled, before the sinister grip of radical groups began to infiltrate the country in an attempt to fill the power vacuum that had been left. ISIS were crossing borders to join forces with those still loyal to the yet-to-be-found Colonel Gaddafi.

Huge battles erupted across the country. Britain and France had intervened to help the rebels against the government forces loyal to Gaddafi. The timely intervention almost stopped the government advance on the rebel stronghold in Benghazi and turned the tide of the coupe.

Travelling to and from the coastal towns of Benghazi, Ajdabiya, Misrata and Tripoli became high risk, not just because of radical fundamentalists, but because of the detritus of war strewn around the towns and cities. These included unexploded munitions, grenades, RPG rounds and mines; all surface laid and buried but not clearly marked.

I had a near miss while staying in a hotel in Tripoli. The hotel itself was damaged from recent fighting but was open for trade and was right on the coast, on the edge of the city centre. I was sleeping when, as we all do, I needed the toilet. I climbed out of bed, started the short journey across the room to my en-suite bathroom, listening to the sporadic gunfire across the city and some closer on the roads outside. I heard a loud bang just as I entered the bathroom. The bang was very quickly, almost instantaneously, followed by what sounded like two smaller bangs that, in my half-asleep state, sounded like they were in my room. Then came a softer noise, almost like a coin dropping on a tiled floor. I used the toilet and quickly went back to bed.

The next morning, I found the culprit of the 'bang' as I drew back the ill-fitting curtains. A 7.62mm bullet had been fired through my window, pierced through the UPVC frame, gone through the open toilet door and hit the wall; the 'coin' was the hard metallic core of the bullet falling to the ground as its kinetic energy was spent. I found it lying next to the toilet bowl. A lucky escape and a very close call. I still have the spent bullet now at home.

Ammunitions were everywhere. The rebels had stormed the military bases where ammunition stores and stockpiles existed. It was a free-for-all. We were called to a particular ammunition storage compound, one that had been bombed by the French. Much had exploded during the initial attack but many tons of munitions, including aircraft bombs, rockets of various types and sizes, anti-tank missiles and small-arms ammunition just sat in open warehouses, and it was a free-for-all as trucks just turned up, loaded up and drove away. The compound security was one man in trousers, sandals and a string vest. He sat on a chair at the entrance gate of the compound (which was pointless, as three of the four walls surrounding the compound had been blasted away) smoking a cigarette, not caring who came and went. It was total chaos.

It wasn't long before the situation in Syria provided the opportunity for my consultancy services to be employed again. The ISIS issues were starting to dominate the landscape in Syria. It was a complex mess there to be sure.

Initially, it was a straightforward rebellion. Following the 'Arab Spring' rebellions, the population peacefully demonstrated against the Bashar al-Assad government regime and were met with violent and deadly force. This led to the creation of a people's rebellion army, the Free Syrian Army or FSA.

This was initially a ragtag collection of people who were prepared to take up arms in an attempt to overthrow Bashar al-Assad and install a democratically elected government. The Syrian army was too strong in the early days for the FSA to have any real success against, but they did gain in strength and numbers. Western governments supported the FSA and supplied weapons and military advisers to train them. Most of the early FSA consisted of ordinary people, some of whom had never fired a weapon before. They were a selection of their society, bankers, lawyers, teachers, grocers, builders, largely the same people you might see on your high street.

With Al Qaeda fighting in Iraq and its transformation into ISIS, the newly appearing void in Syria gave them an important foothold and the start of what would become the caliphate, the base in Syria to expand from and to land-grab across borders to form their new homeland.

The FSA, some would say unwittingly, invited the extremists to join them by sending out a message to all Muslims to come and fight against the tyranny of Al Bashir and his government.

Foreign fighters flooded into Syria. Initially, they joined the FSA to fight the government forces but that was an uneasy relationship at best. Soon there were various factions splitting away from the FSA and looking to gain control for themselves. ISIS was taking over and battled against the FSA and the government to take land and control for their own caliphate. It was rumoured at one point during the war that ISIS, or at least one of its many offshoots, were being paid by the government to fight *for* them, not *against* them. It was hard to keep track of who was fighting who and why.

Many aid organisations had their offices in towns along the Turkey-Syrian border, and teams crossed at safe border crossings, initially on a regular basis. As the fighting intensified, the border crossings closed, only opening for a short window to allow those delivering humanitarian aid to cross into and get out of Syria.

I worked for several major international organisations during the Syria emergency.

One particular organisation was a medical INGO, offering medical support to the hospitals close to Aleppo. Hospitals were frequently attacked by the government forces if it was known that they were treating rebel fighters. Hospitals were usually safe havens, treating casualties regardless of who they were or where they come from. They were supposed to be 'safe areas', as described in the Geneva Convention, meaning that they should never be attacked by any side. It appears that the Geneva Convention did not get any level of application by either the government or the rebels and other fighting factions.

This particular organisation had recruited Syrian nationals, doctors, nurses and others, living in Turkey who were comfortable, to a point, with travelling into Syria and offering assistance to the hospitals. It came to a point where the organisation needed to send in some international specialists, such as surgeons, theatre nurses and other specialist clinicians, to offer a day's training to the hospital staff who had now turned their hospital into a large-scale emergency-treatment   hospital dealing with battlefield casualties, blast injuries and gunshot wounds.

I had to brief the teams and sort out the convoy of vehicles, as we were taking in hospital supplies that were much needed alongside the human support.

I had several Syrian nationals working with me, one of whom was able to get across the border and was very well connected with good people who could relay important information on clear routes and locations of any fighting and give a very good general picture of overall activity in the areas we would travel through to our destination.

Our convoy of three vehicles would travel within line of sight distance, meaning that on open roads we could keep a large distance between us and in towns and villages we would close up to ensure we didn't lose a vehicle, when turning for example. We used VHF handset radios between vehicles for communication and each vehicle had a satellite phone. We had to be very careful not to be seen using the radios, as it could have been misunderstood that we were either government military or one of the FSA or ISIS groups. Suspicion was driving a palpable fear, and anything that looked strange could invite trouble.

I had an earpiece in, which was connected to my satellite phone. (The mobile phone network in Syria was not functioning outside of major cities but you could still pick up the Turkish signal if you were not too far from the border or in an elevated position: for instance, on the top of a building.)

I was in contact with my Syrian national guy who kept me updated on any changes to the situation on the ground.

We arrived safely at the hospital and thanks to my friend's information managed to avoid any road checkpoints on the way.

We parked up and entered the hospital. We were met, as arranged by the hospital administration manager. The clinicians were shown to their work area and met the teams they would be working alongside for the day. Our logistician was shown the storeroom and given a couple of helpers to assist in unloading the much-needed medical supplies we had brought.

I was taken by the administration manager to look over the small hospital's layout and to give advice on their emergency evacuation procedures. I was also asked for any advice I could give for the treatment of chemical casualties and for a suggestion as to where to site an external chemical-casualty treatment room.

The Syrian government had recently been using barrel bombs, but loaded with chemicals, such as nerve agents, onto large residential areas. Apart from it being against the Geneva Convention to use or even hold chemical weapons, they had been used by Bashar al-Assad's government forces against his own people.

Luckily, I had some knowledge of chemical warfare from my military days; I had attended a nuclear, biological and chemical (NBC) warfare instructor's course, a unit NBC training officer's course and an NBC tri-service cell controller's course, which in the world of the military meant I was very well trained in all things NBC.

We looked externally and found a site that would afford shelter from the wind and weather. I talked him through how to set up an airlock entrance and a pressurised environment to triage casualties and briefed him on the equipment he would need. While much of the kit could be improvised, some of it they just didn't have, so it was a case of coping with what they did have.

Walking through the hospital, the administration manager told me of his ultimate fear. The hospital was very close to the front line of fighting on three separate fronts. He was worried that they may receive casualties from opposing sides at the same time. This could cause a battle at the hospital, which it was a realistic scenario.

The hospital had already been hit by rocket fire twice in the previous month, so the fighting was close. There were no lifts to be used in the hospital, so getting to the upper floor and to the basement was by stairs only. This caused a major dilemma concerning the evacuation of bed-ridden patients in a hurry. He confided that during the last rocket attack, all the nurses and staff just abandoned those on the upper floors while they ran to the basement.

My only suggestion was to try, as best as possible, to have all the bed-ridden cases on the ground floor or in the basement and the walking wounded on the upper floors. But knowing that the operating theatres were on the ground floor, they couldn't realistically change much around, particularly as more and more people were coming to the hospital each day; not only the wounded but the sick, the pregnant and the old and infirm. It truly was chaotic.

I started to look at emergency exit points that were away from the front entrance. I noticed that every external door was locked and a metal gates had been built over them for further protection but they were locked with large chains and very robust padlocks. I asked the reason for this. He simply said that it was to keep thieves, who wanted to steal medications in their possession, out.

The windows, too, had steel bars on them for the same reason. I asked who held the keys to the padlocks and how quickly the doors could be opened. He shrugged his shoulders and confessed he had no idea who had the keys or where they were.

I suggested that he either find them, and find them soon, or cut the chains off, as these would be the only method of escape if a gun battle started at the entrance. I also mentioned that in the event of a fire in the hospital, it would be extremely beneficial to be able to leave the building via the windows on the upper floors if the stairs weren't accessible; but with the doors locked and the windows barred, you would burn to death, as there was no way to escape.

I saw the light bulb switch on as the seriousness of what I was saying struck home. He really was between a rock and a hard place and he would, over the following days, have to find a workable solution to the issues he was confronted with.

I finally made my way to the rooftop. I had to stay low, as it was known that snipers often took potshots at anything moving on the roof. It was the only place where I could get a satellite signal. It also gave me a unique vantage point to view all the approaches to the hospital.

After a few minutes, I saw an approaching convoy of vehicles. The vehicle were 4x4s with machine guns mounted and lots of people hanging off the back and clinging to the sides. They were heading to the hospital. Who were they? I had no idea until they got very close and I could see the black flag that was associated with ISIS.

Using the hand-held radios that we had used in the cars and were now with each team in the hospital, I warned them of the approaching threat and told them all to assemble in the basement.

The vehicles were carrying several wounded fighters; some looked close to death. They were manhandled in through the entrance of the hospital. A team of doctors and nurses rushed to help and started working on the most serious cases on the floor in the entranceway.

There was much tension. Those who brought the injured were crying and shouting at the doctors to save their comrades.

Everyone was heavily armed. Just as it started to calm down, another convoy arrived. This time there was no flag. They were dressed, not in the predominantly black garb of the first group, but in a more westernised type of apparel, with some in a mismatched camouflage garb. This, I thought, was the FSA. SHIT!

I radioed the team and told them to stay in the basement and lie on the ground or get behind any hard items that may offer a little cover and hide them from view. I told the logistician to turn off any lights down there and to remove the bulbs, keeping it as dark as possible.

From my vantage point on the roof, I braced myself for a firefight. The administration manager's worst nightmare was about to unfold right below me.

The new arrivals finally arrived at the hospital gates. What I saw next was either a supreme act of bravery or an act of total stupidity. As the vehicles started to drive up the small driveway, I saw the administration manager running towards them, madly waving his hands and shouting. The vehicles stopped. A very heated conversation was now underway. I could clearly see that the vehicles, like the first arrivals, were carrying battle casualties.

Several times, the occupants pushed and shoved the administration manager and pointed their weapons at him. I thought he was going to be shot.

Miraculously, they got back in their vehicles, turned around and drove away. He had stopped their convoy just before the bend in the driveway to the main entrance; if they had gone any further, they would have seen the ISIS vehicles and flags and a battle would have most certainly ensued.

Every person in that hospital, me included, owed their life to the mad but immensely brave administration manager.

I quickly ran down from the rooftop to our assembled team in the basement. I gathered them and told them to be ready to move on my call.

I took our three drivers, all Syrian nationals, and got them to bring our vehicles around to the front entrance. The administration manager had managed to take all the other fighters still in the hospital to a rear room, on the pretext of getting some food, water and rest.

I stood in a recess in the foyer, just out of sight, waiting for the administration manager to come back and give me the thumbs-up to move.

Within moments, our team was rushing up the stairs and calmly, but with a purpose, heading out to the waiting vehicles. I conducted a headcount as they passed me, to ensure we left no one behind in the confusion. The last person up the stairs was a nurse, a semi-retired lady from Sussex. She was a senior theatre nurse and very dedicated to her job. As she came to the top of the stairs, I noticed she wasn't as eager to leave as the others. She stopped and said, "I can't leave. These people need me here. I can help. It's my job to help save lives. I am not leaving."

I couldn't believe what I was hearing. Not leaving? I had no time for this.

"You are leaving. You either walk out that door or I will drag you to the vehicles, even if I have to knock you out first to do so. NOW MOVE!"

I took her by her arm and force-marched her to the waiting vehicles. Once we were all in, we sped off, away from the hospital and back towards the Turkish border.

Situations such as this can often occur in high-pressure, high-stake situations. The desire to do more and go beyond what is realistically safe (thinking that if you do more, you will save more lives) is a strong compulsion but you really need to know when to stay and when to go. If she would have stayed, she would most likely have been identified as being English and possibly kidnapped then killed. By leaving, she lived to help another day. It took several days for her to acknowledge the reality of her emotional outburst but she then came to me and apologised for potentially putting all of us in further danger. She knew she had been wrong but emotions are powerful and can override decisions you know deep down are right.

There were several more instances in my career when I faced such difficulties. I have not related them in this book; to do so would make it rival *War and Peace*, and that's a hell of a long book. They ranged from being forcibly detained in Somaliland and going through a mock execution, (only to be set free with our team 72 hours later) to conducting further safety assessments in locations where organisations had previously worked until it got too dangerous to visiting existing programmes to assess their preparedness and their compliance to strict safety and security guidelines.

My road ended not in a conflict zone but in a deadly epidemic in Africa.

I was at home with my family, casually flicking through the various news channels, when a headline appeared with a tally of deaths caused by Ebola in West Africa. The very next day, I received a phone call from a leading humanitarian organisation who wanted to hire me to look after the safety and security of a new treatment facility that they were about to jointly build, equip and run alongside the British Army. It would provide field medical care and be the main manpower, via the Royal Engineers, to build the site. Doctors and nurses alongside NHS volunteers and INGO staff were to coordinate and run the centre.

A few days later, after a rigorous medical and general health check, I was on a plane bound for Freetown, Sierra Leone.

My initial brief was simple: to oversee the safety aspect (non-medical) and to ensure that the chance of cross-contamination from dirty to clean areas was reduced and was clearly marked and observed. I was also to establish the protocols of safe movement in a highly contagious area within the treatment centre. I was to liaise with the private company that had been contracted to provide perimeter security and main gate-controlled access.

My other task was to assist the country director with his existing programmes across the country. Most locations were very remote, and travel was nearly always on jungle tracks. Every journey had to be well prepared and well briefed.

There was a huge influx of NHS staff along with the medical teams employed by the organisation. I was to brief them on arrival and give them an insight into the country and what to be aware of. I was also to give them an insight into the new treatment centre that was being built and the safeguards that were in place to keep everyone in good health.

At times, it was like herding cats. Many of the NHS staff didn't like the formality of what they were doing. They did a great job but their attitude was at times was extremely poor. Many failed to abide by the protocols that had been agreed, always thinking they knew better. There was a strict 'no handshake, no contact' rule. Many of the staff, particularly the nurses, ignored this ruling. At the Ebola treatment centre (ETC), there was a strict rule regarding transiting between clean and dirty areas. There was also a system for changing out of dirty 'scrubs' into clean 'scrubs' when leaving the infected patient area. I was visiting the centre when I saw a male nurse in his everyday clothes walking through the clean area towards the infected patient area. I shouted for him to stop. He replied that he was a nurse and it was okay for him to be there. I told him to come out the way he had come in, immediately. He told me he would only be a moment as he was looking for his friend Jesus. I told him that if he didn't come out right then, he would be meeting Jesus sooner than he expected.

PPE was also something I assisted with. It was just like the NBC suits in the military. Understanding how to safely remove contaminated PPE suits and replace them with clean ones, and the disposal issues involved, was something I had a great deal of knowledge and know-how about.

At the airport on the way home, many nurses and doctors were openly hugging and exposing skin to skin contact. I had to remind several of them that they could still pass on the infection (many of them had still been caring for the dying a few hours before leaving for the airport).

My overriding memory of the epidemic was taking one of our young female doctors to the Connaught Hospital in Freetown. She was attending a liaison meeting with the local doctors there about treatment and referrals. I decided to accompany her, as she was new to working overseas, never having been to Africa before, and was generally nervous too.

I had been to the hospital before and knew it was always busy to the point of overcrowding. At times, even I had been approached and asked if I could help people; they'd assumed I was a doctor who had come to the hospital to assist with the Ebola outbreak.

I told the doctor to listen to everything I said and to stay by my side, and if I said we had to leave then that's what we'd do. She agreed, and we entered the hospital.

We stopped a nurse and asked for directions to the office of the doctor we were to meet. She kindly pointed us in the right direction, so we set off. The hospital was crowded, and lots of people were pushing by us. We stopped by a desk, when suddenly there was a loud commotion; there was screaming and shouting.

Two young men were half carrying, half dragging an elderly lady towards us at the desk. They were crying and hysterically shouting for help. The woman was bleeding from her nose, mouth and eyes. She was delirious and, it seemed, very close to death. There was a foul smell of human excrement; the woman had voided her bladder and bowels.

The young doctor I was with was transfixed with fear. She froze, her eyes wide, and started to shake as she realised the three were heading straight towards us. They were shouting to us to help. I shouted to the nurse at the desk to call for help. I grabbed the arm of the doctor and told her forcefully to move. She froze, transfixed by the horrific scene unfolding just a few metres in front of her.

"Move now," I shouted as I pulled her back towards the main entrance and out into the daylight.

Once outside, we headed for our vehicle. The doctor was now crying uncontrollably. She was both shocked and totally overwhelmed by the incident.

We sat in the vehicle for a while until she calmed down. We talked through what had happened and she apologised for her behaviour. As a doctor, she should have handled it better, she said. I told her that doctor or not, it would have been a harrowing experience for anyone, let alone someone who had no experience with this type of situation. She thanked me for acting so quickly and getting her out of harm's way. I was glad I'd decided to go with her.

The Ebola crisis in West Africa was horrific, particularly in the rural areas where they were less informed as to why they were seeing family members getting sick. Sons, daughters, mothers and fathers would sit with the sick and wash and care for them, not realising that by doing so they, too, were becoming infected. When a family member died from Ebola, it was tradition to wash the body and prepare it for burial; but the body was still infectious even when life had left it.

It took a while and a whole lot of education, which was delivered in remote villages, to teach them how to handle sick relatives and inform them that they should not touch the deceased, as they were still contaminated.

Many in those areas were too scared to go to the hospital, as they thought that once you were admitted you didn't come out; you died there. So, many infected people stayed at home, unknowingly infecting others.

Once there had been a death in a dwelling, the ambulance would arrive. The medics, all dressed in full PPE (from head to toe in white, reinforced paper suits, with hoods up and face masks and visors on) would take away the body and completely disinfect the dwelling. They soon got the nickname of 'ghosts'. It was easy to see why.

The Ebola crisis for me, on reflection, was one intervention too far. At the airport, while waiting to board, I was standing in line talking to one of the nurses who I recognised from the ETC in Kerrytown. We chatted casually about our experiences, but she seemed distracted, on edge. I put it down to tiredness and her being a bit anxious to get home, as we had a six-hour stopover in Casablanca before we could fly on to Heathrow.

In Casablanca, I found a small hotel within the airport and booked a room. It turned out to be a very small room with a bed that touched the walls on each side, so you had to climb onto the bed from where the footboard would be. It had a wall hanger, to hang a coat on, and a TV; that was it. The showers and washroom were at the top of the corridor and were communal. It was basic but clean and provided an ideal opportunity to catch up on some much-needed sleep.

It was soon time to board the plane home. Once in the air, we were told that on arrival we had to declare we had come from an Ebola-infected country. We would be separated and screened by a doctor before we left the airport. We were part of the first and largest contingent of humanitarian and NHS workers to arrive back in the UK since the epidemic began.

The screening was a temperature check and a series of questions about our health and how we were feeling at that moment. Depending on what role we'd had, we were given a category of risk. Doctors and nurses who'd had direct contact with those with Ebola were high risk, those directly supporting in terms of supplying medication or other services in contaminated areas were medium risk and everyone else was low risk. They couldn't decide on my risk level; while I was not high risk (I had spent most of my time in clean areas), I *had* been in contaminated areas. I was eventually labelled as medium risk.

The procedure at Heathrow was diabolical. It was disorganised, ill-prepared and chaotic. I was one of the first people directed into a very small waiting room. I had my details taken and was told to take a seat. I asked the woman behind the desk if she knew that there were a lot of NHS staff returning, the largest return into the UK of Ebola volunteers, and we would easily fill the small room, with it possibly being a squeeze to get everyone in. She smiled and said it was okay and they had been told what to expect. In the eternal words of Jim Royle, "MY ARSE!"

As the plane emptied, people were questioned at passport control about where they had travelled from. They were then redirected to be screened in the small room. It quickly became apparent that the room was too small. People were crammed against one another, something that had been drilled into us not to do; we had been told to keep a distance and avoid person-to-person contact. This all went to shite at Heathrow. People had to push past each other to register their details at the desk before pushing past people again to join a queue. I was first in and, for some reason, fifth to be seen. It was a very badly organised and dangerously run process.

As I came out of the room to continue my route out of Heathrow, I could see the lines of closely packed people waiting to get into the same room I had just left.

I eventually arrived at baggage claim, retrieved my case and exited through the doors that led into the main airport. I was met by Val and my two kids. It was a strange meeting. Something had changed. For the very first time, Val burst into tears; largely out of relief, I suppose, but she had always been so controlled and calm whenever she picked me up on my return from my travels. I felt it too.

I still had to observe the no-bodily contact rule. That was difficult, as all we wanted to do was hug tightly and kiss, like a normal couple.

I had to endure a 21-day isolation at home. Public Health England was regularly in touch over that time, checking on my condition and offering any support I might need. I didn't need it and the 21-day isolation torture finally came to an end.

During the immediate day or two after arriving home, it was reported that a nurse who'd returned from Sierra Leone had Ebola and was critically ill. They mentioned her name on the news but that didn't ring any bells; I am terrible with remembering names, but faces I never forget. Her name was Pauline Cafferkey. When her photo appeared, I realised that she was the nurse I had stood next to and chatted with at the airport in Freetown. I had noticed then that she looked distracted. Had she known? Was it exhaustion? We all suffered from it at the time of departure. Only she knew, I supposed.

I informed Public Health England that I had been in close proximity to Pauline, but they said that if I came through the isolation without symptoms, I was okay. It stayed on my mind for quite a while.

On reuniting with my family at Heathrow, I knew something had changed. I had lost quite a lot of weight and my hair was longer than it had been since I was sixteen. I was exhausted. Not just from the travel I had just endured, but from the constant high levels of stress caused by being on the edge of dangerous situations, working in hostile environments for 15 years and making decisions and plans that people's lives depended upon. Being a true global journeyman was beginning to show. I felt like the cat with nine lives; I had taken my nine and I didn't think I should chance a tenth. I had been lucky so many times. I'd made good decisions most of the time but I was tired; not just the 'tired' that a good night's sleep would cure but the 'tired' that needed a complete lifestyle change.

At home, I sat with my wife and kids and talked through my feelings without, at first, making a final decision. I listened to their thoughts and arguments. It was unanimous; they wanted me to quit and get a normal job, but they had wanted me to quit before. This was different, though. I felt different.

I paused, took a deep breath and announced that the Ebola intervention was to be my last. I was retiring from the safety-and-security-in-hostile-locations game; this time for good. This was, without doubt, the hardest decision I have ever made. It was the right decision but a really difficult one, nonetheless. I was so emotionally tied to my work; not just the safety and security aspect but to the programmes I had been privileged to support. I had met many of the beneficiary groups, the families and the children, and listened as they told their stories of extreme hardship and the triumphs they'd had, no matter how short-lived. I had been involved at many levels and had fully and emotionally invested in my role as a humanitarian worker.

After a long rest and an attempt to adjust to normal life, I joined my wife in the family business, taking the role of joint owner and operations director. The job still affords me travel opportunities, as we attend education conferences around the world, advertising and gaining business from international schools who buy their school supplies from the UK through our consolidation service. We order it, check it, repack it and ship it to schools all over the world. It's a great business, founded by my wife who built it up and made it the success it is today.

Do I miss the humanitarian sector? Yes, I do. Do I regret my decision to retire from it? No, I don't.

It has been very hard over the years to adapt, probably harder than most would think. I had 22 years in the military, with several operational tours under my belt, both war and post-war. I then fell into the humanitarian sector and was back in hostile locations again, this time without the support of a military force behind me; unarmed and having to, at times, think very quickly on my feet in critical situations. The level of adrenaline-fuelled excitement that it produced always had me on a fine edge. It was almost a drug. I was good at my work; very good. I was once referred to, in a safety and security meeting, as a sector leader; not something I had ever considered myself to be.

I enjoyed working with people from different backgrounds and different countries. I relished the challenges, which were varied and many, and, of course, the camaraderie of my co-workers, many of whom had the same dark sense of humour as me, generated by a tolerance to hardship and experiencing situations most people could not even imagine: death, suffering and poverty affecting adults and, heartbreakingly, children alike.

It is now as I close my journey, that I ask the reader to reflect and direct their thoughts to those who volunteer to undergo hardship in order to bring support and life-saving assistance to those who are in real danger, poverty and suffer real hunger and hardship.

The world of the humanitarian worker is hard, both physically and emotionally, but it has its rewards too: the smiles of children who have every reason not smile, the kindness of those who have nothing but still care and seeing how those who just can't help themselves remain dignified. Joy and sadness squeezed together into your emotional space.

I will always admire the humanitarian workers. Regardless of the faults or stance of the organisations they choose to work for, the individuals are truly golden. They usually opt to stay out of the limelight but we should bring them into the light. We should share in their experiences and understand the selfless service they choose to give.

The unrecognised, and largely unsupported, but dedicated people are out there. They are not hugging trees, but many may, like me, still be emotionally attached to their past experiences; they are burnt into your memory, the good and the bad.

My hat is off to them all. Truly wonderful people.

Chapter 9:

The Lioness's Tale

In 2002, Phil finally retired from 22 years' service in the military. I never thought we would revisit a similar life that I'd assumed we had left behind; the long weeks and months of separation and the anguish of not knowing the details of his situation. I always knew that Phil was keen on exploring work in the humanitarian sector, but if I'm honest, I didn't really think it would amount to anything substantive. Why would he want the pressure of working in those environments again?

Little did I know that just 12 months later, we would be facing our first separation in civilian life, as he was off to Iraq of all places.

I have always fully supported Phil in his career, as he has me, but it has been difficult. I was torn inside between wanting to continue that support and accept that we would spend further time away from each other and stating my many reasons why he shouldn't accept this line of work. I knew it could be dangerous. I knew what I wanted, but I also knew that he needed to do this.

So what were my reasons? The most important issue for me was his safety. He had survived many trials and tribulations in the military and now he was going back to work in those same hostile environments as a civilian. It seemed like madness to a lot of people but I had complete trust in Phil, knowing he would be under no illusions about what he was undertaking; and he had survived far worse situations in his military career.[27] I had complete faith in his judgement.

But where did it leave me and our kids? For me, now working full time after picking up my career when Phil retired from the military, it meant childcare arrangements for our son who was still in primary school. Our daughter, who was 13 at the time, was still too young to take care of him, so I had to either alter my working hours or put them both in the before- and after-school care. It was so much easier for me when Phil was home, as he took care of the children, the chores and the meals, leaving me to sort myself out for work.

Out of school and at weekends, I also had to cope alone. Our son was a member of the local football team and he had to be taken to training and matches. This would fall on just me, when I'd been used to either Phil taking him or both of us going and making an outing of it.

It wasn't going to be easy for any of us but we had been there before and conquered it, so we'd survive it again, I guessed.

In addition to the practical issues above, there was the constant worry about Phil's safety. He didn't tell me everything he was experiencing, of course, but I'd get snippets through his emails or

---

[27] Phil received a citation for his bravery during Operation Granby, when his vehicle, full of ammunition and grenades, developed an electrical fault which made the vehicle turret live, sparking furiously when there was metal on metal contact. It rendered his radio communications unworkable and the failure of the electric supply to the turret and the 30mm Rarden Canon meant that everything had to be done manually, including directing his driver, who had no night sight, and physically relaying his gunner on to several Iraqi targets that threatened the safety of the armoured column. This meant he had to sit 'head up', when the order was to 'batten down', during the various stages of battle, to ensure he could direct and anticipate the platoon and the company's battle plan and the formations required.

phone calls and pick up on the severity of the situations by watching the news, then I'd be left to fill in the blanks and that always made it appear much worse than perhaps it sometimes was. I'd wake in the middle of the night, unable to get back to sleep for worrying about him, so exhaustion played another part in my life as the wife of a humanitarian worker!

I also remember how lonely I felt during the summer months if he was away. I would see friends and family going on holidays or off out for days of fun; although I took our kids to fun places, being alone was never the same as having your husband by your side. I'd hear our neighbours playing in their gardens with their kids and wish Phil was there and we could be a family of four again, instead of three.

It was a very emotional time for me. I had to stay strong for our kids, being the mum and dad at times, and fend off their sometimes very awkward questions about what their dad's job actually was and how much danger was he in. This wasn't something I wanted them to worry about, so I had to play it down and come up with stories to pacify them. I often reassured them that he was staying in a nice hotel away from the danger zones, which was better for them to hear than the reality (which was far from what I'd described to them).

I was a wreck on the inside, worrying every time I took a phone call from a number I didn't recognise in case it was bad news, but I could never let that type of emotion spill over to the kids; they just couldn't see me like that.

This took me back to the same worries and concerns I'd had when Phil was a soldier. Every knock on the front door was answered with trepidation, anticipating that it could be the dreaded visit from the police or some other authority to inform me that something bad had happened to him.

I think that the general public probably don't fully understand that humanitarian workers put themselves in danger almost every day throughout the course of their work.

It is very different to military and public services, as it is extremely rare, in my opinion, that the sector is recognised for its dedication to the causes it undertakes and the dangers it accepts, which directly impacts humanitarian workers' lives. Furthermore, there is no support network for the families of humanitarian workers; there are no family groups for support and no collective like-minded groups on your doorstep to comfort and confide in. Wives and families of humanitarian workers are largely alone, unlike in the military.

Needless to say, we survived it all and, above all else, the kids and I are extremely proud of Phil and all his achievements in the humanitarian sector, as well as his military service.

Reading some of his testimonials, it is clear to see that he was held in extremely high regard by his employers and clients who engaged his consultancy services and all of the people he worked with in the field. Phil is the rock of our family and my soulmate.

*

TESTIMONIAL

medical relief, lasting health care

House 78. Block Number 11 Al West Algazar Street Al Riyad Khartoum Sudan.

Re: Philip Jones

Greetings from Khartoum, Sudan, Merlin North Sudan Mission. I am Taye Dejene, country director of Merlin for North Sudan, and trust you are well.

I just wanted to reflect on the performance and contribution of Phil Jones, who has been providing services in the areas of security and safety consultancy for the mission in Darfur and the management base, Khartoum. Phil has been extremely helpful in providing regular support in advising the management to take appropriate decisions before things get complicated. His vast knowledge and experience in the field have helped us remain safe and secure, as have the results of his updates, reports, phone conversations and what not! His recommendations helped Merlin not only manage day-to-day security situations but also strategize ourselves as to how to cope with the upcoming situations and developments associated with the referendum in Sudan, an historical political milestone for the country, which has implications on our working areas. His thoughts and suggestions have been supportive and have helped make decisions. He has been producing comprehensive updates and reports, taking in to account facts and rumours, through meticulous assessment of situations in the operating environment that could potentially affect Merlin programmes in Sudan. I am personally impressed by his contribution in the field to providing real-time security briefings, updates and reports, working in Sudan and visiting the toughest and most difficult parts of Darfur (and, of course, the most insecure parts of the world) so that we make appropriate decisions when it comes to the security and safety of our staff and beneficiaries and the reputation of the organisation in Sudan. I, as a manager, have been in the field for 18 years, and having worked with so many professionals in various fields, I should be open with you that he is one of the best professionals I have ever worked with.

I am also impressed by his contribution as an excellent team player, working with our team in the field and demonstrating his seriousness and commitment to his roles not just as a consultant but as a concerned member of the team in Darfur. As it is always painful to lose such a personality, who has the utmost conviction and commitment to helping people, we wish him all the best.

Even at this time, when he is about to depart our mission, he recommended staying a few days with our staff in the deep field to help on post Eid situation, professional thinking and decision. Thank you, Phil, and keep it up!

In a nutshell, I thank him so much for his time and significant contribution to our field and mission and hope we will meet once again.

Best,

Liben, Taye Dejene

Country Director

Merlin International - UK

Khartoum, Sudan Tel: ███████████████████
— Zain Skype: ██████████